CODE OF FEDERAL REGULATIONS

Title 4
Accounts

Revised as of January 1, 2019

Containing a codification of documents of general applicability and future effect

As of January 1, 2019

Published by the Office of the Federal Register National Archives and Records Administration as a Special Edition of the Federal Register

Table of Contents

Cite this Code: CFR

To cite the regulations in this volume use title, part and section number. Thus, 4 CFR 2.1 *refers to title 4, part 2, section 1.*

Explanation

The Code of Federal Regulations is a codification of the general and permanent rules published in the Federal Register by the Executive departments and agencies of the Federal Government. The Code is divided into 50 titles which represent broad areas subject to Federal regulation. Each title is divided into chapters which usually bear the name of the issuing agency. Each chapter is further subdivided into parts covering specific regulatory areas.

Each volume of the Code is revised at least once each calendar year and issued on a quarterly basis approximately as follows:

Title 1 through Title 16..........as of January 1
Title 17 through Title 27..........as of April 1
Title 28 through Title 41..........as of July 1
Title 42 through Title 50..........as of October 1

The appropriate revision date is printed on the cover of each volume.

LEGAL STATUS

The contents of the Federal Register are required to be judicially noticed (44 U.S.C. 1507). The Code of Federal Regulations is prima facie evidence of the text of the original documents (44 U.S.C. 1510).

HOW TO USE THE CODE OF FEDERAL REGULATIONS

The Code of Federal Regulations is kept up to date by the individual issues of the Federal Register. These two publications must be used together to determine the latest version of any given rule.

To determine whether a Code volume has been amended since its revision date (in this case, January 1, 2019), consult the "List of CFR Sections Affected (LSA)," which is issued monthly, and the "Cumulative List of Parts Affected," which appears in the Reader Aids section of the daily Federal Register. These two lists will identify the Federal Register page number of the latest amendment of any given rule.

EFFECTIVE AND EXPIRATION DATES

Each volume of the Code contains amendments published in the Federal Register since the last revision of that volume of the Code. Source citations for the regulations are referred to by volume number and page number of the Federal Register and date of publication. Publication dates and effective dates are usually not the same and care must be exercised by the user in determining the actual effective date. In instances where the effective date is beyond the cut-off date for the Code a note has been inserted to reflect the future effective date. In those instances where a regulation published in the Federal Register states a date certain for expiration, an appropriate note will be inserted following the text.

OMB CONTROL NUMBERS

The Paperwork Reduction Act of 1980 (Pub. L. 96–511) requires Federal agencies to display an OMB control number with their information collection request.

Many agencies have begun publishing numerous OMB control numbers as amendments to existing regulations in the CFR. These OMB numbers are placed as close as possible to the applicable recordkeeping or reporting requirements.

PAST PROVISIONS OF THE CODE

Provisions of the Code that are no longer in force and effect as of the revision date stated on the cover of each volume are not carried. Code users may find the text of provisions in effect on any given date in the past by using the appropriate List of CFR Sections Affected (LSA). For the convenience of the reader, a "List of CFR Sections Affected" is published at the end of each CFR volume. For changes to the Code prior to the LSA listings at the end of the volume, consult previous annual editions of the LSA. For changes to the Code prior to 2001, consult the List of CFR Sections Affected compilations, published for 1949-1963, 1964-1972, 1973-1985, and 1986-2000.

"[RESERVED]" TERMINOLOGY

The term "[Reserved]" is used as a place holder within the Code of Federal Regulations. An agency may add regulatory information at a "[Reserved]" location at any time. Occasionally "[Reserved]" is used editorially to indicate that a portion of the CFR was left vacant and not accidentally dropped due to a printing or computer error.

INCORPORATION BY REFERENCE

What is incorporation by reference? Incorporation by reference was established by statute and allows Federal agencies to meet the requirement to publish regulations in the Federal Register by referring to materials already published elsewhere. For an incorporation to be valid, the Director of the Federal Register must approve it. The legal effect of incorporation by reference is that the material is treated as if it were published in full in the Federal Register (5 U.S.C. 552(a)). This material, like any other properly issued regulation, has the force of law.

What is a proper incorporation by reference? The Director of the Federal Register will approve an incorporation by reference only when the requirements of 1 CFR part 51 are met. Some of the elements on which approval is based are:

(a) The incorporation will substantially reduce the volume of material published in the Federal Register.

(b) The matter incorporated is in fact available to the extent necessary to afford fairness and uniformity in the administrative process.

(c) The incorporating document is drafted and submitted for publication in accordance with 1 CFR part 51.

What if the material incorporated by reference cannot be found? If you have any problem locating or obtaining a copy of material listed as an approved incorporation by reference, please contact the agency that issued the regulation containing that incorporation. If, after contacting the agency, you find the material is not available, please notify the Director of the Federal Register, National Archives and Records Administration, 8601 Adelphi Road, College Park, MD 20740-6001, or call 202-741-6010.

CFR INDEXES AND TABULAR GUIDES

A subject index to the Code of Federal Regulations is contained in a separate volume, revised annually as of January 1, entitled CFR INDEX AND FINDING AIDS. This volume contains the Parallel Table of Authorities and Rules. A list of CFR titles, chapters, subchapters, and parts and an alphabetical list of agencies publishing in the CFR are also included in this volume.

An index to the text of "Title 3—The President" is carried within that volume.

The Federal Register Index is issued monthly in cumulative form. This index is based on a consolidation of the "Contents" entries in the daily Federal Register.

A List of CFR Sections Affected (LSA) is published monthly, keyed to the revision dates of the 50 CFR titles.

REPUBLICATION OF MATERIAL

There are no restrictions on the republication of material appearing in the Code of Federal Regulations.

INQUIRIES

For a legal interpretation or explanation of any regulation in this volume, contact the issuing agency. The issuing agency's name appears at the top of odd-numbered pages.

For inquiries concerning CFR reference assistance, call 202–741–6000 or write to the Director, Office of the Federal Register, National Archives and Records Administration, 8601 Adelphi Road, College Park, MD 20740-6001 or e-mail *fedreg.info@nara.gov.*

SALES

The Government Publishing Office (GPO) processes all sales and distribution of the CFR. For payment by credit card, call toll-free, 866-512-1800, or DC area, 202-512-1800, M-F 8 a.m. to 4 p.m. e.s.t. or fax your order to 202-512-2104, 24 hours a day. For payment by check, write to: US Government Publishing Office – New Orders, P.O. Box 979050, St. Louis, MO 63197-9000.

ELECTRONIC SERVICES

The full text of the Code of Federal Regulations, the LSA (List of CFR Sections Affected), The United States Government Manual, the Federal Register, Public Laws, Public Papers of the Presidents of the United States, Compilation of Presidential Documents and the Privacy Act Compilation are available in electronic format via *www.govinfo.gov*. For more information, contact the GPO Customer Contact Center, U.S. Government Publishing Office. Phone 202-512-1800, or 866-512-1800 (toll-free). E-mail, *ContactCenter@gpo.gov.*

The Office of the Federal Register also offers a free service on the National Archives and Records Administration's (NARA) World Wide Web site for public law numbers, Federal Register finding aids, and related information. Connect to NARA's web site at *www.archives.gov/federal-register.*

The e-CFR is a regularly updated, unofficial editorial compilation of CFR material and Federal Register amendments, produced by the Office of the Federal Register and the Government Publishing Office. It is available at *www.ecfr.gov.*

OLIVER A. POTTS,
Director,
Office of the Federal Register
January 1, 2019

THIS TITLE

Title 4—ACCOUNTS is composed of one volume. This volume contains chapter I—Government Accountability Office (GAO). The contents of this volume represent all current regulations codified under this title of the CFR as of January 1, 2019.

For this volume, Cheryl E. Sirofchuck was Chief Editor. The Code of Federal Regulations publication program is under the direction of John Hyrum Martinez, assisted by Stephen J. Frattini.

Title 4—Accounts

CHAPTER I—GOVERNMENT ACCOUNTABILITY OFFICE

EDITORIAL NOTE: Nomenclature changes to chapter I appear at 70 FR 17583, Apr. 7, 2005.

SUBCHAPTER A—PERSONNEL SYSTEM

SUBCHAPTER B—GENERAL PROCEDURES

SUBCHAPTER A—PERSONNEL SYSTEM

PART 1 [RESERVED]

PART 2—PURPOSE AND GENERAL PROVISION

AUTHORITY: 31 U.S.C. 732.

SOURCE: 45 FR 68375, Oct. 15, 1980, unless otherwise noted.

§ 2.1 Purpose, scope, and applicability.

(a) This regulation establishes and sets forth the basic policy for the Government Accountability Office (GAO) personnel system. Personnel management is a primary responsibility of all who plan, direct, or supervise the work of employees. The objective of personnel management is to contribute to the effective accomplishment of GAO's mission through proper acquisition, development, fair treatment, motivation, compensation and productive utilization f employees.

(b) Nothing in this regulation prohibits or restricts any lawful effort to achieve equal employment opportunity through affirmative action.

§ 2.2 References.

(a) Subchapters III and IV of Chapter 7 of Title 31 U.S.C.

(b) Title 5, United States Code.

[45 FR 68375, Oct. 15, 1980, as amended at 47 FR 56979, Dec. 22, 1982]

§ 2.3 GAO Personnel Appeals Board.

The Government Accountability Office Personnel Appeals Board is established by 31 U.S.C. 751. This board will promulgate regulations providing for employee appeals and establishing its operating procedures.

[47 FR 56979, Dec. 22, 1982]

§ 2.4 Merit system principles.

(a) Merit personnel systems are based on the principle that an organization is best served by motivated, competent, honest and productive workers. In a merit system, employees are hired, promoted, rewarded, and retained on the basis of individual ability and fitness for employment without regard to race, color, sex, religion, age, or national origin. Central to this principle is the protection of employees from discrimination, improper political influence and personal favoritism.

(b) Equal employment opportunity is an integral part of every merit system. Affirmative action plans, designed to provide a work force reflective of the Nation's diversity, must assure that both in operation and results the merit system reflects equal opportunity at every step of the personnel process.

(c) GAO personnel systems shall embody the following merit system principles:

(1) Recruitment should be from qualified individuals from appropriate sources in an endeavor to achieve a work force from all segments of society, and selection and advancement should be determined solely on the basis of relative ability, knowledge, and skills, after fair and open competition which assures that all receive equal opportunity.

(2) All employees and applicants for employment should receive fair and equitable treatment in all aspects of personnel management without regard to political affiliation, race, color, religion, national origin, sex, marital status, age, or handicapping condition, and with proper regard for their privacy and constitutional rights.

(3) Equal pay should be provided for work of substantially equal value, with appropriate consideration of both national and local rates paid by employers in the private sector, and appropriate incentives and recognition should be provided for excellence in performance.

(4) All employees should maintain high standards of integrity, conduct, and concern for the public interest.

(5) The work force should be used efficiently and effectively.

(6) Employees should be retained on the basis of the adequacy of their performance, inadequate performance should be corrected, and employees should be separated who cannot or will not improve their performance to meet required standards.

(7) Employees should be provided effective education and training in cases in which such education and training would result in better organizational and individual performance.

(8) Employees should be protected against arbitrary action, personal favoritism, or coercion from partisan political purposes and prohibited from using their official authority or influence for the purpose of interfering with or affecting the results of an election or a nomination for election.

(9) Employees should be protected against reprisal for the lawful disclosure of information which the employee reasonably believes evidences: a violation of any law, rule or regulation; or mismanagement, a gross waste of funds, an abuse of authority, or a substantial and specific danger to public health or safety.

§ 2.5 Prohibited personnel practices.

Any GAO employee who has authority to take, direct others to take, recommend, or approve any personnel action, shall not, with respect to such authority engage in the following prohibited personnel practices.

(a) *Discrimination.* GAO employees shall not discriminate for or against any employee or applicant for employment—

(1) On the basis of race, color, religion, sex, or national origin, as prohibited under section 717 of the Civil Rights Act of 1964 (42 U.S.C. 2000 e–16);

(2) On the basis of age, as prohibited under section 12 and 15 of the Age Discrimination in Employment Act of 1967 (29 U.S.C. 631, 633a);

(3) On the basis of sex, as prohibited under section 6(d) of the Fair Labor Standards Act of 1938 (29 U.S.C. 206(d));

(4) On the basis of handicapping condition, as prohibited under section 501 of the Rehabilitation Act of 1973 (29 U.S.C. 791); or

(5) On the basis of marital status or political affiliation, as prohibited under any law, rule, or regulation.

(b) *Recommendations or statements.* GAO employees shall not solicit or consider any recommendation or statement, oral or written, with respect to any individual who requests or is under consideration for any personnel action unless such recommendation or statement is based on the personal knowledge or records of the person furnishing it and consists of—

(1) An evaluation of the work performance, ability, aptitude, or general qualifications of such individual, or

(2) An evaluation of the character, loyalty, or suitability of such individual.

(c) *Political activity.* GAO employees shall not coerce the political activity of any person (including the providing of any political contribution or service), or take any action against any employee or applicant for employment as a reprisal for the refusal of any person to engage in such political activity.

(d) *Compete for employment.* GAO employees shall not deceive or willfully obstruct any person with respect to such person's right to compete for employment.

(e) *Influencing competition.* GAO employees shall not influence any person to withdraw from competition for any position for the purpose of improving or injuring the prospects of any other person for employment.

(f) *Preference or advantage.* GAO employees shall not grant any preference or advantage not authorized by law, rule, or regulation to any employee or applicant for employment (including defining the scope or manner of competition or the requirements for any position) for the purpose of improving or injuring the prospects of any particular person for employment.

(g) *Relatives.* GAO employees who are serving as public officials (as defined in section 3110(a)(2) of title 5, United States Code) shall not appoint, employ, promote, advance, or advocate for appointment, employment, promotion, or advancement, in or to a GAO position any individual who is a relative (as defined in section 3110(a)(3) of title 5, U.S. Code) of such employee.

(h) *Reprisals.* GAO employees shall not take or fail to take a personnel action with respect to any employee or applicant for employment as a reprisal for—

(1) A disclosure of information by an employee or applicant which the employee or applicant reasonably believes evidences—

(i) A violation of any law, rule, or regulation, or

(ii) Mismanagement, a gross waste of funds, an abuse of authority, or a substantial and specific danger to public health or safety, if such disclosure is not specifically prohibited by law and if such information is not specifically required by Executive order to be kept secret in the interest of national defense or the conduct of foreign affairs; or

(2) A disclosure to the General Counsel of the GAO Personnel Appeals Board of information which the employee or applicant reasonably believes evidences—

(i) A violation of any law, rule, or regulation, or

(ii) Mismanagement, a gross waste of funds, an abuse of authority, or a substantial and specific danger to public health or safety.

(i) *Reprisals for appeals.* GAO employees shall not take or fail to take any personnel action against any employee or applicant for employment as a reprisal for the exercise of any appeal right granted by any law, rule, or regulation.

(j) *Discrimination for conduct.* GAO employees shall not discriminate for or against any employee or applicant for employment on the basis of conduct which does not adversely affect the performance of the employee or applicant or the performance of others; except that nothing in this paragraph shall prohibit an agency from taking into account in determining suitability or fitness any conviction of the employee or applicant for any crime under the laws of any State, or the District of Columbia, or of the United States.

(k) *Other personnel actions.* GAO employees shall not take or fail to take any other personnel action if the taking of or failure to take such action violates any law, rule or regulation implementing, or directly concerning, the merit system principles described in §2.4.

(l) *Information to the Congress.* Nothing in this section shall be construed to authorize the withholding of information from the Congress or the taking of any personnel action against an employee who discloses information to the Congress.

§2.6 Veterans' preference.

(a) GAO will provide preference, for any individual who would be a preference eligible in the executive branch, in a manner and to an extent consistent with preference eligibles in the executive branch.

(b) Appeals from preference decisions will be heard by the GAO Personnel Appeals Board.

PART 3—EMPLOYMENT

AUTHORITY: 31 U.S.C. 732.

SOURCE: 45 FR 68376, Oct. 15, 1980, unless otherwise noted.

§3.1 Appointment, promotion, and assignment.

Employees of GAO shall be appointed, promoted and assigned solely on the basis of merit and fitness, but without regard to the provisions of title 5, United States Code, governing appointments and other personnel actions in the competitive service.

§3.2 Oath of office.

The provisions of subchapter II of chapter 33 of title 5, U.S. Code, and Office of Personnel Management implementing regulations apply to Government Accountability Office employees.

§3.3 Assignments to and from States.

The provisions of subchapter VI of chapter 33 of title 5, U.S. Code, and Office of Personnel Management implementing regulations apply to Government Accountability Office employees.

PART 4—EMPLOYEE PERFORMANCE AND UTILIZATION

AUTHORITY: 31 U.S.C. 732.

SOURCE: 45 FR 68376, Oct. 15, 1980, unless otherwise noted.

§ 4.1 Training.

The provisions of chapter 41, of title 5, United States Code, and Office of Personnel Management implementing regulations apply to Government Accountability Office employees.

§ 4.2 Performance appraisal.

(a) The GAO shall develop one or more performance appraisal systems which provide for periodic appraisals of job performance of employees; encourages employee participation in establishing performance standards; and uses the results of performance appraisal as a basis for training, rewarding, reassigning, promoting, reducing in grade, retaining, and removing employees.

(b) Each performance appraisal system shall provide for—

(1) Establishing performance standards which will, to the maximum extent feasible, permit the accurate evaluation of job performance on the basis of job-related criteria (which may include the extent of courtesy demonstrated to the public) for each GAO employee.

(2) As soon as practicable, but not later than October 1, 1981, with respect to initial appraisal periods, and thereafter at the beginning of each following appraisal period, communicating to reach GAO employee the performance standards and the critical elements of the employee's position.

(3) Annually evaluating each employee during the appraisal period on such standards.

(4) Recognizing and rewarding employees whose performance so warrants.

(5) Assisting employees in improving unacceptable performance.

(6) Reassigning, reducing in grade, or removing employees who continue to have unacceptable performance but only after an opportunity to demonstrate acceptable performance.

§ 4.3 Removal for unacceptable performance.

GAO may reduce in grade/pay level or remove an employee for unacceptable performance in accordance with the provisions of this section.

(a) *Employee entitlement.* A GAO employee whose reduction in grade/pay level or removal is proposed under this section is entitled to—

(1) An advance written notice of the proposed action which identifies—

(i) Specific instances of unacceptable performance by the employee on which the proposed action is based; and

(ii) The critical elements of the employee's position involved in each instance of unacceptable performance.

(2) Be represented by an attorney or other representative.

(3) A reasonable time to answer orally and in writing.

(4) A written decision which—

(i) Specifies the instances of unacceptable performance by the employee on which the reduction in grade/pay level or removal is based.

(ii) Unless proposed by the Comptroller General or by a senior manager (e.g., the Deputy Comptroller General, an Assistant Comptroller General, or a Division or Office Director) has been concurred in by an employee who is in a higher position than the employee who proposed the action.

(b) *Decisions to retain, reduce in grade/pay level or remove.* The decision to retain, reduce in grade or remove a GAO employee—

(1) Shall be made within 30 days after the date of expiration of the notice period, and

(2) In the case of reduction in grade/pay level or removal, may be based only on those instances of unacceptable performance by the employee—

(i) Which occurred during the 1-year period ending on the date of the notice of the proposed action.

(ii) For which the notice and other requirements of this section are complied with.

(c) *Performance improvement.* If because of performance improvement by the employee during the notice period, the employee is not reduced in grade/pay level or removed, and the employee's performance continues to be acceptable for 1 year from the date of advance written notice, any records shall be retained only as prescribed by other recordkeeping requirements, such as grievances, adverse action appeals, or discrimination complaints. In these circumstances any entry or notation of unacceptable performance shall be removed from the employee's official personnel folder and maintained in separate files to be used only in connection with an employee initiated complaint.

(d) *Appeals.* A GAO employee who has been reduced in grade/pay level or removed under this section is entitled to appeal the action to the GAO Personnel Appeals Board.

(e) *Nonapplicability.* This section does not apply to—

(1) The reduction to the grade/pay level previously held of a supervisor or manager who has not completed the trial period.

(2) The reduction in grade/pay level or removal of a GAO employee who is serving a trial period under an initial appointment or who has not completed 1 year of current continuous employment under other than a temporary appointment limited to 1 year or less.

(3) Employees in the GAO Senior Executive Service.

§4.4 Incentive awards.

The provisions of chapter 45 of title 5, United States Code and Office of Personnel Management implementing regulations apply to Government Accountability Office employees.

PART 5—COMPENSATION

Sec.

AUTHORITY: 31 U.S.C. 732.

SOURCE: 45 FR 68377, Oct. 15, 1980, unless otherwise noted.

§5.1 Pay.

(a) *Pay principles.* Pay of the employees of GAO shall be fixed by the Comptroller General consistent with the principles that—

(1) There be equal pay for work of substantially equal value.

(2) Pay distinctions be maintained in keeping with work and performance distinctions.

(3) Pay rates be comparable with private enterprise pay rates for the same levels of work.

(4) Pay levels be interrelated to the General Schedule.

(b) *Pay rates.* (1) The Comptroller General shall publish a schedule of pay rates which shall apply to GAO employees. Except as provided in paragraph (b) (2) of this section, and regulations for the GAO Senior Executive Service, the highest rate under such schedule shall not exceed the highest rate of basic pay payable for grade GS–15 under the General Schedule.

(2) Such schedule may provide for rates which do not exceed the maximum rate payable for grade GS–18 of the General Schedule for up to one hundred employees, reduced by the number of employees who are in the GAO Senior Executive Service, other than those in such service pursuant to 31 U.S.C. 733(c).

(c) *Pay adjustments.* Except as provided in regulations for the GAO Senior Executive Service and the Merit Pay System, the pay of GAO employees shall be adjusted at the same time and to the same extent as rates of basic pay are adjusted for the General Schedule.

[45 FR 68377, Oct. 15, 1980, as amended at 47 FR 56979, Dec. 22, 1982]

§5.2 Grade and pay retention.

(a) *Change of positions.* Any GAO employee who is placed in a lower grade position as a result of a reduction-in-force may be entitled to the retained grade of the higher position he or she previously held. The employee receives this entitlement (which is for a period of 2 years) if he or she has served for at least 52 consecutive weeks in one or more positions at a grade or grades higher than the new position. The 2-year period begins on the date of placement to the lower grade position.

(b) *Reclassification.* Any GAO employee who is in a position which is reduced in grade is entitled to have the grade of such position before reduction be treated as the retained grade of such employee for the 2-year period beginning on the date of reduction in grade. However, this section shall not apply to any reduction in the grade of a position which had not been classified at the higher grade for a continuous period of at least 1 year immediately before such reduction.

(c) *Retained grade.* For the 2-year period referred to in paragraphs (a) and (b) of this section, the retained grade of GAO employees shall be treated as the grade of the employee's position for all purposes (including pay and pay administration, retirement, life insurance and eligibility for training and promotion) except—

(1) For purposes of § 5.2(a).

(2) For purposes of applying any reduction-in-force procedures.

(3) For purposes of determining whether the employee is covered by a merit pay system.

(4) For such other purposes as the Comptroller General may provide by regulation.

(d) *Termination of retained grade.* The foregoing provisions of this section shall cease to apply to any GAO employee who—

(1) Has a break in service of 1 workday or more;

(2) Is demoted for personal cause or at the employee's request;

(3) Is placed in, or declines, a reasonable offer of, a position the grade of which is equal or higher than the retained grade; or

(4) Elects in writing to have the benefits of this chapter terminate.

(e) *Pay retention.* (1) Any GAO employee: who ceases to be entitled to a retained grade by reason of the expiration of the 2-year period; or who (but for this paragraph) would be subject to a reduction in pay under circumstances prescribed by the Comptroller General by regulation to warrant the application of this paragraph is entitled to—

(2) Basic pay at a rate equal to the employee's allowable former rate of basic pay, plus 50 percent of the amount of each increase in the maximum rate of basic pay payable for the employee's position immediately after such reduction in pay if such allowable former rate exceeds such maximum rate for such grade.

(f) "*Allowable former rate of basic pay.*" This means the lower of—

(1) The rate of basic pay payable to the employee immediately before the reduction in pay; or

(2) 150 percent of the maximum rate of basic pay payable for the grade of the employee's position immediately after such reduction in pay.

(g) *Termination of retained pay.* The pay retention provisions in § 5.2(e) shall cease to apply to a GAO employee who—

(1) Has a break in service of 1 workday or more.

(2) Is entitled by operation of §§ 5.1, 5.2, and 5.3 to a rate of basic pay which is equal to or higher than, or declines a reasonable offer of a position the rate of basic pay for which is equal to or higher than, the rate to which the employee is entitled under § 5.2(e); or

(3) Is demoted for personal cause or at the employee's request.

(h) *Remedial actions.* Under regulations prescribed by the Comptroller General, Personnel shall—

(1) Obtain and make available to employees receiving benefits under this section, information on vacancies in other Federal agencies.

(2) Take such steps as may be appropriate to assure employees receiving benefits under this section have the opportunity to obtain necessary qualifications for the selection to positions which would minimize the need for the application of this section; and

(3) Establish a program under which employees receiving benefits under this section are given priority in the consideration for or placement in positions which are equal to their retained grade or pay.

(i) *Appeals.* In the case of the termination of any benefits to a GAO employee under this section on the grounds that such employee declined a reasonable offer of a position the grade or pay of which was equal to or greater than their retained grade or pay, after administrative remedies have been exhausted, such termination may be appealed to the GAO Personnel Appeals Board under procedures prescribed by the Board.

§5.3 Merit pay.

The Comptroller General may promulgate regulations establishing a merit pay system for such employees of the Government Accountability Office as the Comptroller General considers appropriate. The merit pay system shall be designed to carry out purposes consistent with those set forth in section 5401(a) of title 5, United States Code, which provides—

§5401. Purpose

(a) It is the purpose of this chapter to provide for—

(1) A merit pay system which shall—

(A) Within available funds, recognize and reward quality performance by varying merit pay adjustments;

(B) Use performance appraisals as the basis for determining merit pay adjustments;

(C) Within available funds, provide for training to improve objectivity and fairness in the evaluation of performance; and

(D) Regulate the costs of merit pay by establishing appropriate control techniques; and

(2) A cash award program which shall provide cash awards for superior accomplishment and special service.

§5.4 Pay administration.

The provisions of chapter 55 of title 5, U.S. Code and the Office of Personnel Management implementing regulations apply to Government Accountability Office employees.

§5.5 Travel, transportation, and subsistence.

The provisions of chapter 57 of title 5, U.S. Code and the implementing regulations for the Executive Branch apply to Government Accountability Office employees.

§5.6 Allowances.

The provisions of chapter 59 of title 5, U.S. Code and the implementing regulations for the Executive Branch apply to Government Accountability Office employees.

PART 6—ATTENDANCE AND LEAVE

AUTHORITY: 31 U.S.C. 732.

§6.1 Applicable law and regulations.

The provision of subpart E, title 5, United States Code and the Office of Personnel Management implementing regulations regarding "Attendance and Leave" apply to Government Accountability Office employees. This includes hours of work, annual leave, sick leave, and other paid leave.

[45 FR 68378, Oct. 15, 1980, as amended at 47 FR 56979, Dec. 22, 1982]

PART 7—PERSONNEL RELATIONS AND SERVICES

Sec.

AUTHORITY: 31 U.S.C. 732.

SOURCE: 45 FR 68378, Oct. 15, 1980, unless otherwise noted.

§7.1 Labor management relations.

(a) *Policy.* Each employee of GAO has the right, freely and without fear of penalty or reprisal, to form, join, or assist an employee organization, or to refrain from such activity.

(b) *Labor relations program.* A labor relations program consistent with chapter 71 of title 5, United States Code will be developed for the Government Accountability Office.

§7.2 Equal employment opportunity.

(a) *Policy.* All personnel actions affecting employees or applicants for employment in GAO shall be taken without regard to race, color, religion, age, sex, national origin, political affiliation, marital status or handicapping condition.

(b) *Equal opportunity recruiting program.* GAO shall conduct continuing programs for the recruitment of members of minorities and women for positions in GAO in a manner designed to eliminate underrepresentation of minorities and women in the various categories of employment in GAO. Special efforts will be directed at recruiting in minority communities, in educational institutions, and from other sources from which minorities can be recruited. GAO will conduct a continuing program of evaluation and oversight of such recruiting programs to determine their effectiveness in eliminating minority and women underrepresentation.

(c) *Statutory rights and remedies.* Nothing in this order shall be construed to abolish or diminish any right or remedy granted to employees of or applicants for employment in GAO—

(1) By section 717 of the Civil Rights Act of 1964 (42 U.S.C. 2000e–16);

(2) By sections 12 and 15 of the Age Discrimination in Employment Act of 1967 (29 U.S.C. 631, 633a);

(3) By section 6(d) of the Fair Labor Standards Act of 1938 (29 U.S.C. 206(d));

(4) By sections 501 and 505 of the Rehabilitation Act of 1973 (29 U.S.C. 791, 794a); or

(5) By any other law prohibiting discrimination in Federal employment on the basis of race, color, religion, age, sex, national origin, political affiliation, marital status or handicapping condition.

(d) Authorities granted thereunder to the Equal Employment Opportunity Commission, Office of Personnel Management, the Merit Systems Protection Board, or any other agency in the executive branch concerning oversight and appeals shall be exercised by the GAO Personnel Appeals Board. Other responsibilities shall be exercised by the Comptroller General.

§ 7.3 Political activities.

(a) In this section:

(1) *Contribution* means any gift, subscription, loan, advance, deposit of money, allotment of money, or anything of value given or transferred by one person to another, including in cash, by check, by draft, through a payroll deduction or allotment plan, by pledge or promise, whether or not enforceable, or otherwise.

(2) *Election* includes a primary, special, and general election.

(3) *Employee* means an individual who occupies a position in the Government Accountability Office.

(4) *Employer* or *employing authority* means the Comptroller General, his principals, or an employee's supervisor.

(5) *Federal workplace* means any place, site, installation, building, room, or facility in which any department or agency conducts official business, including, but not limited to, office buildings, forts, arsenals, navy yards, post offices, vehicles, ships, and aircraft.

(6) *Nonpartisan election* means—

(i) An election at which none of the candidates is to be nominated or elected as representing a political party any of whose candidates for presidential elector received votes in the last preceding election at which presidential electors were selected; and

(ii) An election involving a question or issue which is not specifically identified with a political party, such as a constitutional amendment, referendum, approval of a municipal ordinance, or any question or issue of a similar character.

(7) *Partisan* when used as an adjective refers to a political party.

(8) *Political fund* means any fund, organization, political action committee, or other entity that, for purposes of influencing in any way the outcome of any partisan election, receives or expends money or anything of value or transfers money or anything of value to any other fund, political party, candidate, organization, political action committee, or other entity.

(9) *Political party* means a national political party, a state political party, and an affiliated organization.

(b) All employees are free to engage in political activity to the widest extent consistent with the restrictions imposed by law and this section. Each employee retains the right to—

(1) Register and vote in any election;

(2) Express his opinion as an individual privately and publicly on political subjects and candidates;

(3) Display a political picture, sticker, badge, or button;

(4) Participate in the nonpartisan activities of a civic, community, social, labor, or professional organization, or of a similar organization;

(5) Be a member of a political party or other political organization and participate in its activities to the extent consistent with law;

(6) Attend a political convention, rally, fund-raising function, or other political gathering;

(7) Sign a political petition as an individual;

(8) Make a financial contribution to a political fund, political party, or organization;

(9) Take an active part, as an independent candidate, or in support of an independent candidate in a partisan election covered by paragraphs (h), (i), and (j) of this section;

(10) Take an active part, as a candidate or in support of a candidate, in a nonpartisan election;

(11) Be politically active in connection with a question which is not specifically identified with a political party, such as a constitutional amendment, referendum, approval of a municipal ordinance or any other question or issue of a similar character;

(12) Serve as an election judge or clerk, or in a similar position to perform nonpartisan duties as prescribed by state or local law; and

(13) Otherwise participate fully in public affairs, except as prohibited by law, in a manner which does not materially compromise his/her efficiency or integrity as an employee or the neutrality, efficiency, or integrity of the agency.

(c) Paragraph (b) of this section does not authorize an employee to engage in political activity in violation of law, while on duty. The Comptroller General may prohibit or limit the participation of an employee or class of employees in an activity permitted by paragraph (b) of this section, if participation in the activity would interfere with the efficient performance of official duties, or create a conflict or apparent conflict of interests.

(d) An employee may not use his/her official authority or influence for the purpose of interfering with or affecting the result of an election.

(e) An employee may not take an active part in political management or in a political campaign, except as permitted by this section.

(f) Activities prohibited by paragraph (e) of this section include but are not limited to—

(1) Serving as an officer of a political party, a member of a national, state, or local committee of a political party, an officer or member of a committee of a partisan political club, or being a candidate for any of these positions;

(2) Organizing or reorganizing a political party organization or political club;

(3) Directly or indirectly soliciting, receiving, collecting, handling, disbursing, or accounting for assessments, contributions, or other funds for a partisan political purpose;

(4) Organizing, selling tickets to, promoting, or actively participating in a fund-raising activity of a candidate in a partisan election or of a political party, or political club;

(5) Taking an active part in managing the political campaign of a candidate for public office in a partisan election or a candidate for political party office;

(6) Becoming a candidate for, or campaigning for, an elective public office in a partisan election;

(7) Soliciting votes in support of or in opposition to a candidate for public office in a partisan election or a candidate for political party office;

(8) Acting as recorder, watcher, challenger, or similar officer at the polls on behalf of a political party or a candidate in a partisan election;

(9) Driving voters to the polls on behalf of a political party or a candidate in a partisan election;

(10) Endorsing or opposing a candidate for public office in a partisan election or a candidate for political party office in a political advertisement, a broadcast, campaign, literature, or similar material;

(11) Serving as a delegate, alternate, or proxy to a political party convention;

(12) Addressing a convention, caucus, rally, or similar gathering of a political party in support of or in opposition to a partisan candidate for public office or political party office;

(13) Initiating or circulating a partisan nominating petition;

(14) Soliciting, collecting, or receiving a contribution at or in the federal

workplace from any employee for any political party, political fund, or other partisan recipient;

(15) Paying a contribution at or in the federal workplace to any employee who is the employer or employing authority of the person making the contribution for any political party, political fund, or other partisan recipient; and

(16) Soliciting, paying, collecting, or receiving a contribution at or in the federal workplace from any employee for any political party, political fund, or other partisan recipient.

(g) Paragraph (f) of this section does not apply to—

(1) The Comptroller General or the Deputy Comptroller General;

(2) An employee who resides in a municipality or other political subdivision designated under paragraph (i), subject to the conditions of paragraphs (i) and (j) of this section; or

(3) An employee who works on an irregular or occasional basis, on the days that he/she performs no services.

(h) Paragraph (f) of this section does not prohibit activity in political management or in a political campaign by an employee in connection with—

(1) A nonpartisan election, or

(2) Subject to the conditions and limitations established by the Comptroller General, an election held in a municipality or political subdivision designated under paragraph (i) of this section.

(i) For the purpose of paragraph (h)(2) of this section, the Comptroller General may designate a municipality or political subdivision in Maryland or Virginia in the immediate vicinity of the District of Columbia or a municipality in which the majority of voters are employed by the Government of the United States, when the Comptroller General determines that, because of special or unusual circumstances, it is in the domestic interest of employees to participate in local elections. The following municipalities and political subdivisions have been designated:

In Maryland

Annapolis
Anne Arundel County
Berwyn Heights
Bethesda
Bladensburg
Bowie
Brentwood
Capitol Heights
Cheverly
Chevy Chase, sections 1, 2, 3, and 4 Martin's Additions 1, 2, 3, and 4 to Chevy Chase
Chevy Chase View
College Park
Cottage City
District Heights
Edmonston
Fairmont Heights
Forest Heights
Garrett Park
Glendarden
Glen Echo
Greenbelt
Howard County
Hyattsville
Kensington
Landover Hills
Montgomery County
Morningside
Mount Rainier
New Carrollton
North Beach
North Brentwood
North Chevy Chase
Northwest Park
Prince Georges County
Riverdale
Rockville
Seat Pleasant
Somerset
Takoma Park
University Park
Washington Grove

In Virginia

Alexandria
Arlington County
Clifton
Fairfax County
Town of Fairfax
Falls Church
Herndon
Loudoun County
Manassas
Manassas Park
Portsmouth
Prince William County
Stafford County
Vienna

Other Municipalities

Anchorage, AK
Benicia, CA
Bremerton, WA
Centerville, GA
Crane, IN
District of Columbia
Elmer City, WA
Huachuca City, AZ
New Johnsonville, TN
Norris, TN
Port Orchard, WA

Sierra Vista, AZ
Warner Robins, GA

(j) An employee who resides in a municipality or political subdivision listed in paragraph (i) of this section may take an active part in political management and political campaigns in connection with partisan elections for local offices of the municipality or political subdivision, subject to the following limitations:

(1) Participation in politics shall be as an independent candidate or on behalf of, or in opposition to, an independent candidate.

(2) Candidacy for, and service in, an elective office shall not result in neglect of or interference with the performance of the duties of the employee or create a conflict, or apparent conflict, of interests.

[53 FR 26421, July 13, 1988]

§7.4 Employment limitations, foreign gifts and decorations, and misconduct.

The provisions of subchapters II, IV, and V of chapter 73 of title 5, United States Code and implementing regulations thereunder continue to apply to this office.

§7.5 Adverse actions: Suspensions for 14 days or less.

(a) *Policy.* A GAO employee may be suspended for 14 days or less for such cause as will promote the efficiency of GAO (including discourteous conduct to the public confirmed by an immediate supervisor's report of four such instances within any 1-year period or any other pattern of discourteous conduct). Suspension means placing an employee, for disciplinary reasons, temporarily in a status without duties and pay.

(b) *Employee entitlement.* An employee against whom a suspension for 14 days or less is proposed is entitled to—

(1) An advance written notice stating the specific reasons for the proposed action;

(2) A reasonable time to answer orally and in writing and to furnish affidavits and other documentary evidence in support of the answer;

(3) Be represented by an attorney or other representative; and

(4) A written decision and the specific reasons therefore at the earliest practicable date.

(c) *Documentation.* Copies of the notice of proposed action, the answer of the employee if written, a summary thereof if made orally, the notice of decision and reasons therefor, and any order effecting the suspension, together with any supporting material, shall be maintained by Personnel and shall be furnished to the employee affected upon the employee's request.

(d) *Nonapplicability.* This section is not applicable to—(1) An employee who is serving a trial period under an initial appointment in GAO or who has not completed 1 year of current continuous employment in the same or similar positions in GAO under other than a temporary appointment limited to 1 year or less.

(2) A suspension in the interest of national security.

§7.6 Adverse actions: Removal, suspension for more than 14 days, reduced in grade, reduced in pay or furloughed for 30 days or less.

(a) *Policy.* A GAO employee may be removed, suspended for more than 14 days, reduction in grade or pay, or furlough for 30 days or less for such cause as will promote the efficiency of GAO. Furloughed means placing an employee in a temporary status without duties and pay because of lack of work or funds or other nondisciplinary reasons.

(b) *Employee entitlement.* An employee against whom an action is proposed under this section is entitled to—

(1) At least 30 days' advance written notice, unless there is reasonable cause to believe the employee has committed a crime for which a sentence of imprisonment may be imposed, stating the specific reasons for the proposed action,

(2) A reasonable time to answer orally and in writing and to furnish affidavits and other documents in support of the answer.

(3) Be represented by an attorney or other representative; and

(4) A written decision and the specific reasons therefor at the earliest practicable date.

(c) *Appeals.* After administrative remedies have been exhausted, an employee against whom an action is taken under this section is entitled to appeal to the GAO Personnel Appeals Board.

(d) *Documentation.* Copies of the notice of proposed action, the answer of the employee if written, a summary thereof when made orally, the notice of decision and reasons therefor, and any order affecting an action covered by this section, together with any supporting material, shall be maintained by Personnel and shall be furnished to the GAO Personnel Appeals Board upon its request and to the employee affected upon the employee's request.

(e) *Nonapplicability.* This section does not apply to—

(1) Employees who are serving a trial period under an initial appointment or who has not completed 1 year of current continuous employment under other than a temporary appointment limited to 1 year or less.

(2) A suspension or removal of an employee in the interests of national security.

(3) A reduction in force.

(4) The reduction in grade of a supervisor or manager who has not completed the probationary period.

(5) A reduction in grade or removal for unacceptable performance under part 4.

(6) An action ordered by the GAO Personnel Appeals Board.

§ 7.7 Other appeals and grievances.

The personnel system shall provide procedures for the processing of complaints and grievances which are not otherwise provided for.

§ 7.8 Services to employees.

The provisions of chapter 79 of title 5, United States Code, and the Office of Personnel Management implementing regulations apply to Government Accountability Office employees.

PART 8—INSURANCE AND ANNUITIES

AUTHORITY: 31 U.S.C. 732.

§ 8.1 Applicable law and regulations.

The provisions of subpart G, title 5, United States Code and implementing regulations for the Executive Branch covering compensation for work injuries, retirement, unemployment compensation, life insurance, and health insurance apply to Government Accountability Office employees.

[45 FR 68380, Oct. 15, 1980, as amended at 47 FR 56979, Dec. 22, 1982]

PART 9—SENIOR EXECUTIVE SERVICE

AUTHORITY: 31 U.S.C. 733.

§ 9.1 GAO Senior Executive Service.

(a) The Comptroller General may promulgate regulations establishing a Government Accountability Office Senior Executive Service which meets the requirements set forth in section 3131 of title 5, United States Code, which provides—

§ 3131 The GAO Senior Executive Service

The Senior Executive Service shall be administered so as to—

(1) Provide for a compensation system, including salaries, benefits, and incentives, and for other conditions of employment, designed to attract and retain highly competent senior executives;

(2) Ensure that compensation, retention, and tenure are contingent on executive success which is measured on the basis of individual and organizational performance (including such factors as improvements in efficiency, productivity, quality of work or service, cost efficiency, and timeliness of performance and success in meeting equal employment opportunity goals);

(3) Assure that senior executives are accountable and responsible for the effectiveness and productivity of employees under them;

(4) Recognize exceptional accomplishment;

(5) Enable the head of an agency to reassign senior executives to best accomplish the agency's mission;

(6) Provide for severance pay, early retirement, and placement assistance for senior executives who are removed from the Senior Executive Service for nondisciplinary reasons;

(7) Protect senior executives from arbitrary or capricious actions;

(8) Provide for program continuity in the management of GAO programs;

(9) Maintain a merit personnel system free of prohibited personnel practices;

(10) Ensure accountability for honest, economical, and efficient Government;

(11) Ensure compliance with all applicable personnel laws, rules, and regulations, including those related to equal employment opportunity, political activity, and conflicts of interest;

(12) Provide for the initial and continuing systematic development of highly competent senior executives;

(13) Provide for an executive system which is guided by the public interest and free from improper political interference; and

(14) Appoint career executives to fill Senior Executive Service positions to the extent practicable, consistent with the effective and efficient implementation of agency policies and responsibilities.

(b) Requirements for positions included in the GAO Senior Executive System. The GAO Senior Executive Service may include—

(1) The 100 positions authorized by 31 U.S.C. 732(c)(4);

(2) The position of the General Counsel authorized by 31 U.S.C. 731(c);

(3) The 5 positions authorized by 31 U.S.C. 731(d); and

(4) The 10 positions authorized by 31 U.S.C. 731(e)(2).

[45 FR 68380, Oct. 15, 1980, as amended at 47 FR 56979, Dec. 22, 1982]

PART 11—RECOGNITION OF ATTORNEYS AND OTHER REPRESENTATIVES

Sec.

AUTHORITY: 31 U.S.C. 711.

SOURCE: 41 FR 35155, Aug. 20, 1976, unless otherwise noted. Redesignated at 45 FR 68374, Oct. 15, 1980.

§11.1 Right to representation before the Government Accountability Office.

Each person having a claim or other rights assertable in the Government Accountability Office may pursue such claim or right individually or through an attorney or other representative.

§11.2 Practice by attorneys.

Any person who is a member in good standing of the bar of the Supreme Court of the United States or of the highest court of any State, territory, or the District of Columbia, and is not under any order of any court suspending, enjoining, restraining, disbarring, or otherwise restricting him in the practice of law, may represent others before the Government Accountability Office.

§11.3 Authority to represent in payment cases.

In the prosecution of claims involving payments to be made by the United States, a proper power of attorney is required before an attorney or other representative may be recognized. A power of attorney from the principal may also be requested in other cases.

§11.4 Authority to represent in other cases.

When an attorney acting in a representative capacity appears in person or signs a document submitted to the Government Accountability Office in connection with a matter other than one involving a payment to be made by the United States, his personal appearance or signature shall constitute a representation that he is authorized and qualified to represent the particular party in whose behalf he acts. In the case of representatives other than attorneys, a simple written declaration from the principal will be accepted as evidence of the authority of the representative to act on behalf of the principal.

§11.5 Revocation of authority to represent.

Prior to the conclusion of action by the Government Accountability Office on a matter in which a principal is represented by another person whose authority to act is established under either §11.3 or §11.4, the principal may revoke the authority of his representative. Such revocation is not effective unless it is in writing and signed by the principal and until the written revocation is received by the Government Accountability Office. Upon notification of the death of the principal during the pendency of any matter involving representation of the principal by an attorney or other party, the Government Accountability Office will consider the representative's authority to have been automatically revoked.

SUBCHAPTER B—GENERAL PROCEDURES

PART 21—BID PROTEST REGULATIONS

AUTHORITY: 31 U.S.C. 3551–3556.

SOURCE: 61 FR 39042, July 26, 1996, unless otherwise noted.

EDITORIAL NOTE: Nomenclature changes to part 21 appear at 73 FR 32429, June 9, 2008.

§ 21.0 Definitions.

(a)(1) *Interested party* means an actual or prospective bidder or offeror whose direct economic interest would be affected by the award of a contract or by the failure to award a contract.

(2) In a public-private competition conducted under Office of Management and Budget (OMB) Circular A–76 regarding performance of an activity or function of a Federal agency, or a decision to convert a function performed by Federal employees to private sector performance without a competition under OMB Circular A–76, *interested party* also means

(i) The official responsible for submitting the Federal agency tender, and

(ii) Any one individual, designated as an agent by a majority of the employees performing that activity or function, who represents the affected employees.

(b)(1) *Intervenor* means an awardee if the award has been made or, if no award has been made, all bidders or offerors who appear to have a substantial prospect of receiving an award if the protest is denied.

(2) If an interested party files a protest in connection with a public-private competition conducted under OMB Circular A–76 regarding an activity or function of a Federal agency, the official responsible for submitting the Federal agency tender, or the agent representing the Federal employees as described in paragraph (a)(2)(ii) of this section, or both, may also be *intervenors*.

(c) *Federal agency* or *agency* means any executive department or independent establishment in the executive branch, including any wholly owned government corporation, and any establishment in the legislative or judicial branch, except the Senate, the House of Representatives, and the Architect of the Capitol and any activities under the Architect's direction.

(d) *Days* are calendar days. In computing any period of time described in Subchapter V, Chapter 35 of Title 31, United States Code, including those described in this part, the day from which the period begins to run is not counted, and when the last day of the period is a Saturday, Sunday, or Federal holiday, the period extends to the next day that is not a Saturday, Sunday, or Federal holiday. Similarly, when the Government Accountability Office (GAO), or another Federal agency where a submission is due, is closed for all or part of the last day, the period extends to the next day on which the agency is open.

(e) *Adverse agency action* is any action or inaction by an agency that is prejudicial to the position taken in a protest filed with the agency, including a decision on the merits of a protest; the opening of bids or receipt of proposals, the award of a contract, or the rejection of a bid or proposal despite a pending protest; or contracting agency acquiescence in continued and substantial contract performance.

(f) *Electronic Protest Docketing System (EPDS)* is GAO's web-based electronic docketing system. GAO's website [*https://epds.gao.gov/login*] includes instructions and guidance on the use of EPDS.

(g) A document is *filed* on a particular day when it is received in EPDS by 5:30 p.m., Eastern Time. Delivery of a protest or other document by means other than those set forth in the online EPDS instructions does not constitute a filing. Filing a document in EPDS constitutes notice to all parties of that filing.

(h) *Alternative dispute resolution* encompasses various means of resolving cases expeditiously, without a written decision, including techniques such as outcome prediction and negotiation assistance.

[61 FR 39042, July 26, 1996, as amended at 67 FR 79835, Dec. 31, 2002; 70 FR 19681, Apr. 14, 2005; 73 FR 32429, June 9, 2008; 83 FR 13823, Apr. 2, 2018]

§ 21.1 Filing a protest.

(a) An interested party may protest a solicitation or other request by a Federal agency for offers for a contract for the procurement of property or services; the cancellation of such a solicitation or other request; an award or proposed award of such a contract; and a termination of such a contract, if the protest alleges that the termination was based on improprieties in the award of the contract.

(b) Protests must be filed through the EPDS.

(c) A protest filed with GAO shall:

(1) Include the name, street address, email address, and telephone and facsimile numbers of the protester,

(2) Be signed by the protester or its representative,

(3) Identify the agency and the solicitation and/or contract number,

(4) Set forth a detailed statement of the legal and factual grounds of protest including copies of relevant documents,

(5) Set forth all information establishing that the protester is an interested party for the purpose of filing a protest,

(6) Set forth all information establishing the timeliness of the protest,

(7) Specifically request a ruling by the Comptroller General of the United States, and

(8) State the form of relief requested.

(d) In addition, a protest filed with GAO may:

(1) Request a protective order,

(2) Request specific documents, explaining the relevancy of the documents to the protest grounds, and

(3) Request a hearing, explaining the reasons that a hearing is needed to resolve the protest.

(e) The protester shall furnish a complete copy of the protest, including all attachments, to the individual or location designated by the agency in the solicitation for receipt of protests, or if there is no designation, to the contracting officer. The designated individual or location (or, if applicable, the contracting officer) must receive a complete copy of the protest and all attachments not later than 1 day after the protest is filed with GAO. The protest document must indicate that a complete copy of the protest and all attachments are being furnished within 1 day to the appropriate individual or location.

(f) No formal briefs or other technical forms of pleading or motion are required. Protest submissions should be concise and logically arranged, and should clearly state legally sufficient grounds of protest. Protests of different procurements should be separately filed.

(g) Unless precluded by law, GAO will not withhold material submitted by a protester from any party outside the government after issuing a decision on the protest, in accordance with GAO's rules at 4 CFR part 81. If the protester believes that the protest contains information which should be withheld, a statement advising of this fact must be on the front page of the submission. This information must be identified wherever it appears, and within 1 day after the filing of its protest, the protester must file a final redacted copy of the protest which omits the information.

(h) Protests and other documents containing classified information shall not be filed through the EPDS. Parties who intend to file documents containing classified information should notify GAO in advance to obtain advice regarding procedures for filing and handling the information.

(i) A protest may be dismissed for failure to comply with any of the requirements of this section, except for the items in paragraph (d) of this section. In addition, a protest shall not be dismissed for failure to comply with paragraph (e) of this section where the contracting officer has actual knowledge of the basis of protest, or the agency, in the preparation of its report, was not prejudiced by the protester's noncompliance.

[61 FR 39042, July 26, 1996, as amended at 67 FR 79835, Dec. 31, 2002; 73 FR 32430, June 9, 2008; 83 FR 13823, Apr. 2, 2018]

§21.2 Time for filing.

(a)(1) Protests based upon alleged improprieties in a solicitation which are apparent prior to bid opening or the time set for receipt of initial proposals shall be filed prior to bid opening or the time set for receipt of initial proposals. In procurements where proposals are requested, alleged improprieties which do not exist in the initial solicitation but which are subsequently incorporated into the solicitation must be protested not later than the next closing time for receipt of proposals following the incorporation. If no closing time has been established, or if no further submissions are anticipated, any alleged solicitation improprieties must be protested within 10 days of when the alleged impropriety was known or should have been known.

(2) Protests other than those covered by paragraph (a)(1) of this section shall be filed not later than 10 days after the basis of protest is known or should have been known (whichever is earlier), with the exception of protests challenging a procurement conducted on the basis of competitive proposals under which a debriefing is requested and, when requested, is required. In such cases, with respect to any protest basis which is known or should have been known either before or as a result of the debriefing, and which does not involve an alleged solicitation impropriety covered by paragraph (a)(1) of this section, the initial protest shall not be filed before the debriefing date offered to the protester, but shall be filed not later than 10 days after the date on which the debriefing is held.

(3) If a timely agency-level protest was previously filed, any subsequent protest to GAO must be filed within 10 days of actual or constructive knowledge of initial adverse agency action, provided the agency-level protest was filed in accordance with paragraphs (a)(1) and (2) of this section, unless the agency imposes a more stringent time for filing, in which case the agency's time for filing will control. In cases where an alleged impropriety in a solicitation is timely protested to an agency, any subsequent protest to GAO will be considered timely if filed within the 10-day period provided by this paragraph, even if filed after bid opening or the closing time for receipt of proposals.

(b) Protests untimely on their face may be dismissed. A protester shall include in its protest all information establishing the timeliness of the protest; a protester will not be permitted to introduce for the first time in a request for reconsideration information necessary to establish that the protest was timely.

(c) GAO, for good cause shown, or where it determines that a protest raises issues significant to the procurement system, may consider an untimely protest.

[61 FR 39042, July 26, 1996, as amended at 83 FR 13823, Apr. 2, 2018]

§21.3 Notice of protest, communications among parties, submission of agency report, and time for filing of comments on report.

(a) GAO shall notify the agency within 1 day after the filing of a protest, and, unless the protest is dismissed under this part, shall promptly provide a written confirmation to the agency and an acknowledgment to the protester. The agency shall immediately give notice of the protest to the awardee if award has been made or, if no award has been made, to all bidders or offerors who appear to have a substantial prospect of receiving an award. The agency shall provide copies of the protest submissions to those parties, except where disclosure of the information is prohibited by law, with instructions to communicate further directly with GAO. All parties shall provide copies of all communications with GAO to the agency and to other participating parties either through EPDS or by email. GAO's website [*https://epds.gao.gov/login*] includes guidance regarding when to file through EPDS versus communicating by email or other means.

(b) A agency or intervenor which believes that the protest or specific protest allegations should be dismissed before submission of an agency report should file a request for dismissal as soon as practicable.

(c) The agency shall file a report on the protest within 30 days after receiving notice of the protest from GAO. The report need not contain documents which the agency has previously provided or otherwise made available to the parties in response to the protest. At least 5 days prior to the filing of the report, in cases in which the protester has filed a request for specific documents, the agency shall file a response to the request for documents. If the fifth day prior to the filing of the report falls on a weekend or Federal holiday, the response shall be filed by the last business day that precedes the weekend or holiday. The agency's response shall, at a minimum, identify whether the requested documents exist, which of the requested documents or portions thereof the agency intends to produce, which of the requested documents or portions thereof the agency intends to withhold, and the basis for not producing any of the requested documents or portions thereof. Any objection to the scope of the agency's proposed disclosure or nondisclosure of documents must be filed within 2 days of receipt of this response.

(d) The report shall include the contracting officer's statement of the relevant facts (including a best estimate of the contract value), a memorandum of law, and a list and a copy of all relevant documents, or portions of documents, not previously produced, including, as appropriate: the bid or proposal submitted by the protester; the bid or proposal of the firm which is being considered for award, or whose bid or proposal is being protested; all evaluation documents; the solicitation, including the specifications; the abstract of bids or offers; and any other relevant documents. In appropriate cases, a party may file a request that another party produce relevant documents, or portions of documents, that are not in the agency's possession.

(e) Where a protester or intervenor does not have counsel admitted to a protective order and documents are withheld from the protester or intervenor on that basis, the agency shall file redacted documents that adequately inform the protester and/or intervenor of the basis of the agency's arguments in response to the protest. GAO's website [*https://epds.gao.gov/login*] provides guidance regarding filing documents where no protective order is issued or where a protester or intervenor does not have counsel admitted to a protective order.

(f) The agency may file a request for an extension of time for the submission of the response to be filed by the agency pursuant to §21.3(c) or for the submission of the agency report. Extensions will be granted on a case-by-case basis.

(g) The protester may file a request for additional documents after receipt of the agency report when their existence or relevance first becomes evident. Except when authorized by GAO, any request for additional documents must be filed not later than 2 days after their existence or relevance is known or should have been known, whichever is earlier. The agency shall file the requested documents, or portions of documents, within 2 days or explain why it is not required to produce the documents.

(h) Upon a request filed by a party, GAO will decide whether the agency must file any withheld documents, or portions of documents, and whether this should be done under a protective order. When withheld documents are provided, the protester's comments on the agency report shall be filed within the original comment filing period unless GAO determines that an extension is appropriate.

(i)(1) Comments on the agency report shall be filed within 10 days after the agency has filed the report, except where GAO has granted an extension of time, or where GAO has established a shorter period for filing of comments.

Extensions will be granted on a case-by-case basis.

(2) The protest shall be dismissed unless the protester files comments within the period of time established in §21.3(i)(1).

(3) GAO will dismiss any protest allegation or argument where the agency's report responds to the allegation or argument, but the protester's comments fail to address that response.

(j) GAO may request or permit the submission of additional statements by the parties and by other parties participating in the protest as may be necessary for the fair resolution of the protest. The agency and other parties must receive GAO's approval before submitting any additional statements. GAO reserves the right to disregard material submitted without prior approval.

[61 FR 39042, July 26, 1996, as amended at 67 FR 79835, Dec. 31, 2002; 73 FR 32430, June 9, 2008; 83 FR 13823, Apr. 2, 2018]

§21.4 Protective orders.

(a) At the request of a party or on its own initiative, GAO may issue a protective order controlling the treatment of protected information. Such information may include proprietary, confidential, or source-selection-sensitive material, as well as other information the release of which could result in a competitive advantage to one or more firms. The protective order shall establish procedures for application for access to protected information, identification and safeguarding of that information, and submission of redacted copies of documents omitting protected information. Because a protective order serves to facilitate the pursuit of a protest by a protester through counsel, it is the responsibility of protester's counsel to request that a protective order be issued and to submit timely applications for admission to that order. GAO generally does not issue a protective order where an intervenor retains counsel, but the protester does not.

(b) Any agency or party filing a document that the agency or party believes to contain protected material shall, if requested by another party, provide to the other parties (unless they are not admitted to the protective order) an initial proposed redacted version of the document within 2 days of the request. Where appropriate, the exhibits to the agency report or other documents may be proposed for redaction in their entirety. The party that authored the document shall file the final redacted version of the document that has been agreed to by all of the parties. Only the final agreed-to version of a redacted document must be filed. If the parties are unable to reach an agreement regarding redactions, the objecting party may submit the matter to GAO for resolution. Until GAO resolves the matter, the disputed information must be treated as protected.

(c) If no protective order has been issued, or a protester or intervenor does not have counsel admitted to a protective order, the agency may withhold from the parties those portions of its report that would ordinarily be subject to a protective order, provided that the requirements of §21.3(e) are met. GAO will review in camera all information not released to the parties.

(d) After a protective order has been issued, counsel or consultants retained by counsel appearing on behalf of a party may apply for admission under the order by filing an application. The application shall establish that the applicant is not involved in competitive decision-making for any firm that could gain a competitive advantage from access to the protected information and that there will be no significant risk of inadvertent disclosure of protected information. Objections to an applicant's admission shall be filed within 2 days after the application is filed, although GAO may consider objections filed after that time.

(e) Any violation of the terms of a protective order may result in the imposition of such sanctions as GAO deems appropriate, including referral to appropriate bar associations or other disciplinary bodies, restricting the individual's practice before GAO, prohibition from participation in the remainder of the protest, or dismissal of the protest.

[61 FR 39042, July 26, 1996, as amended at 67 FR 79835, Dec. 31, 2002; 73 FR 32430, June 9, 2008; 83 FR 13824, Apr. 2, 2018]

§ 21.5 Protest issues not for consideration.

A protest or specific protest allegations may be dismissed any time sufficient information is obtained by GAO warranting dismissal. Where an entire protest is dismissed, no agency report need be filed; where specific protest allegations are dismissed, an agency report shall be filed on the remaining allegations. Among the protest bases that shall be dismissed are the following:

(a) *Contract administration.* The administration of an existing contract is within the discretion of the agency. Disputes between a contractor and the agency are resolved pursuant to the disputes clause of the contract and the Contract Disputes Act of 1978. 41 U.S.C. 7101–7109.

(b) *Small Business Administration (SBA) issues*—(1) *Small business size standards and North American Industry Classification System (NAICS) standards.* Challenges of established size standards or the size status of particular firms, and challenges of the selected NAICS code may be reviewed solely by the SBA. 15 U.S.C. 637(b)(6).

(2) *Small Business Certificate of Competency Program.* Referrals made to the SBA pursuant to sec. 8(b)(7) of the Small Business Act, or the issuance of, or refusal to issue, a certificate of competency under that section will generally not be reviewed by GAO. The exceptions, which GAO will interpret narrowly out of deference to the role of the SBA in this area, are protests that show possible bad faith on the part of government officials, or that present allegations that the SBA failed to follow its own published regulations or failed to consider vital information bearing on the firm's responsibility due to the manner in which the information was presented to or withheld from the SBA by the procuring agency. 15 U.S.C. 637(b)(7).

(3) *Procurements under sec. 8(a) of the Small Business Act.* Under that section, since contracts are entered into with the SBA at the contracting officer's discretion and on such terms as are agreed upon by the procuring agency and the SBA, the decision to place or not to place a procurement under the 8(a) program is not subject to review absent a showing of possible bad faith on the part of government officials or that regulations may have been violated. 15 U.S.C. 637(a).

(c) *Affirmative determination of responsibility by the contracting officer.* Because the determination that a bidder or offeror is capable of performing a contract is largely committed to the contracting officer's discretion, GAO will generally not consider a protest challenging such a determination. The exceptions are protests that allege that definitive responsibility criteria in the solicitation were not met and those that identify evidence raising serious concerns that, in reaching a particular responsibility determination, the contracting officer unreasonably failed to consider available relevant information or otherwise violated statute or regulation.

(d) *Procurement integrity.* For any Federal procurement, GAO will not review an alleged violation of subsections (a), (b), (c), or (d) of sec. 27 of the Office of Federal Procurement Policy Act, 41 U.S.C. 2101-2107, as amended by sec. 4304 of the National Defense Authorization Act for Fiscal Year 1996, Public Law 104–106, 110 Stat. 186, February 10, 1996, where the protester failed to report the information it believed constituted evidence of the offense to the Federal agency responsible for the procurement within 14 days after the protester first discovered the possible violation.

(e) Protests not filed either with GAO or the agency within the time limits set forth in § 21.2.

(f) Protests that lack a detailed statement of the legal and factual grounds of protest as required by § 21.1(c)(4), or that fail to clearly state legally sufficient grounds of protest as required by § 21.1(f).

(g) *Procurements by agencies other than Federal agencies as defined by sec. 3 of the Federal Property and Administrative Services Act of 1949, 40 U.S.C. 102.* Protests of procurements or proposed procurements by agencies such as the U.S. Postal Service, the Federal Deposit Insurance Corporation, and non-appropriated fund activities are beyond GAO's bid protest jurisdiction as established in 31 U.S.C. 3551–3556.

(h) *Subcontract protests.* GAO will not consider a protest of the award or proposed award of a subcontract except where the agency awarding the prime contract has filed a request that subcontract protests be decided pursuant to §21.13.

(i) *Suspensions and debarments.* Challenges to the suspension or debarment of contractors will not be reviewed by GAO. Such matters are for review by the agency in accordance with the applicable provisions of the Federal Acquisition Regulation.

(j) *Competitive range.* GAO will not consider protests asserting that the protester's proposal should not have been included or kept in the competitive range.

(k) *Decision whether or not to file a protest on behalf of Federal employees.* GAO will not review the decision of an agency tender official to file a protest or not to file a protest in connection with a public-private competition.

(l) *Protests of orders issued under task or delivery order contracts.* As established in 10 U.S.C. 2304c(e) and 41 U.S.C. 4106(f), GAO does not have jurisdiction to review protests in connection with the issuance or proposed issuance of a task or delivery order except for the circumstances set forth in those statutory provisions.

(m) *Protests of awards, or solicitations for awards, of agreements other than procurement contracts.* GAO generally does not review protests of awards, or solicitations for awards, of agreements other than procurement contracts, with the exception of awards or agreements as described in §21.13; GAO does, however, review protests alleging that an agency is improperly using a non-procurement instrument to procure goods or services.

[61 FR 39042, July 26, 1996, as amended at 67 FR 79835, Dec. 31, 2002; 70 FR 19681, Apr. 14, 2005; 73 FR 32430, June 9, 2008; 83 FR 13824, Apr. 2, 2018]

§21.6 Withholding of award and suspension of contract performance.

When a protest is filed, the agency may be required to withhold award and to suspend contract performance. The requirements for the withholding of award and the suspension of contract performance are set forth in 31 U.S.C. 3553(c) and (d); GAO does not administer the requirements to withhold award or suspend contract performance. An agency shall file a notification in instances where it overrides a requirement to withhold award or suspend contract performance, and it shall file either a copy of any issued determination and finding, or a statement by the individual who approved the determination and finding that explains the statutory basis for the override.

[83 FR 13824, Apr. 2, 2018]

§21.7 Hearings.

(a) Upon a request filed by a party or on its own initiative, GAO may conduct a hearing in connection with a protest. The request shall set forth the reasons why a hearing is needed to resolve the protest.

(b) Prior to the hearing, GAO may hold a pre-hearing conference to discuss and resolve matters such as the procedures to be followed, the issues to be considered, and the witnesses who will testify.

(c) Hearings generally will be conducted as soon as practicable after receipt by the parties of the agency report and relevant documents. Although hearings ordinarily will be conducted at GAO in Washington, DC, hearings may, at the discretion of GAO, be conducted at other locations, or by telephone or other electronic means.

(d) All parties participating in the protest shall be invited to attend the hearing. Others may be permitted to attend as observers and may participate as allowed by GAO's hearing official. In order to prevent the improper disclosure of protected information at the hearing, GAO's hearing official may restrict attendance during all or part of the proceeding.

(e) GAO does not provide for hearing transcripts. If the parties wish to have a hearing transcribed, they may do so at their own expense, so long as a copy of the transcript is provided to GAO at the parties' expense.

(f) If a witness whose attendance has been requested by GAO fails to attend the hearing or fails to answer a relevant question, GAO may draw an inference unfavorable to the party for whom the witness would have testified.

(g) If a hearing is held, each party shall file comments with GAO within 5 days after the hearing was held or as specified by GAO. If the protester has not filed comments by the due date, GAO shall dismiss the protest.

(h) In post-hearing comments, the parties should reference all testimony and admissions in the hearing record that they consider relevant, providing specific citations to the testimony and admissions referenced.

[61 FR 39042, July 26, 1996, as amended at 67 FR 79836, Dec. 31, 2002; 83 FR 13825, Apr. 2, 2018]

§ 21.8 Remedies.

(a) If GAO determines that a solicitation, cancellation of a solicitation, termination of a contract, proposed award, or award does not comply with statute or regulation, it shall recommend that the agency implement any combination of the following remedies:

(1) Refrain from exercising options under the contract;

(2) Terminate the contract;

(3) Recompete the contract;

(4) Issue a new solicitation;

(5) Award a contract consistent with statute and regulation; or

(6) Such other recommendation(s) as GAO determines necessary to promote compliance.

(b) In determining the appropriate recommendation(s), GAO shall, except as specified in paragraph (c) of this section, consider all circumstances surrounding the procurement or proposed procurement including the seriousness of the procurement deficiency, the degree of prejudice to other parties or to the integrity of the competitive procurement system, the good faith of the parties, the extent of performance, the cost to the government, the urgency of the procurement, and the impact of the recommendation(s) on the agency's mission.

(c) If the head of the procuring activity determines that performance of the contract notwithstanding a pending protest is in the government's best interest, GAO shall make its recommendation(s) under paragraph (a) of this section without regard to any cost or disruption from terminating, recompeting, or reawarding the contract.

(d) If GAO determines that a solicitation, proposed award, or award does not comply with statute or regulation, it may recommend that the agency pay the protester the costs of:

(1) Filing and pursuing the protest, including attorneys' fees and consultant and expert witness fees; and

(2) Bid and proposal preparation.

(e) *Recommendation for reimbursement of costs.* If the agency decides to take corrective action in response to a protest, GAO may recommend that the agency pay the protester the reasonable costs of filing and pursuing the protest, including attorneys' fees and consultant and expert witness fees. The protester shall file any request that GAO recommend that costs be paid not later than 15 days after the date on which the protester learned (or should have learned, if that is earlier) that GAO had closed the protest based on the agency's decision to take corrective action. The agency shall file a response within 15 days after the request is filed. The protester shall file comments on the agency response within 10 days of receipt of the response. GAO shall dismiss the request unless the protester files comments within the 10-day period, except where GAO has granted an extension or established a shorter period.

(f) *Recommendation on the amount of costs.* (1) If GAO recommends that the agency pay the protester the costs of filing and pursuing the protest and/or of bid or proposal preparation, the protester and the agency shall attempt to reach agreement on the amount of costs. The protester shall file its claim for costs, detailing and certifying the time expended and costs incurred, with the agency within 60 days after receipt of GAO's recommendation that the agency pay the protester its costs. Failure to file the claim within that time may result in forfeiture of the protester's right to recover its costs.

(2) The agency shall issue a decision on the claim for costs as soon as practicable after the claim is filed.

(3) If the protester and the agency cannot reach agreement regarding the amount of costs within a reasonable time, the protester may file a request that GAO recommend the amount of costs to be paid, but such request shall

be filed within 10 days of when the agency advises the protester that the agency will not participate in further discussions regarding the amount of costs.

(4) Within 15 days after receipt of the request that GAO recommend the amount of costs to be paid, the agency shall file a response. The protester shall file comments on the agency response within 10 days of receipt of the response. GAO shall dismiss the request unless the protester files comments within the 10-day period, except where GAO has granted an extension or established a shorter period.

(5) In accordance with 31 U.S.C. 3554(c), GAO may recommend the amount of costs the agency should pay. In such cases, GAO may also recommend that the agency pay the protester the costs of pursuing the claim for costs before GAO.

(6) Within 60 days after GAO recommends the amount of costs the agency should pay the protester, the agency shall file a notification of the action the agency took in response to the recommendation.

[61 FR 39042, July 26, 1996, as amended at 67 FR 79836, Dec. 31, 2002; 83 FR 13825, Apr. 2, 2018]

§21.9 Time for decision by GAO.

(a) GAO shall issue a decision on a protest within 100 days after it is filed. GAO will attempt to resolve a request for recommendation for reimbursement of protest costs under §21.8(e), a request for recommendation on the amount of protest costs under §21.8(f), or a request for reconsideration under §21.14 within 100 days after the request is filed.

(b) In protests where GAO uses the express option procedures in §21.10, GAO shall issue a decision on a protest within 65 days after it is filed.

(c) GAO, to the maximum extent practicable, shall resolve a timely supplemental protest adding one or more new grounds to an existing protest, or a timely amended protest, within the time limit established in paragraph (a) of this section for decision on the initial protest. If a supplemental or an amended protest cannot be resolved within that time limit, GAO may resolve the supplemental or amended protest using the express option procedures in §21.10.

[61 FR 39042, July 26, 1996, as amended at 83 FR 13825, Apr. 2, 2018]

§21.10 Express options, flexible alternative procedures, accelerated schedules, summary decisions, and status and other conferences.

(a) Upon a request filed by a party or on its own initiative, GAO may decide a protest using an express option.

(b) The express option will be adopted at the discretion of GAO and only in those cases suitable for resolution within 65 days.

(c) Requests for the express option shall be filed not later than 5 days after the protest or supplemental/amended protest is filed. GAO will promptly notify the parties whether the case will be handled using the express option.

(d) When the express option is used, the following schedule applies instead of those deadlines in §21.3 and §21.7:

(1) The agency shall file a complete report within 20 days after it receives notice from GAO that the express option will be used.

(2) Comments on the agency report shall be filed within 5 days after receipt of the report.

(3) Where circumstances demonstrate that a case is no longer suitable for resolution using the express option, GAO shall establish a new schedule for submissions by the parties.

(e) GAO, on its own initiative or upon a request filed by the parties, may use flexible alternative procedures to promptly and fairly resolve a protest, including alternative dispute resolution, establishing an accelerated schedule, and/or issuing a summary decision.

(f) GAO may conduct status and other conferences by telephone or in person with all parties participating in a protest to promote the expeditious development and resolution of the protest.

[61 FR 39042, July 26, 1996, as amended at 67 FR 79836, Dec. 31, 2002; 83 FR 13825, Apr. 2, 2018]

§21.11 Effect of judicial proceedings.

(a) A protester must immediately advise GAO of any court proceeding which involves the subject matter of a pending protest and must file copies of all relevant court documents.

(b) GAO will dismiss any case where the matter involved is the subject of litigation before, or has been decided on the merits by, a court of competent jurisdiction. GAO may, at the request of a court, issue an advisory opinion on a bid protest issue that is before the court. In these cases, unless a different schedule is established, the times provided in this part for filing the agency report (§ 21.3(c)), filing comments on the report (§ 21.3(i)), holding a hearing and filing comments (§ 21.7), and issuing a decision (§ 21.9) shall apply.

[61 FR 39042, July 26, 1996, as amended at 67 FR 79836, Dec. 31, 2002; 83 FR 13825, Apr. 2, 2018]

§ 21.12 Distribution of decisions.

(a) Unless it contains protected information, a copy of a decision shall be provided to the protester, any intervenors, and the agency involved; a copy also shall be made available to the public. A copy of a decision containing protected information shall be provided only to the agency and to individuals admitted to any protective order issued in the protest. A public version omitting the protected information shall be prepared wherever possible.

(b) Decisions will be distributed to the parties through the EPDS.

[61 FR 39042, July 26, 1996, as amended at 67 FR 79836, Dec. 31, 2002; 73 FR 32430, June 9, 2008; 83 FR 13825, Apr. 2, 2018]

§ 21.13 Nonstatutory protests.

(a) GAO will consider protests concerning awards of subcontracts by or for a Federal agency, sales by a Federal agency, or procurements by agencies of the government other than Federal agencies as defined in § 21.0(c) if the agency involved has agreed in writing to have protests decided by GAO.

(b) The provisions of this part shall apply to nonstatutory protests except for:

(1) Section 21.8(d) and (e) pertaining to recommendations for the payment of costs; and

(2) Section 21.6 pertaining to the withholding of award and the suspension of contract performance pursuant to 31 U.S.C. 3553(c) and (d).

[61 FR 39042, July 26, 1996, as amended at 83 FR 13825, Apr. 2, 2018]

§ 21.14 Request for reconsideration.

(a) The protester, any intervenor, and any Federal agency involved in the protest may request reconsideration of a bid protest decision. GAO will not consider a request for reconsideration that does not contain a detailed statement of the factual and legal grounds upon which reversal or modification is deemed warranted, specifying any errors of law made or information not previously considered.

(b) A request for reconsideration of a bid protest decision shall be filed not later than 10 days after the basis for reconsideration is known or should have been known, whichever is earlier.

(c) GAO will summarily dismiss any request for reconsideration that fails to state a valid basis for reconsideration or is untimely. To obtain reconsideration, the requesting party must show that GAO's prior decision contains errors of either fact or law, or must present information not previously considered that warrants reversal or modification of the decision; GAO will not consider a request for reconsideration based on repetition of arguments previously raised.

[61 FR 39042, July 26, 1996, as amended at 73 FR 32430, June 9, 2008; 83 FR 13825, Apr. 2, 2018]

PART 22—RULES OF PROCEDURE OF THE GOVERNMENT ACCOUNTABILITY OFFICE CONTRACT APPEALS BOARD

AUTHORITY: Sec. 1501, Public Law 110–161, 121 Stat. 2249.

SOURCE: 73 FR 36258, June 26, 2008, unless otherwise noted.

§22.1 Applicability of Rules [Rule 1].

The Government Accountability Office Contract Appeals Board is authorized to hear appeals from decisions of contracting officers with respect to any contract entered into by a legislative branch agency. These rules shall apply to all appeals filed with the Board on or after October 1, 2007.

§22.2 Board Consideration [Rule 2].

(a) *Offices.* The office of the Board shall be at the Government Accountability Office, 441 G Street, NW., Washington, DC 20548, or in such other place as may from time to time hereafter be assigned for its use. All files and records of the Board shall be kept at such office. All communications, pleadings, and/or documents addressed to the Board shall be addressed or delivered to the Board at the Government Accountability Office, 441 G Street, NW., Room 7182, Washington, DC 20548; Telephone: 202–512–3342; Facsimile: 202–512–9749; E-mail: *cab@gao.gov.*

(b) *Three member panel.* Generally, all appeals will be assigned to a panel of three members of the Board appointed by the Chairman of the Board; said panel may or may not include the Chairman of the Board as a member. Each panel will include a presiding member who is responsible for case management, including scheduling, and who may, without participation of the other panel members, rule on non-dispositive motions and resolve procedural disputes. Hearings on appeals may be held by one or more of the panel members of the Board. Appeals resolved under the Board's small claims or accelerated procedures (see §22.22 of this part [Rule 22]) may be decided by a single member of the Board. Requests for consideration of a matter by all members of the Contract Appeals Board will not be granted in any appeal filed under these rules.

(c) *Absence or disability of Chairman.* The activities of the Board shall be performed under the supervision of the Chairman of the Board. In the absence of, or during the disability of, the Chairman, the Vice Chairman of the Board shall act as the Chairman.

§22.3 Appeals—How Taken [Rule 3].

(a) *Form.* An appeal by the contractor shall be filed with the Board in the form of a written notice of appeal. The notice shall identify the contract by number, the name of the government agency and/or department against which the claim is asserted, the contracting officer for the subject dispute, the decision from which the appeal is taken, an estimate of the amount of money in controversy, if any, and shall be signed personally by the appellant (the contractor making the appeal) or by his representative or attorney. The complaint referred to in §22.5(a) of this part [Rule 5(a)] may be filed with the notice of appeal or the appellant may designate the notice of appeal as a complaint if it otherwise fulfills the requirements of a complaint. The appellant shall promptly provide a copy of the appeal and complaint to the contracting officer.

(b) *Timeliness.* (1) For claims where a contracting officer has issued a final decision, the contractor may file an appeal no later than 90 days after it receives the contracting officer's final decision.

(2) For certified claims submitted to the contracting officer in excess of $50,000 where the contracting officer has not issued a final decision within a

reasonable time, taking into account such factors as the size and complexity of the claim, the contractor may file a notice of appeal citing the failure of the contracting officer to issue a decision.

(3) For claims submitted to the contracting officer in the amount of $50,000 or less where the contracting officer has not issued a final decision within 60 days of the contractor's request that a final decision be issued within that time, the contractor may file a notice of appeal citing the failure of the contracting officer to issue a decision.

(4) In lieu of a notice of appeal filed under paragraphs (b)(2) or (b)(3) of this section [Rules 3(b)(2) or 3(b)(3)], the contractor may request that the Board direct a contracting officer to issue a decision within a specified period of time, as determined by the Board, in the event of undue delay by the contracting officer in issuing a decision.

(5) An appeal filed with the Board will be deemed "filed" on the date actually received by the Board if received by 5:30 p.m. local time in Washington, DC, or on the next business day if received after 5:30 p.m.

(c) *Service of the appeal; copies.* An original plus 3 copies of the appeal shall be filed with the Board by hand delivery, express or priority mail, approved commercial carrier (e.g., UPS or FedEx), facsimile, or e-mail, although e-mail is the preferred method of delivery in all Board matters. The use of first class or parcel post mail is strongly discouraged because the delivery delays and screening process for government mail could result in untimely filed appeals. If filed by e-mail or facsimile, the appellant shall provide the original plus 3 copies to the Board by hand delivery or commercial carrier within 2 business days of the e-mailed or facsimile transmitted filing. The appellant shall furnish a copy of the appeal to the contracting officer from whose decision, or failure to issue the decision, the appeal is taken using the same method or service as for the Board, or an equal or more expeditious method of service. For service of documents once an appeal has commenced, see § 22.7(b) of this part [Rule 7(b)].

(d) *Docketing.* When the Board receives a notice of appeal from the appellant, the Board will promptly docket the appeal and provide written notice of docketing to all parties, or their counsel, with a copy of these rules.

(e) *Consolidation.* The Board, in its discretion, may consolidate cases involving common issues of law or fact.

[73 FR 36258, June 26, 2008, as amended at 73 FR 60610, Oct. 14, 2008]

§ 22.4 Appeal File [Rule 4].

(a) *Duties of the Contracting Officer.* (1) Within 30 days after receipt of the complaint, or within such other period of time as may be established by the Board, the contracting officer shall assemble and transmit to the Board an appeal file consisting of all documents pertinent to the appeal, including:

(i) The decision from which the appeal is taken;

(ii) The contract, including relevant specifications, amendments, plans, and drawings;

(iii) All correspondence between the parties relevant to the appeal, including the letter or letters of claim in response to which the decision was issued;

(iv) All documents and other tangible things on which the contracting officer relied in making the decision, and any correspondence relating thereto;

(v) Transcripts of any testimony taken during the course of proceedings, and affidavits or statements of any witnesses on the matter in dispute made prior to the filing of the notice of appeal with the Board; and

(vi) Any additional information or evidence considered relevant to the appeal.

(2) Within the same time specified above, the contracting officer shall furnish the appellant a copy of each document he or she transmits to the Board, except those in paragraph (a)(1)(ii) of this section [Rule 4(a)(1)(ii)]. As to the latter, a list furnished to the appellant indicating specific contractual documents transmitted will suffice. Documents filed under this rule, and any supplements, shall be organized and filed in accordance with paragraph (d) of this section [Rule 4(d)].

(b) *Duties of the appellant.* Within 30 days after receipt of a copy of the appeal file provided pursuant to paragraph (a) of this section [Rule 4(a)], or within such other period of time as may be established by the Board, the appellant shall transmit to the Board for inclusion in the appeal file any documents not contained therein which the appellant considers to be relevant to the appeal. Within the same period of time, the appellant shall furnish a copy of such documents to the contracting officer or counsel for the government. Documents filed under this rule shall be organized and filed in accordance with paragraph (d) of this section [Rule 4(d)].

(c) *Continuing duty to supplement the record.* All parties have a continuing duty to supplement the record with relevant documents and tangible things, and the appeal file may be supplemented by any party at any time before the closing of the record. In cases where a hearing is requested, these supplements shall be provided well in advance of the pre-hearing conference so that objections to admissibility may be heard and resolved, to the maximum extent possible, in advance of the hearing. All supplements to the appeal file shall be organized and filed in accordance with paragraph (d) of this section [Rule 4(d)].

(d) *Organization of appeal file.* Only relevant documents and tangible things should be provided as part of the appeal file. Appeal file documents may be originals or true, legible, and complete copies or facsimiles. The appeal file shall be arranged in chronological order with the earliest documents first; bound in a 3-ring binder (or binders) or similar loose-leaf binder(s) no larger than 4 inches in width, except where size or shape makes such binding impracticable; numbered; tabbed; and indexed. Numbering of pages shall be consecutive and continuous from one page to the next (*i.e.*, "Bates" numbered), so that the complete file, including any supplements, will consist of one set of consecutively numbered pages. Preceding each Bates number shall be a designation "A" for appellant or "R" for respondent, indicating which party provided the document. Multiple binders shall be consecutively numbered and include references on the outside cover and binding that state the range of tab numbers and Bates numbers contained therein. Within each binder, tabs shall separate each document; multiple documents shall not be placed behind a single tab, unless each document is separated by a divider. The appeal file shall include an index identifying each document included in the appeal file by date, brief description of the document, and the tab and Bates numbers where the document can be located in the appeal file. The Board may, in its discretion or upon request of a party, order an alternative organization of the appeal file. If an alternative organization of the appeal file is permitted, such as by document type or topic, documents within that grouping must be presented in chronological order to the extent possible. The Board may impose special requirements on the production of electronic documents and, if any portion of the §22.4 [Rule 4] file or supplement contains electronic documents, the party submitting such documents shall contact the Board before submission for guidance.

(e) *Submissions on order of the Board.* The Board may, at any time during the pendency of the appeal, require any party to file documents or tangible things as additional exhibits. The Board may also require a party to file printed versions of electronic records or, conversely, may require electronic versions of printed documents.

(f) *Status of documents in the record.* Documents contained in the appeal file are considered, without further action by the parties, as part of the record upon which the Board will render its decision. However, a party may object to consideration of a particular document or documents by filing a written objection. Such objections shall be raised by motion pursuant to §22.6 of this part [Rule 6] and shall be filed as early as necessary to allow the Board, to the maximum extent possible, to resolve the objection in advance of a scheduled hearing, or before the record is closed if no hearing is held.

§22.5 Pleadings [Rule 5].

(a) *Complaint.* Within 15 days after receipt of the docketing notice from the Board, or within such other period of time as may be established by the Board, the appellant will file with the Board, if not previously filed with the notice of appeal, a complaint setting forth simple, concise, and direct statements of each of its claims showing that it is entitled to relief; identifying the contract provision or provisions under which relief is claimed; and stating the amount in controversy or an estimate thereof, if known, and/or the relief requested. The complaint shall be limited to those requests for relief which have been presented to the contracting officer and were either denied or not ruled upon by the contracting officer in accordance with § 22.3 of this part [Rule 3]. No technical form is required, but each claim should be separately identified. In the event that the complaint is not filed within the time stated above, the appeal may be dismissed by the Board for lack of prosecution.

(b) *Answer.* Within 30 days after receipt of the complaint, or within such other period of time as may be established by the Board, the contracting officer or counsel for the government shall prepare and file with the Board an answer thereto. The answer shall set forth simple, concise, and direct statements of the government's defenses to each claim asserted by the appellant. Each defense shall be stated with as much particularity as is practicable. Defenses which go to the Board's jurisdiction may be included in the answer, or may be raised by motion pursuant to the provisions of § 22.6 of this part [Rule 6]. Motions in lieu of an answer may be filed only with the advance permission of the Board.

(c) *Small claims and accelerated procedures.* When an appellant elects to use the small claims or accelerated procedures described in § 22.22 of this part [Rule 22], the Board may shorten the time for filing the complaint and answer.

(d) *Amendment of pleadings.* At any time before a hearing on the merits, or before the closing of the record when a hearing is not held, the Board in its discretion may permit a party to amend its complaint or answer concerning matters that are within the proper scope of the appeal, upon conditions that are just to both parties. The Board, upon its own initiative or upon application by a party, may in its discretion order a party to make a more definite statement of its complaint or answer, or to reply to an answer. When issues within the proper scope of the appeal, but not raised by the complaint and answer, are determined by express or implied consent of the parties as having been raised, they shall be treated in all respects as if they had been raised in the pleadings. Such amendment of the complaint and answer as may be necessary to cause them to conform to the evidence may be made upon motion at any time, but failure to so amend does not affect the result of the hearing of these issues. If evidence is objected to at the hearing on the ground that it is not within the issues raised by the complaint and answer, the Board may allow the pleadings to be amended within the proper scope of the appeal and shall do so freely when the presentation of the merits of the action will be served thereby and the objecting party fails to satisfy the Board that the admission of such evidence would prejudice it in maintaining its appeal or defense on the merits. The Board may, however, grant a continuance to enable the objecting party to respond to such evidence.

§ 22.6 Motions, Briefs, and Other Statements [Rule 6].

(a) *Motions, generally.* Motions shall be made in writing, indicate the relief sought and include the grounds therefor, and be filed with the Board as soon as practicable after the grounds therefor are known and as early as necessary to allow the Board to rule on the motion in advance of a scheduled hearing. Except for motions submitted under paragraph (d) of this section [Rule 6(d)], any party may respond to a motion by submitting a written response to the motion within 10 days of receipt of the motion, and the moving party may reply to the response within 5 days of receipt of the response, except that the Board, in its discretion, may shorten or lengthen the time for the response and reply based on the nature of the motion, the nature and timing of the case, and the scheduling needs of the Board. The Board may request additional submissions from the parties and may decide motions on the written submissions without oral argument.

The Board shall decide all motions before the hearing on the merits unless the Board determines that a ruling be deferred pending a hearing on both the merits and the motion. Jurisdictional and procedural defenses may be raised at any time by motion, but should be raised as soon as the grounds therefor are known; and the Board, at any time and on its own initiative, may raise an issue of jurisdiction and may decline to proceed with an appeal in which it lacks authority to decide the issues. All motions, responses, replies, and additional submissions required by the Board shall be filed in accordance with paragraphs (b) and (c) of this section [Rules 6(b) and 6(c)].

(b) *Briefs and citations.* In addition to submissions required by these rules, the Board may require the parties to file legal or factual briefs concerning any matter that may aid in the disposition of the appeal. When such briefs or submissions are required (by rule or by the Board), the brief or submission shall contain citations to the record and legal authority as appropriate, and follow such other format as may be directed by the Board. Citations to the record must be specific (*i.e.*, to Bates number or other similar designation) so that the Board can locate the exact proposition or matter to which the party is referring. The parties should not expect the Board to search the record for evidence in support of either party's position. Briefs and submissions that are not submitted in the required format, or which do not contain adequate citations to the record or legal authority, may be rejected by the Board or returned to the party with an order that the party resubmit the brief or submission with appropriate revisions.

(c) *Declarations, affidavits, or other statements.* Any declaration, affidavit, or other statement that is submitted to explain the record must, to the maximum extent possible, include citations to the record in support of the statement, argument, or analysis made. Citations to the record must be specific (*i.e.*, to Bates number or similar designation). Declarations, affidavits, or other statements containing inadequate citations may be returned to the party with an order that the party resubmit the statement with appropriate revisions.

(d) *Motions for summary judgment*—(1) *Generally.* Motions for summary judgment or partial summary judgment shall be filed only when a party believes, based on uncontested material facts, that it is entitled to relief, in whole or in part, as a matter of law. Such motions shall be filed as soon as practicable to allow the Board to rule on the motion in advance of a scheduled hearing. In considering a motion, or partial motion, for summary judgment, the Board will consider the pleadings, depositions, answers to interrogatories, admissions of record, and affidavits provided, and will grant such motion if there is no genuine issue of material fact and the moving party is entitled to judgment as a matter of law. In deciding motions for summary judgment, the Board will look to Rule 56 of the Federal Rules of Civil Procedure for guidance.

(2) *Requirements.* Where both parties agree that disposition by summary judgment or partial summary judgment is appropriate, they shall file a stipulation of all material facts necessary for the Board to rule on the motion. Otherwise, the moving party shall file with its motion a "Statement of Undisputed Material Facts" setting forth the claimed undisputed material facts in separately numbered paragraphs, each of which shall be supported by citations to the § 22.4 [Rule 4] file or other evidence establishing the facts. The non-moving party shall file a "Statement of Genuine Issues of Material Facts," responding to each numbered paragraph, demonstrating the existence of genuine issues of material facts where appropriate, and including for each fact citations to the § 22.4 [Rule 4] file or other evidence in support. A fact properly proposed by one party may be accepted by the Board as undisputed unless the opposing party properly responds and establishes that the fact is in dispute. An opposing party may not rely on mere allegations or denials in its pleadings to demonstrate the existence of a genuine issue of material fact. Either party may rely on affidavits, depositions, answers to interrogatories, or admissions of record to establish the existence of,

or to dispute, a material fact. The moving party and non-moving party each shall submit a memorandum of law supporting or opposing summary judgment, and the moving party may file a reply to the non-moving party's opposition of the motion.

(3) *Time.* Generally, the non-moving party shall file its opposition to a motion for summary judgment or partial summary judgment within 20 days of receipt of the motion, and the moving party's reply is due within 10 days of receipt of the opposition, except that the Board, in its discretion, may shorten or lengthen the time for opposition and reply based on the nature of the motion, the nature and timing of the case, and the scheduling needs of the Board.

(4) *Citations.* All motions for summary judgment, oppositions to such motions, briefs, and statements in support of the motions or opposition to the motions shall be filed in conformance with paragraphs (b) and (c) of this section [Rules 6(b) and 6(c)].

§ 22.7 Copies and Service Thereof [Rule 7].

(a) *Rule 4 file.* For documents provided pursuant to § 22.4 of this part [Rule 4], the original and one copy shall be provided to the Board, and one copy shall be provided to each party. Documents shall be provided by hand delivery, express or priority mail, or approved commercial carrier (e.g., UPS or FedEx); first class and parcel post mail are not permitted unless authorized by the Board.

(b) *Other submissions filed with the Board.* Except as otherwise authorized by the Board, all correspondence and submissions, other than documents provided pursuant to § 22.4 of this part [Rule 4] and appeals filed under § 22.3(c) of this part [Rule 3(c)], shall be provided to the Board by e-mail at *cab@gao.gov*, with a courtesy copy of the submission provided by e-mail to each of the members of the Board. All e-mails to *cab@gao.gov* must identify the case name and docket number in the subject line of the e-mail. In addition, unless the Board directs otherwise, the original plus 3 copies of the e-mailed submission also shall be provided to the Board by hand delivery, express or priority mail, or approved commercial carrier (e.g., UPS or FedEx) within 2 business days of the e-mailed filing (except that the original and one copy are required for appeals involving small claims or using accelerated procedures). Delivery to the Board by first class or parcel post mail is not permitted. However, the Board may at any time modify the number of copies required or authorize alternative methods of delivery to the Board.

(c) *Service on parties.* All correspondence and submissions to the Board must be provided to all other parties using the same method of service as used for the Board, or an equal or more expeditious method of service. Except for documents provided pursuant to § 22.4 of this part [Rule 4], e-mail service is preferred. However, where the parties agree to other methods of service, such other methods of service to parties are permitted.

(d) *Proof of service.* A party sending a document to the Board must represent to the Board that a copy has been sent to the other parties, identify the date on which service was made, and identify the method of delivery used. This may be done by certificate of service, by notation of a photostatic copy (cc:), or by any other means that can reasonably be expected to show the Board that the other party has been provided a copy, the date on which the copy was provided, and the method of delivery used to provide the copy. Proof of service must be provided to the Board at the time of filing. If proof of service is not provided, the Board may decline to consider the document in the appeal.

§ 22.8 General Discovery Procedures [Rule 8].

(a) *General policy and methods of discovery.* The parties are encouraged to engage in voluntary discovery procedures and may obtain discovery by one or more of the following methods: Depositions; written interrogatories; requests for admissions; and requests for production of documents, electronically stored information, other tangible things, or entry onto land.

(b) *Scope of discovery.* Except as otherwise limited by order of the Board, the parties may obtain discovery regarding any matter, not privileged, which is relevant to the subject matter involving the pending appeal, whether it relates to a claim or defense of a party, including the existence, description, nature, custody, condition, and location of any books, documents, electronically stored information, or other tangible things, and the identity and location of persons having knowledge of any discoverable matter. It is not a ground for objection that the information sought will be inadmissible if the information sought appears reasonably calculated to lead to the discovery of admissible evidence.

(c) *Discovery plan, conferences, and orders.* Within 30 days of the initial filing of documents in accordance with § 22.4(a) of this part [Rule 4(a)], the parties shall confer and file with the Board a proposed discovery plan, which shall include estimated time frames and proposed dates for completing discovery and when the parties anticipate that a hearing can be scheduled. Upon request of a party or on its own initiative, the Board may at any time hold an informal meeting or telephone conference with the parties to identify outstanding issues relating to discovery; establish a plan and schedule for discovery; set limitations on discovery; compel compliance with discovery; and issue such orders or determine such other matters as are necessary for the proper management of discovery, including imposing sanctions on the parties as may be appropriate.

(d) *Discovery limits.* On motion or on its own initiative, the Board may make any order necessary to protect a party or person from annoyance, embarrassment, oppression, or undue burden or expense. Such order may impose limitations on the scope, method, time and place for discovery, and include provisions for protecting the secrecy of confidential information or documents.

(e) *Discovery objections.* Unless otherwise ordered by the Board, any objection to a discovery request must be filed with the Board within 15 days of receipt of the request. Objections must be filed in writing and state with specificity the grounds therefor. Upon receipt, the Board will establish a schedule for resolving the objections, which may include additional briefing by the parties or oral argument, and will determine the extent to which discovery will be permitted. A party shall fully respond to any discovery request to which it does not file a timely objection, in accordance with paragraph (f) of this section [Rule 8(f)]. The parties are required to make a good faith effort to resolve objections to discovery requests informally prior to seeking relief from the Board.

(f) *Discovery responses.* Unless otherwise ordered by the Board, a party is required to respond to written interrogatories, requests for admission, and requests for production of documents, electronically stored information, other tangible things, or entry onto land within 30 days of receipt.

(g) *Duty to supplement discovery responses.* A party that has responded to written interrogatories, requests for admission, or requests for production of documents, electronically stored information, or other tangible things, upon becoming aware of deficiencies or inaccuracies in its original responses, or upon acquiring additional information or documents relevant thereto, shall, as quickly as practicable, and as often as necessary, supplement its responses to the requesting party with correct and sufficient additional information and such additional documents as are necessary to give a complete and accurate response to the request.

(h) *Voluntary cooperation.* Each party is expected to cooperate by making available witnesses and evidence under its control when requested by another party, and to secure the voluntary attendance of third-party witnesses and production of evidence by third parties, when practicable.

(i) *Motions to compel discovery.* If a party refuses to comply with a discovery request, or a party's response to a discovery request is incomplete or entirely absent, any other party may file a motion to compel a response. However, such motion must include a representation that the moving party has tried in good faith, prior to filing the motion, to resolve the matter informally. The motion to compel shall include a copy of each discovery request at issue and the response, if any.

(j) *Sanctions.* If, after being properly served with such discovery request, a party fails to appear for deposition, respond to interrogatories or requests for admissions, or respond to a request for production of documents, electronically stored information, other tangible things, or entry onto land, the party seeking discovery may move the Board to impose sanctions under § 22.10 of this part [Rule 10].

(k) *Discovery motions, timing.* All motions concerning discovery, including motions to compel discovery, shall be filed on or before the scheduled end date of discovery to the maximum extent practicable. Motions that are filed after the end date of discovery will not be considered except for good cause shown.

[73 FR 36258, June 26, 2008, as amended at 73 FR 60610, Oct. 14, 2008]

§ 22.9 Subpoenas [Rule 9].

(a) *Issuance.* Upon the written request of any party, or on the initiative of the Board, a subpoena may be issued that commands the person to whom it is directed to attend and give testimony at a deposition or hearing, and/or produce documents or electronically stored information (including writings, papers, books, accounts, photographs, drawings, graphs, charts, recordings, and other data or data compilations) or other tangible things designated in the subpoena, or to permit entry onto designated premises for inspection or other purposes. Requests for subpoenas shall identify the Board and state the name and docket number of the appeal; identify the name of the person to whom the subpoena is directed; command the person to whom the subpoena is directed to, at a specific place and time, appear and testify, or produce designated documents, electronically stored information, or other tangible things, or permit the inspection of designated premises; and state the scope and relevance of the requested testimony or evidence to the appeal. All requests for subpoenas shall be filed at least 15 days before the testimony or evidence is to be provided, except that the Board may, in its discretion, honor requests for subpoenas not made within this time limitation.

(b) *Service.* The party requesting the subpoena shall cause the subpoena to be served upon the person named in the subpoena as soon as practicable after the subpoena has been issued and shall provide proof of service to the Board. Service shall be made by any person who is not a party and not less than 18 years of age by personal delivery to the person named in the subpoena, and shall include tender of the fees for one day attendance and the mileage allowed by 28 U.S.C. 1821 or other applicable law; however, where the subpoena is issued on behalf of the government, money payments need not be tendered in advance of attendance.

(c) *Motions to quash.* Upon written motion of the person named in the subpoena or a party, the Board may quash or modify the subpoena if it is unreasonable and oppressive or for other good cause shown, or the Board may require the party in whose behalf the subpoena was issued to advance the reasonable costs of producing subpoenaed evidence. Motions to quash or modify a subpoena must be filed within 10 days of service of the subpoena or by the date and time specified in the subpoena for compliance, whichever is earlier.

(d) *Contumacy.* In the case of contumacy or refusal to obey a subpoena by a person who resides, is found, or transacts business within the jurisdiction of a United States district court, the Board may apply to the court through the Attorney General of the United States for an order requiring the person to appear before the Board to give testimony, produce evidence, or both.

§ 22.10 Sanctions [Rule 10].

(a) *Standards.* All parties and their representatives, attorneys, and any experts/consultants retained by them or their attorneys, must obey directions and orders prescribed by the Board and adhere to standards of conduct applicable to such parties and persons. As to an attorney, the standards include the rules of professional conduct and ethics of the jurisdictions in which an attorney is licensed to practice, to the extent that those rules are relevant to conduct affecting the integrity of the Board, its process, and its proceedings.

The Board will also look to professional guidelines in evaluating an individual's conduct.

(b) *Imposition of sanctions.* (1) When a party or its representative or attorney or any expert/consultant fails to comply with any direction or order issued by the Board (including an order to provide or permit discovery), or engages in misconduct affecting the Board, its process, or its proceedings, the Board may make such orders as are just, including the imposition of appropriate sanctions. The sanctions may include:

(i) Taking the facts pertaining to the matter in dispute to be established for the purpose of the appeal in accordance with the contention of the party submitting the discovery request;

(ii) Forbidding challenge of the accuracy of any evidence;

(iii) Refusing to allow the noncompliant party to support or pose designated claims or defenses;

(iv) Prohibiting the noncompliant party from introducing in evidence designated documents or items of testimony;

(v) Striking pleadings or parts thereof, or staying further proceedings until the order is obeyed;

(vi) Dismissing the appeal or any part thereof; and/or

(vii) Imposing such other sanctions as the Board deems appropriate.

(2) Prior to imposing sanctions, the Board will provide the noncompliant party with notice and an opportunity to be heard on the issue of whether sanctions should be imposed. The opportunity to be heard does not mean that the party is entitled to a hearing; the opportunity to provide written argument shall satisfy this requirement.

(c) *Disciplinary proceedings.* In addition to the above procedures, the Board may discipline individual party representatives, attorneys, and experts/consultants for a violation of any Board order or direction or standard of conduct applicable to such individual where the violation affects the integrity of the Board's process or proceedings. Sanctions may be public or private and may include admonishment, disqualification from a particular matter, referral to an appropriate licensing authority, or such other action as circumstances may warrant. The Board, in its discretion, may suspend an individual from appearing before the Board as a party representative, attorney, or expert/consultant if, after affording such individual notice and an opportunity to be heard, a majority of all members of the Contact Appeals Board determines that such sanction is warranted.

§22.11 Depositions [Rule 11].

(a) *When depositions may be taken.* After an appeal has been docketed by the Board and a complaint has been filed, either party may take the testimony of any person by deposition upon oral examination or written questions, for the purpose of discovery or for use as evidence in the appeal proceedings, or for both purposes.

(b) *Time, place, and manner of taking.* The time, place, and manner of taking depositions shall be as mutually agreed to by the parties or, failing such agreement, be governed by order of the Board.

(c) *Limits.* The number of depositions taken shall not be limited except as the Board may require to protect a party from annoyance, burden, or harassment.

(d) *Use as evidence.* No testimony taken by deposition shall be considered as part of the evidence in the hearing of an appeal unless and until such testimony is offered and received in evidence at the hearing. Depositions ordinarily will not be received in evidence if the deponent is present and can testify personally at the hearing; however, depositions may be used to contradict or impeach the testimony of a deponent as a witness. If only a part of a deposition is offered in evidence by a party, an adverse party may require the offering party to introduce any other part which in fairness ought to be considered with the part introduced. In any case, the Board, upon the agreement of the parties, may permit the introduction of relevant portions of depositions as designated by the parties. If no hearing has been conducted and the appeal has been submitted on the record pursuant to §22.17 of this part [Rule 17], the Board, in its discretion, may receive depositions in evidence to supplement the record.

§22.12 Interrogatories [Rule 12].

(a) *When interrogatories may be served.* After an appeal has been docketed by the Board and a complaint has been filed, a party may serve on an adverse party written interrogatories to be answered by the party served or, if the party served is a public or private corporation or a partnership or association, by any officer or agent who shall furnish such information as is available to the party.

(b) *Answers.* The interrogatories shall be answered separately and fully in writing, signed under oath by the person answering them, and served on the party submitting the interrogatories. Objections to the interrogatories shall be signed by counsel for the party responding to the interrogatories. An interrogatory is not necessarily objectionable merely because an answer to the interrogatory may involve an opinion or contention that relates to fact or the application of law to fact; however, the Board may order that such interrogatory need not be answered until after discovery has been completed or some other event has occurred.

(c) *Scope and use as evidence.* Interrogatories may relate to any matters which can be inquired into under §22.11 of this part [Rule 11] (Depositions), and the answers may be used to the same extent as provided for the use of the deposition of a party.

(d) *Limits.* The number of interrogatories or sets of interrogatories to be served shall not be limited except as the Board may require to protect a party from annoyance, burden, or harassment.

(e) *Option to produce business records.* Where the answer to an interrogatory may be derived or ascertained from the business records of the party upon which the interrogatory has been served, and the burden of deriving or ascertaining the answer is substantially the same for the party serving the interrogatory as for the party served, it is a sufficient answer to such interrogatory to specify the record(s) from which the answer may be derived or ascertained and to afford the party serving the interrogatory a reasonable opportunity to examine, audit, or inspect such records and to make copies thereof. Such specification shall be in sufficient detail to permit the interrogating party to locate and to identify, as readily as can the party served, the record(s) from which the answer may be ascertained.

§22.13 Requests for Admission [Rule 13].

(a) *When requests for admission may be served.* (1) After an appeal has been docketed by the Board and a complaint has been filed, a party may serve on the opposing party a written request for the admission by the latter of the genuineness of any relevant documents described in and exhibited with the request, or of the truth of any relevant matters of fact set forth in the request. Each of the matters for which an admission is requested shall be deemed admitted unless, within the period designated in §22.8(c) and §22.8(f) of this part [Rules 8(e) and 8(f)] for responding to discovery requests, the party to whom the request is directed serves upon the party requesting the admission either:

(i) A sworn statement denying specifically the matters for which an admission is requested or setting forth in detail the reasons why he or she cannot truthfully admit or deny those matters, or

(ii) Written objections on the ground that some or all of the requested admissions are privileged or irrelevant or that the request is otherwise improper in whole or in part.

(2) If written objections to a part of the request are made, the remainder of the request shall be answered within the period designated in Rule 8(f). A denial shall fairly meet the substance of the requested admission and, when good faith requires that a party deny only a part of a matter for which an admission is requested, he or she shall specify so much of it as is true and deny only the remainder.

(b) *Limits.* The number of requests for admissions served shall not be limited except as the Board may require to protect a party from annoyance, burden, or harassment.

(c) *Use as evidence.* Any matter admitted is conclusively established for the purpose of the pending action, unless the Board, on motion, permits withdrawal or amendment of the admission.

[73 FR 36258, June 26, 2008, as amended at 73 FR 60610, Oct. 14, 2008]

§22.14 Production of Documents, Electronically Stored Information, Other Tangible Things, or Entry Onto Land [Rule 14].

(a) *When documents, electronically stored information, other tangible things, or entry onto land may be requested.* After an appeal has been docketed by the Board and a complaint has been filed, any party may serve on any other party a request—

(1) To produce and permit the inspection, copying, or photographing of any designated documents or electronically stored information (including writings, papers, books, accounts, photographs, drawings, graphs, charts, recordings, and other data or data compilations), or other tangible things, not privileged, which are in his, her, or its possession, custody, or control and which are within the scope of discovery as described in §22.8(b) of this part [Rule 8(b)]; or

(2) To permit entry onto designated land or other property in his or its possession or control for the purpose of inspecting, measuring, surveying, filming, or photographing the property or any designated object or operation thereon which is within the scope of discovery as described in §22.8(b) of this part [Rule 8(b)].

(b) *Time, place, and manner.* The request shall specify the time, place, and manner of making the inspection and taking the copies and photographs. The Board may make an order that the inspection, copying, measuring, surveying, filming, or photographing shall be limited to certain matters; or the Board may make any other order which, in its discretion, it deems appropriate to protect the party from annoyance, burden, or harassment.

§22.15 Conferences and Orders [Rule 15].

(a) *Initial status conference.* As soon as practicable after the filing of the complaint and answer, the Board shall schedule an initial status conference to discuss the issues of the case, the procedures available under the Board's rules of resolution of the case, and a tentative schedule for such resolution, including the plan for possible discovery required by Rule 8(c), the possibility of alternative dispute resolution (see Rule 24), and the possibility of dispositive motions.

(b) *Status conferences and reports.* At any time during the appeal, the Board, upon its own initiative or upon the request of one of the parties, may call upon the parties or their attorneys or representatives to appear before the Board (or one or more members thereof) for a status conference to consider or report on whatever matters are necessary to aid in the disposition of the appeal. Such matters may include, for example, the simplification or clarification of issues, the necessity or desirability of amendments to the pleadings, agreements and rulings to facilitate discovery, progress reports during discovery, and pre-hearing procedures and scheduling. Status conferences may be conducted in person or by telephone, and the Board generally will make an order which recites the action taken at the conference(s). From time to time, the Board also may require one or more of the parties, either jointly or individually, to provide status reports concerning any matter that aids in the disposition of the appeal.

(c) *Rulings, orders, and directions.* The Board may make such rulings and issue such orders and directions as are necessary to secure the informal, expeditious, and inexpensive resolution of every case before the Board. Any ruling, order, or direction that the Board may make or issue pursuant to the rules of this Board may be made on the motion of any party or on the initiative of the Board. The Board may also amend, alter, or vacate a ruling, order, or direction upon such terms as it deems appropriate. In making rulings and issuing orders and directions, the Board will take into consideration those Federal Rules of Civil Procedure and Federal Rules of Evidence which address matters not specifically covered herein.

[73 FR 60610, Oct. 14, 2008]

§22.16 Hearings [Rule 16].

(a) *Election of hearing or record submission.* Each party shall inform the

Board, in writing, whether it elects a hearing or submission of the case on the record pursuant to § 22.17 of this part [Rule 17]. Such election shall occur no later than 15 days after the conclusion of discovery, unless the Board directs otherwise. In the event that only one party waives a hearing and submits its case on the record, the Board shall proceed with a hearing attended by the remaining parties.

(b) *Pre-hearing schedule.* (1) Within 30 days of the conclusion of discovery, the parties shall meet and confer and provide the Board with a joint proposed schedule for pre-hearing and hearing disclosures, submissions, and key events. In the absence of agreement, each party shall submit its own proposed schedule. The schedule shall address, at a minimum, deadlines for submitting the following:

(i) Dispositive motions, motions for summary judgment, and motions in limine, which allow sufficient time for the Board to resolve the motions before the hearing;

(ii) Pre-hearing briefs or statements of the case;

(iii) The identification of lay and expert witnesses for hearing, the general substance of testimony to be offered by each witness, and any depositions that will be used in lieu of witness testimony;

(iv) The exchange of expert reports and statements (if not done during discovery);

(v) Proposed stipulations of fact;

(vi) The exchange of hearing exhibit books;

(vii) The production of any additional documents to be used at the hearing that are not already part of the § 22.4 [Rule 4] file;

(viii) Objections to proposed evidence or § 22.4 [Rule 4] file submissions;

(ix) Date for conducting a pre-hearing conference;

(x) Dates and duration of the hearing; and

(xi) Any other matter necessary for resolution before the hearing.

(2) As soon as practicable after receipt of the parties' proposed schedule(s), the Board will issue an order establishing a schedule for pre-hearing submissions and events, taking into account the parties' proposed schedule, the nature of the case, and the scheduling needs of the Board.

(c) *Pre-hearing conference.* Prior to the hearing, the Board will conduct a pre-hearing conference to discuss such matters as may be necessary to conduct an orderly and efficient hearing. Objections to evidence may be resolved during the pre-hearing conference or at such other time as established by the Board.

(d) *Pre-hearing briefs.* At least 20 days before a scheduled hearing, each party shall file, in accordance with § 22.6(b) of this part [Rule 6(b)], a pre-hearing statement of the case, which shall include the party's legal and factual analysis of the relevant issues, and how the party intends to prove its case.

(e) *Location of hearing.* Hearings will be held at 441 G Street, NW., Washington, DC 20548, unless otherwise ordered by the Board. The Board will consider a request for a hearing at another location if compelling reasons are timely presented.

(f) *Notice of hearing.* The parties, or their counsel, will be given at least 15 days notice of the time and place of a hearing on the merits, provided that the parties may, with the approval of the Board, waive notice and fix a mutually satisfactory time for the hearing. Continuances will not be granted except upon written request and for good cause.

(g) *Nature of hearing.* Hearings may be held by one or more of the panel members of the Board and shall be as informal as may be reasonable and appropriate under the circumstances. Each party may offer the testimony of witnesses, who shall be subject to cross-examination by the opposing party, and such relevant and material evidence as they deem appropriate and as would be admissible under paragraph (h) of this section [Rule 16(h)], subject, however, to the sound discretion of the presiding Board member in supervising the extent and manner of presentation of such evidence. Stipulations of fact agreed upon by the parties must be in writing, must be filed with the Board, and may be used as evidence at the hearing. The parties may also stipulate to the testimony that would be given by a witness if the witness were present. The Board may at any time during the hearing require evidence or argument in addition to that put forth by the parties.

(h) *Admissibility and weight of evidence.* In general, any relevant and material evidence that would be admissible under the Federal Rules of Evidence will be admitted to the record. However, evidence which may not be admissible under the Federal Rules of Evidence, including hearsay, may be admitted at the discretion of the presiding Board member. The Board may also exclude evidence to avoid unfair prejudice, confusion of the issues, undue delay, waste of time, or needless presentation of cumulative evidence. The weight to be attached to evidence and credibility to be accorded witnesses will be determined by the Board, in its discretion.

(i) *Examination of witnesses.* Witnesses before the Board will be examined orally under oath or affirmation, unless the facts are stipulated or the Board shall otherwise order. If the testimony of a witness is not given under oath, the Board may warn the witness that his or her statements may be subject to the provisions of title 18, United States Code, secs. 287 and 1001, and any other provisions of law imposing penalties for knowingly making false representations in connection with claims against the United States or in any matter within the jurisdiction of any department or agency thereof.

(j) *Availability of witnesses, documents, and other tangible things.* It is the responsibility of a party desiring to call any witness, or to use any document or other tangible thing as an exhibit in the course of a hearing, to ensure that whoever it wishes to call and whatever it wishes to use is available at the hearing. In the event that a witness does not appear or refuses to answer a question, or evidence requested by the Board is not produced, the Board may draw an adverse inference of the fact in question against the party responsible for providing the witness or evidence.

(k) *Issues not raised by the pleadings.* If evidence is objected to at a hearing on the ground that it is not within the issues raised by the pleadings, it may nevertheless be admitted by the Board, in its discretion, if it is within the proper scope of the appeal. If such evidence is admitted, the pleadings may be amended to conform to the evidence. The Board may also grant the objecting party a continuance to enable it to respond to the evidence.

(l) *Delay by the parties.* If the Board determines that the hearing is being unreasonably delayed by the failure of a party to produce evidence, or by the undue prolongation of the presentation of evidence, it may, by written order or by ruling from the bench, prescribe a time or times within which the presentation of evidence must be concluded, establish time limits on the direct or cross-examination of witnesses, and enforce such order or ruling by appropriate sanctions.

(m) *Exhibits.* Unless otherwise directed by the Board, each party shall prepare (jointly or individually) hearing exhibit books for use during the hearing, and shall provide such books to the Board and opposing counsel at least 3 days before the hearing commences. The books shall consist of documents (or relevant excerpts from documents) placed in a 3-ring binder or similar loose-leaf binder bound on the left margin, separated by numbered tabs, with an index of the documents in the front of each binder. The index shall identify the document by name and, where applicable, the §22.4 [Rule 4] file citation (tab and Bates numbers). Each document page included in the exhibit books must be marked with the corresponding Bates number or applicable numerical markings used in the §22.4 [Rule 4] file. Documents not contained within the hearing books shall be marked by the Board during the hearing. Documents contained in the hearing book that are not admitted into evidence during the hearing will not become part of the record unless already part of the §22.4 [Rule 4] file, or unless their inclusion in the record is requested by the presenting party and permitted by the Board.

(n) *Copies.* Copies of documents may be offered and received into evidence as exhibits, provided that they are of equal legibility and quality as the originals, and such copies shall have the same force and effect as if they were the originals. If the Board so directs, the party offering a copy of a document as an exhibit shall have the original available at the hearing for examination by the Board and any other party. When the original of a document has been received in evidence, an accurate copy thereof may be substituted in evidence for the original by leave of the Board at any time.

(o) *Absence of parties or counsel.* The unexcused absence of a party or his authorized representative at the time and place set for the hearing will not be occasion for delay. In such event, the hearing will proceed and the case will be regarded as submitted by the absent party unless he or she appears before the conclusion of the hearing and offers additional evidence.

(p) *Transcripts.* Unless the Board orders otherwise, all hearings will be stenographically or electronically recorded and transcribed. Other conferences and proceedings may be recorded or transcribed by order of the Board. Generally, the Board will arrange for the stenographer to record and transcribe the proceeding. Each party is responsible for purchasing its own copy of the transcript(s) or recording(s). Waiver of recordation and transcription may be especially suitable for appeals resolved under the small claims procedure prescribed in § 22.22(c) of this part [Rule 22(c)].

(q) *Post-hearing briefs.* The Board may require the submission of post-hearing briefs. In such case, briefs shall be filed within 30 days after receipt of the transcript of the hearing, and reply briefs shall be filed within 15 days after receipt of the initial post-hearing briefs, unless such other time period has been established by the Board. Post-hearing briefs shall be filed in accordance with the requirements of § 22.6(b) of this part [Rule 6(b)].

(r) *Post-hearing evidence.* No evidence shall be submitted by any party after the hearing has concluded, including but not limited to post-hearing declarations, unless authorized by the Board in its discretion.

[73 FR 36258, June 26, 2008, as amended at 73 FR 60610, Oct. 14, 2008]

§ 22.17 Submission on the Record Without a Hearing [Rule 17].

(a) *General requirements.* Pursuant to § 22.16(a) of this part [Rule 16(a)], either party may elect to submit its case on the record without a hearing. Submission of a case without a hearing does not relieve the parties from the necessity of proving the facts supporting their claims or defenses.

(b) *Conference in lieu of hearing.* If neither side desires a hearing, either party may request that a conference be held in lieu of a hearing with one or more members of the panel designated to decide the appeal, and such request may be granted at the discretion of the Board. The purpose of the conference is not to introduce new matters or evidence, but to permit explanations and argument of matters of record. If any new matter is introduced at the conference by either party, consideration of the appeal will be deferred until the opposing party has been apprised thereof and has had an opportunity to reply. Both parties will be afforded the right to be present at any such conference. At the request of a party, or on the Board's initiative, the conference may be stenographically or electronically recorded and transcribed pursuant to § 22.16(p) of this part [Rule 16(p)].

(c) *Statement of the case.* The Board, at its discretion, may order a party that submits its case on the record without a hearing to submit a written statement of the case, including a legal and factual analysis of the relevant issues, within such period of time as the Board allows. The Board may also order parties to submit reply briefs. Briefs will be filed in accordance with the requirements of § 22.6(b) of this part [Rule 6(b)].

§ 22.18 Closing the Record [Rule 18].

(a) *Closing the record.* The record will be closed on a date announced by the Board by written notice.

(b) *Supplementing the record after the record is closed.* Except as the Board may otherwise order in its discretion, no evidence shall be received after the record is closed. However, at any time after the closing of the record and prior to a decision of the appeal by the Board, at the request of a party or upon its own initiative, the Board may reopen the record for the purpose of receiving newly discovered evidence or for such other reason as may appear to the Board to be appropriate.

§ 22.19 Findings and Decisions of the Board [Rule 19].

(a) *Generally.* All proceedings shall be concluded and appeals disposed of as expeditiously as possible, commensurate with sound adjudicatory procedure. The findings and decision in each appeal shall be made by the members of the panel which considered that appeal, and the findings and decision of the majority thereof shall constitute the findings and decision of the Board. The absence or withdrawal of one member of the panel which considered that appeal shall not invalidate the proceedings, and the decision of the remaining panel members shall constitute the decision of the Board. All decisions and findings of the Board shall be made in writing and copies thereof shall be forwarded to the parties or their counsel.

(b) *Record upon which findings and decisions are based.* (1) The record upon which any decision of the Board will be rendered consists of the following:

(i) Notice of appeal;

(ii) Pleadings, motions, written briefs and statements, and responses thereto;

(iii) Rule 4 file and any supplements other than those to which an objection has been sustained;

(iv) Hearing exhibits other than those to which an objection has been sustained;

(v) Orders, rulings, and directions to the parties issued by the Board;

(vi) Written transcripts and electronic recordings of proceedings;

(vii) Stipulations, party admissions, depositions or parts thereof received in evidence, and written interrogatories and responses received in evidence;

(viii) Anything else that the Board may designate.

(2) All other documents and electronically stored information are part of the administrative record of the proceedings and are not included in the record upon which the Board's decision will be rendered.

§ 22.20 Mistakes and Corrections [Rule 20].

(a) *To decisions and orders.* Clerical mistakes in decisions or orders of the Board may be corrected at any time on the Board's own initiative or upon motion of a party, except that if an appeal has been filed with another tribunal, such mistakes may be corrected only with leave of that tribunal.

(b) *To the official transcript.* Corrections to an official transcript of a hearing will be made only when they involve errors affecting its substance. The Board may order such corrections on motion or on its own initiative and only after notice to the parties giving them an opportunity to object. Such corrections will ordinarily be made either by hand with pen and ink or by the appending of an errata sheet, or the Board may require that the reporter provide substitute or additional pages.

§ 22.21 Motion for Reconsideration [Rule 21].

A motion for reconsideration, if filed by either party, shall set forth specifically the ground or grounds relied upon to sustain the motion, and shall be filed within 15 days of receipt of a copy of the Board's decision. Mere disagreement with a decision, re-argument of points already made, or the presentation of new evidence that could have been presented during the appeal but was not, are not sufficient grounds for reconsideration. A motion pending under § 22.21 [Rule 21] does not affect the finality of a decision or suspend its operation.

§ 22.22 Accelerated and Small Claims Procedures [Rule 22].

(a) *Variation from standard proceedings.* The ultimate purpose of any Board proceeding is to resolve fairly and expeditiously any dispute properly before the Board. The Board may at any time during an appeal modify the procedures contained in these rules if it is deemed feasible and furthers the resolution of the issue(s) in controversy.

(b) *Accelerated procedure.* The accelerated procedure is available solely at the appellant's election, and only when the monetary amount in dispute is $100,000 or less. Such election shall be made no later than 15 days after receipt of the government's answer to the complaint, unless the Board enlarges the time for good cause shown. Promptly after receiving a timely filed election, the Board shall establish a schedule of proceedings that will allow for the timely resolution of the appeal. Pleadings may be simplified, discovery and other pre-hearing activities may be restricted or eliminated, and the appeal may be decided by a single member of the Board. Either party's failure to adhere to the Board's schedule may result in the Board drawing evidentiary inferences adverse to the party at fault. Whenever possible, the Board shall resolve an appeal under this procedure within 180 days from the Board's receipt of the election.

(c) *Small claims procedure.* The small claims procedure is available solely at the appellant's election, and only when the monetary amount in dispute is $50,000 or less (or in the case of a small business concern is $150,000 or less). Such election shall be made no later than 15 days after receipt of the government's answer to the complaint, unless the Board enlarges the time for good cause shown. Promptly after receiving a timely filed election, the Board shall establish a schedule of proceedings that will allow for the timely resolution of the appeal. Pleadings may be simplified, discovery and other prehearing activities may be restricted or eliminated, and the appeal may be decided by a single member of the Board. Either party's failure to adhere to the Board's schedule may result in the Board drawing evidentiary inferences adverse to the party at fault. Whenever possible, the Board shall resolve an appeal under this procedure within 120 days from the Board's receipt of the election.

§ 22.23 Suspension of Proceedings [Rule 23].

At any time, the Board may suspend the proceedings by agreement of the parties for settlement discussions, or for good cause shown.

§ 22.24 Alternative Dispute Resolution [Rule 24].

(a) *Docketed appeals.* The Board considers Alternative Dispute Resolution (ADR) to be an efficient way to timely resolve many contract disputes, and therefore encourages the parties to use ADR as an effective means to resolve their contract dispute. ADR with Board participation is available at the initiative of the Board or upon the joint motion of both parties. Guidelines, procedures, and requirements for implementing ADR will be prescribed by agreement of the parties and the Board. Ordinarily, ADR will be performed by a Board member, designated by the Chairman of the Board, that is not one of the three panel members deciding the dispute.

(b) *Other matters.* Upon request and in the Board's discretion, the Board can make an ADR neutral available for an ADR proceeding, even if the contracting officer's decision has not been issued or is not contemplated. Such a request should be directed to the Chairman of the Board.

§ 22.25 Protective Orders and In Camera Review [Rule 25].

(a) *Protective orders.* Upon motion of any party, or on the Board's initiative, the Board may issue a protective order to hold materials under conditions that would limit access to them on the ground that such documents are privileged or confidential, or sensitive in some other way. Any motion filed under this rule must state with specificity the grounds for such limited access. The manner in which such materials will be held, the persons that shall have access to them, and the conditions under which such access will be allowed will be specified in an order of the Board.

(b) *In camera review.* Generally, all documents and evidence provided to the Board must also be provided to all other parties to the appeal or their legal counsel or representative. However, in limited circumstances, such as in deciding matters of privilege, it may be appropriate for the Board to review documents or evidence in camera. In camera review may be requested upon motion to the Board, or on the Board's initiative. Any motion filed under this rule must state with specificity the grounds for seeking in camera review.

§ 22.26 Representation of Parties [Rule 26].

(a) *The appellant.* Any appellant may appear before the Board represented by an attorney duly licensed in any State, Commonwealth, Territory, or in the District of Columbia. An individual appellant may appear before the Board in person; a corporation may be represented by an officer thereof; a partnership or joint venture may be represented by a member thereof. Under special circumstances, the Board may authorize a contractor to appear before the Board represented by a duly authorized representative other than those mentioned herein for the purposes of that appeal only.

(b) *The respondent.* The respondent may appear before the Board represented by an attorney duly licensed in any State, Commonwealth, Territory, or in the District of Columbia. Such attorney shall be designated with authority to represent the government's interests before the Board. Alternatively, if not otherwise prohibited, the respondent may appear before the Board represented by the contracting officer or the contracting officer's authorized representative.

(c) *Others.* The Board may, on motion, in its discretion, permit a special or limited appearance, such as by amicus curiae. Permission to appear, if granted, will be for such purposes and in such manner as established by the Board.

(d) *Notice of appearance.* An attorney or other duly authorized representative representing a party before the Board shall file a notice of appearance. Such notice shall provide the person's name, address, direct dial telephone number, fax number, and e-mail address. If multiple attorneys or law firms represent a party, the contact information for each attorney shall be provided to the Board. In such instances, the party shall designate a single attorney or individual as the primary point of contact for the party. Notices of appearance shall be filed at the commencement of the appeal and shall be updated as necessary during the appeal.

§ 22.27 Ex Parte Communications [Rule 27].

No member of the Board shall entertain, nor shall any person directly or indirectly involved in an appeal submit to the Board, any evidence, explanation, analysis, or advice, whether written or oral, regarding any matter at issue in an appeal without the knowledge and consent of the adverse party. This provision does not apply to consultation among Board members or to ex parte communications concerning the Board's administrative functions or procedures.

§ 22.28 Time [Rule 28].

In computing any period of time described in these rules, "days" refer to calendar days, unless otherwise specified in these rules. The first day from which the period begins to run is not counted, and when the last day of the period is Saturday, Sunday, or a Federal holiday, the period extends to the next day that is not a Saturday, Sunday, or a Federal holiday. Documents shall be deemed "filed" on the date and time received by the Board if received before 5:30 p.m. local time in Washington, DC, or the next business day if received after 5:30 p.m.

[73 FR 60610, Oct. 14, 2008]

§ 22.29 Inspection of the Record [Rule 29].

The notice of appeal, the complaint, the answer, the documents required to be filed therewith pursuant to § 22.4 of this part [Rule 4], all papers filed by the parties with the Board pursuant to these rules, and all correspondence exchanged between the Board and the parties or their attorneys shall be available for inspection at the offices of the Board. Prior arrangements for inspection of the file should be made with a member of the Board.

PART 25—CONDUCT IN THE GOVERNMENT ACCOUNTABILITY OFFICE BUILDING AND ON ITS GROUNDS

Sec.

25.15 Nondiscrimination.
25.16 Penalties.

AUTHORITY: 31 U.S.C. 783.

SOURCE: 55 FR 2359, Jan. 24, 1990, unless otherwise noted.

§ 25.1 Applicability and governing laws.

These rules and regulations, and the laws of the United States and the District of Columbia, apply to the Government Accountability Office (GAO) Building and its grounds, 441 G Street NW., in the District of Columbia, and to all persons while in the building or while entering or leaving it.

§ 25.2 Inspection.

Packages, briefcases, and other containers as well as vehicles and their contents are subject to inspection while in or when being brought into, or when being removed from the GAO Building. A full search of a person may accompany an arrest or apprehension.

§ 25.3 Admission to the GAO building.

A person may be admitted to the GAO Building after presentation of personal identification to conduct lawful business with GAO, its employees, or other tenants of the GAO Building and for any other purposes authorized by the Comptroller General or his designee. During normal working hours, the GAO Building shall be open to the public unless specific circumstances require it to be closed to the public to ensure the orderly conduct of government business. Outside of normal working hours, the GAO Building shall be closed to the public unless the Comptroller General or his designee has approved the after-normal-working-hours use of the Building or portions thereof. When the Building, or a portion thereof, is closed to the public, admission will be restricted to authorized persons who shall register upon entry and exit, and shall, when requested, display government or other identifying credentials to the guards, security staff, or other authorized individuals. Failure to comply with such a request is a violation of these regulations.

§ 25.4 Preservation of property.

The improper disposal of rubbish in the GAO Building or on its grounds, the willful destruction of or damage to the GAO Building or to its grounds or fixtures, the theft of property, the creation of any hazard to persons or things in the GAO Building or on its grounds, the throwing of articles of any kind from or at the GAO Building, or the climbing on any part of the GAO Building, is prohibited.

§ 25.5 Conformity with signs and directions.

Persons in the GAO Building or on its grounds shall at all times comply with official signs of a prohibitory, regulatory, or directory nature and with the direction of the guards, security staff, or other authorized individuals.

§ 25.6 Disturbances.

Loitering, disorderly conduct, or other conduct in the GAO Building or on its grounds which creates loud or unusual noise or a nuisance; which unreasonably obstructs the usual use of entrances, foyers, lobbies, corridors, offices, elevators, escalators, stairways, or parking areas; which otherwise impedes or disrupts the performance of official duties by government employees; or which prevents the general public from obtaining the administrative services provided in the GAO Building in a timely manner, is prohibited.

§ 25.7 Gambling.

Participating in games for money or other personal property or operating gambling devices, conducting a lottery or pool, or selling or purchasing numbers tickets in the GAO Building or on its grounds is prohibited. This prohibition shall not apply to the vending or exchange of chances by licensed blind operators of vending facilities for any lottery set forth in a law of the District of Columbia and conducted by the District of Columbia and authorized by section 2(a)(5) of the Randolph-Sheppard Act (20 U.S.C. 107, *et seq.*).

§ 25.8 Alcoholic beverages and narcotics.

Operating a motor vehicle while in the GAO Building, its grounds or on its entry ramps by a person under the influence of alcoholic beverages, narcotic drugs, hallucinogens, marijuana, barbiturates, or amphetamines is prohibited. It is prohibited for anyone to enter or be in the GAO Building or to be on its grounds while under the influence of, or using, possessing, selling or distributing any narcotic drug, hallucinogen, marijuana, barbiturate, or amphetamine. This prohibition shall not apply in cases where the drug is being used as prescribed for a patient by a licensed physician. It is prohibited for anyone to enter the GAO Building or its grounds, or be on the premises while under the influence of alcoholic beverages. The use of alcoholic beverages in the GAO Building is prohibited except when specifically authorized by the Comptroller General or his designee for a particular event. The Comptroller General or his designee shall be advised of such events and shall inform the guards and other security staff of the time and precise locations of these events.

§25.9 Soliciting, vending, and debt collection.

Soliciting alms, commercial or political soliciting, and vending of all kinds, displaying or distributing commercial advertising, or collecting private debts in the GAO Building is prohibited. This rule does not apply to:

(a) National or local drives for funds for welfare, health, or other purposes as authorized by the "Manual on Fund Raising Within the Federal Service," issued by the U.S. Office of Personnel Management;

(b) Concessions or personal notices posted by employees on authorized bulletin boards;

(c) Solicitation of labor organization membership or dues authorized by occupant agencies under the Civil Service Reform Act of 1978 (Pub. L. 95–454) or the General Accounting Office Personnel Act of 1980, Public Law 96–191 (31 U.S.C. sec. 732(e));

(d) Occupants of space leased for commercial purposes, or made available for cultural, educational, or recreational use under section 1 of Public Law 100–545, October 28, 1988, 102 Stat. 2727, 2728 (31 U.S.C. 782).

§25.10 Posting and distributing materials.

Posting or affixing materials, such as pamphlets, handbills or flyers, on bulletin boards or elsewhere in the GAO Building or on its grounds is prohibited, except as authorized by these rules and regulations or when such displays are conducted as part of authorized government activities. Distribution of materials, such as pamphlets, handbills or flyers is prohibited, unless conducted as part of authorized government activities. Any person or organization proposing to post or distribute materials in any part of the GAO Building or on its grounds shall first obtain a permit from the Comptroller General or his designee and shall conduct the posting or distribution in accordance with the guidelines provided by the Comptroller General or his designee. Failure to comply with those guidelines is a violation of these regulations.

§25.11 Photographs for news, advertising, or commercial purposes.

Photographs may be taken in the GAO Building only with the approval or authorization of the Comptroller General or his designee.

§25.12 Dogs and other animals.

Dogs and other animals, except seeing eye dogs or other guide dogs, shall not be brought into the GAO Building or on its grounds for other than official purposes.

§25.13 Vehicular and pedestrian traffic.

(a) Drivers of all vehicles entering, leaving or while on GAO property or in the GAO Building shall drive in a careful and safe manner at all times and shall comply with all posted traffic signs and with the signals and directions of the guards, security staff, or other authorized individuals;

(b) The blocking of entrances, driveways, walks, loading platforms or fire hydrants on GAO property is prohibited; and

(c) Except in emergencies, parking on GAO property or in the GAO Building is not allowed without a permit. Parking in unauthorized locations or in locations reserved for other persons, or parking contrary to the direction of posted signs or instructions of guards is prohibited. Vehicles parked in violation of posted restrictions or warning signs shall be subject to removal at the owners' risk and expense.

(d) The Comptroller General or his designee may supplement this paragraph from time to time by issuing and posting such specific traffic directives as may be required. When issued and posted, such directives shall have the same force and effect as if made a part hereof. Proof that a motor vehicle was parked in violation of these regulations or directives may be taken as prima facie evidence that the registered owner was responsible for the violation.

§ 25.14 Weapons and explosives.

No person while entering or in the GAO Building or on its grounds shall carry or possess firearms, other dangerous or deadly weapons, explosives or items intended to be used to fabricate an explosive or incendiary device, either openly or concealed, except for official purposes.

§ 25.15 Nondiscrimination.

There shall be no discrimination by segregation or otherwise against any person or persons because of race, creed, sex, color, or national origin in furnishing or by refusing to furnish the use of any facility of a public nature, including all services, privileges, accommodations and activities provided in the GAO Building.

§ 25.16 Penalties.

Whoever shall be found guilty of violating any rule or regulation governing the GAO Building is subject to a fine of not more than $500, or imprisonment for not more than 6 months, or both. Nothing in these rules and regulations shall be construed to abrogate any other Federal laws applicable to the GAO Building.

PART 27—GOVERNMENT ACCOUNTABILITY OFFICE PERSONNEL APPEALS BOARD; ORGANIZATION

Sec.

AUTHORITY: 31 U.S.C. 753.

SOURCE: 58 FR 61992, Nov. 23, 1993, unless otherwise noted.

§ 27.1 The Board.

The Government Accountability Office Personnel Appeals Board, hereinafter the Board, is composed of five members appointed by the Comptroller General, in accordance with the provisions of 31 U.S.C. 751. For purposes of the regulations in this part and 4 CFR part 28, a simple majority of the Board shall constitute a quorum and a majority of a quorum may act for the Board. The Board may designate a panel of its members or an individual Board member to take any action within the scope of the Board's authority, subject to later review by the Board.

[64 FR 15125, Mar. 30, 1999, as amended at 68 FR 69297, Dec. 12, 2003]

§ 27.2 The Chair, Vice Chair.

The members of the Board shall select from among its membership a Chairperson, hereinafter the Chair, who shall serve as the chief executive and administrative officer of the Board. The Members of the Board may select from among its membership a Vice Chairperson, hereinafter the Vice Chair, who shall serve in the absence of the Chair and in other matters delegated by the Chair.

§ 27.3 The General Counsel.

The Chair shall select an individual and the Comptroller General shall appoint the individual selected by the Chair to serve as the General Counsel of the Board. The General Counsel, at the request of the Board, shall investigate matters under the jurisdiction of the Board, and otherwise assist the Board in carrying out its functions.

[58 FR 61992, Nov. 23, 1993, as amended at 68 FR 69297, Dec. 12, 2003]

PART 28—GOVERNMENT ACCOUNTABILITY OFFICE PERSONNEL APPEALS BOARD; PROCEDURES APPLICABLE TO CLAIMS CONCERNING EMPLOYMENT PRACTICES AT THE GOVERNMENT ACCOUNTABILITY OFFICE

Subpart A—Purpose, General Definitions, and Jurisdiction

Subpart B—Procedures

Subpart C—Oversight Procedures

Subpart D—Special Procedures; Equal Employment Opportunity (EEO) Cases

Subpart E—Special Procedures; Representation Proceedings

AUTHORITY: 31 U.S.C. 753.

SOURCE: 58 FR 61992, Nov. 23, 1993, unless otherwise noted.

EDITORIAL NOTE: Nomenclature changes to part 28 appear at 76 FR 76873, Dec. 9, 2011.

Subpart A—Purpose, General Definitions, and Jurisdiction

§ 28.1 Purpose and scope.

(a) The regulations in this part implement the Board's authority with respect to employment practices within the Government Accountability Office (GAO), pursuant to the General Accounting Office Personnel Act of 1980 (GAOPA), 31 U.S.C. 751–755.

(b) The purpose of the rules in this part is to establish the procedures to be followed by:

(1) The GAO, in its dealings with the Board;

(2) Employees of the GAO or applicants for employment with the GAO, or groups or organizations claiming to be affected adversely by the operations of the GAO personnel system;

(3) Employees or organizations petitioning for protection of rights or extension of benefits granted to them under subchapters III and IV of Chapter 7 of title 31, United States Code; and

(4) The Board, in carrying out its responsibilities under Subchapters III and IV of chapter 7 of title 31, United States Code.

(c) The scope of the Board's operations encompasses the investigation and adjudication of cases arising under 31 U.S.C. 753. In addition, the Board has authority for oversight of the equal employment opportunity program at GAO. This includes the review of policies and evaluation of operations as they relate to EEO objectives and, where necessary, the ordering of corrective action for violation of or inconsistencies with equal employment opportunity laws.

(d) In considering any procedural matter not specifically addressed in these rules, the Board will be guided, but not bound, by the Federal Rules of Civil Procedure.

[59 FR 59105, Nov. 16, 1994, as amended at 68 FR 69297, Dec. 12, 2003]

§ 28.2 Jurisdiction.

(a) The Board has jurisdiction to hear and decide the following:

(1) Proceedings in which the General Counsel seeks to stay a personnel action based upon an alleged prohibited personnel practice that has occurred or is about to occur;

(2) Proceedings in which the General Counsel seeks corrective action for an alleged prohibited personnel practice; and

(3) Proceedings in which the General Counsel seeks discipline for a GAO employee who has allegedly committed a prohibited personnel practice or who has engaged in prohibited political activity.

(b) The Board has jurisdiction to hear any action brought by any person or group of persons in the following subject areas:

(1) An officer or employee petition involving a removal, suspension for more than 14 days, reduction in grade or pay, or furlough of not more than 30 days;

(2) A prohibited personnel practice under 31 U.S.C. 732(b)(2);

(3) The appropriateness of a unit of employees for collective bargaining;

(4) An election or certification of a collective bargaining representative;

(5) A matter appealable to the Board under the labor-management relations program under 31 U.S.C. 732(e), including an unfair labor practice under 31 U.S.C. 732(e)(1);

(6) An action involving discrimination prohibited under 31 U.S.C. 732(f)(1); and

(7) An issue about GAO personnel which the Comptroller General by regulation decides the Board shall resolve.

(c) *Special jurisdictional rules where matters are covered by a negotiated grievance procedure.* If a GAO employee is covered by a collective bargaining agreement containing a negotiated grievance procedure that permits the employee to grieve matters that would otherwise be appealable to the Board, the following special rules apply:

(1) *Matters involving discrimination, performance-based reduction in grade or removal, or adverse action.* If the negotiated grievance procedure permits the employee to grieve matters involving prohibited discrimination (as defined in §28.95), performance-based reduction in grade or removal (as described in 5 U.S.C. 4303) or an adverse action (as described in 5 U.S.C. 7512), then the employee may elect to raise the matter either under the negotiated grievance procedure or under the Board's procedures, but not both. The employee will be deemed to have elected the Board's procedures if the employee files a timely charge with the Board's General Counsel or files a timely written EEO complaint with GAO before filing a timely written grievance.

(2) *Matters involving prohibited personnel practices.* If the negotiated grievance procedure permits the employee to grieve an appealable action involving a prohibited personnel practice other than prohibited discrimination (as defined in §28.95), such an action may be raised under either, but not both, of the following procedures:

(A) The Board's procedures; or

(B) The negotiated grievance procedure.

The employee will be deemed to have elected the Board's procedures if the employee files a timely charge with the Board's Office of General Counsel before filing a timely grievance.

(3) *Other matters.* If the negotiated grievance procedure permits the employee to grieve any matters which would otherwise be appealable to the Board, other than those listed in paragraphs (c)(1) or (c)(2) of this section, then those matters may only be raised under the negotiated grievance procedure and not before the Board.

(4) *Board review of final decisions from the negotiated grievance procedure involving discrimination.* If an employee elects to pursue a matter involving prohibited discrimination (as defined in §28.95) through the negotiated grievance procedure, the employee may ask the Board to review the final decision of the negotiated grievance procedure as it relates to the issue of discrimination. A petition seeking such review shall be filed with the Clerk of the Board within 20 days of receipt of the final decision of the negotiated grievance procedure. The Board will not review any final decisions of the negotiated grievance procedure other than those where prohibited discrimination was raised as an issue in the grievance.

(d) Except for actions involving prohibited discrimination (under §28.95) or any other prohibited personnel practice, any appealable action that is excluded from the application of the negotiated grievance procedure may be raised only under the Board's procedures.

[58 FR 61992, Nov. 23, 1993, as amended at 68 FR 69298, Dec. 12, 2003; 76 FR 76873, Dec. 9, 2011]

§28.3 General definitions.

In this part—

Administrative judge means any individual designated by the Board to preside over a hearing conducted on matters within its jurisdiction. An administrative judge may be a member of the Board, an employee of the Board, or any individual qualified by experience or training to conduct a hearing who is appointed to do so by the Board. When a panel of members or the full Board is hearing a case, the Chair shall designate one of the members to exercise the responsibilities of the administrative judge in the proceedings.

Appeal means a request filed with the full Board for review of an initial decision.

Board means the Government Accountability Office Personnel Appeals Board as established by 31 U.S.C. 751 and explained in 4 CFR 27.1.

Charge means any request filed with the PAB Office of General Counsel to investigate any matter within the jurisdiction of the Board, under the provisions of Subchapter IV of chapter 7 of Title 31, United States Code.

Charging Party means any person filing a charge with the PAB Office of General Counsel for investigation.

Clerk of the Board means the Clerk of the Personnel Appeals Board.

Comptroller General means the Comptroller General of the United States.

Days means calendar days.

Director of EEO Oversight means the Personnel Appeals Board Director of EEO Oversight.

Executive Director means the Executive Director of the Personnel Appeals Board.

GAO means the Government Accountability Office.

General Counsel means the General Counsel of the Board, as provided for under 31 U.S.C. 752.

Initial Decision means the adjudicatory statement of a case that is issued by an administrative judge who is a member of or appointed by the Board.

Notice of Appeal means a pleading requesting that the full Board review an initial decision.

Person means an employee, an applicant for employment, a former employee, a labor organization or the GAO.

Petition means any request filed with the Board for action to be taken on matters within the jurisdiction of the Board, under the provisions of Subchapter IV of Chapter 7 of title 31, United States Code.

Petitioner means any person filing a petition for Board consideration.

Pleading means a document that initiates a cause of action before the Board, responds to a cause of action, amends a cause of action, responds to an amended cause of action, requests reconsideration of a decision, responds to such a request, requests appellate review by the full Board or responds to such a request.

Reduction in Force (RIF) means the release of an employee from a job group by separation, demotion, reassignment requiring displacement, or furlough for more than 30 days when the cause of action is lack of work, shortage of funds, insufficient personnel ceiling, reorganization or realignment, an individual's exercise of reemployment or reinstatement rights, correction of skills imbalances, or reduction of high-grade supervisory, or managerial positions.

Request for Reconsideration means a request, filed with the administrative judge who rendered the initial decision, to reconsider that decision in whole or part.

Solicitor means the attorney appointed by the Board to provide advice and assistance to the Board in carrying out its adjudicatory functions and to otherwise provide assistance as directed by the Board.

[68 FR 69298, Dec. 12, 2003]

§ 28.4 Computation of time.

(a) To compute the number of days for filing under these rules, the first day shall be the day after the event from which the time period begins to run and the last day for filing shall be included in the computation. When the last day falls on a Saturday, Sunday or federal government holiday, then the filing deadline will be the next regular federal government workday.

(b) Whenever a party has the right or is required to do some act within a prescribed period after the service of a notice or other paper upon him or her and the notice or paper is served by mail, five (5) days shall be added to the prescribed period. Only two (2) days shall be added when a document is served by express mail or other form of expedited delivery.

(c) Except as otherwise provided by law, whenever an act is required or allowed to be done at or within a specified period of time, the time fixed or the period of time prescribed may for good cause be extended or shortened by the Board or administrative judge.

(d) No written submission shall be accepted by the Clerk of the Board after 4 p.m., Monday through Friday.

[58 FR 61992, Nov. 23, 1993, as amended at 68 FR 69298, Dec. 12, 2003]

Subpart B—Procedures

§28.8 Informal procedural advice.

(a) Persons may seek informal advice on all aspects of the Board's procedures by contacting the Board's Executive Director, Director of EEO Oversight, Solicitor, General Counsel or the Clerk of the Board.

(b) Informal procedural advice will be supplied within the limits of available time and staff.

[58 FR 61992, Nov. 23, 1993, as amended at 68 FR 69298, Dec. 12, 2003]

§28.9 Procedures; general.

(a) The procedures described in this subpart are generally applicable to the processing of all matters presented for consideration by the Board. Where special procedures are to be followed, they will be prescribed in those subsequent subparts to which they are particularly applicable.

(b) No pleading, motion or supporting memorandum filed with the Board shall exceed 60 pages, exclusive of attachments. The Board or the administrative judge may waive this limitation for good cause shown. Pleadings, motions and supporting memoranda, and attachments thereto, shall be on standard letter-size paper (8½x11).

§28.10 Notice of petition rights.

(a) The GAO shall be responsible for ensuring that employees are routinely advised of their rights to petition the Board and that employees who are the object of an adverse or performance-based action are, at the time of the action, adequately advised of their rights to petition the Board. The notice in adverse or performance-based actions must be accompanied by proof of service.

(b) The notice in adverse or performance-based actions shall include:

(1) Time limits for filing a petition with the Board and the address of the Board;

(2) A copy of the Board's regulations; and

(3) Notice of the right to representation, and the availability of a hearing before the Board where factual issues are in dispute.

[58 FR 61992, Nov. 23, 1993, as amended at 68 FR 69298, Dec. 12, 2003]

§28.11 Filing a charge with the Office of General Counsel.

(a) *Who may file.* (1) Any person claiming to be affected adversely by GAO action or inaction which is within the Board's jurisdiction under Subchapter IV of Chapter 7 of Title 31, United States Code, may file a charge with the General Counsel.

(2) Non-EEO class actions. One or more persons may file a charge as representative of a class in any matter within the Board's jurisdiction. See §28.97 for EEO class actions.

(3) Unfair labor practice proceedings. Any person may file a charge alleging that the GAO or a labor organization has engaged or is engaging in an unfair labor practice. (The types of allegations which may be included in an unfair labor practice charge are discussed at §28.121(a)).

(b) *When to file.* (1) Charges relating to adverse and performance-based actions must be filed within 30 days after the effective date of the action.

(2) Charges relating to other personnel actions must be filed within 30 days after the effective date of the action or 30 days after the charging party knew or should have known of the action.

(3) Charges which include an allegation of prohibited discrimination shall be filed in accordance with the special rules set forth in §28.98.

(4) Charges relating to continuing violations may be filed at any time.

(c) *How to file.* Charges may be filed with the Office of General Counsel by personal delivery (including commercial carrier) or by mail.

(1) A charge may be filed by personal delivery at the Office of General Counsel, Personnel Appeals Board, Room 1562, 441 G Street NW., Washington, DC 20548.

(2) A charge may be filed by mail addressed to the Office of General Counsel, Personnel Appeals Board, Room 1562, 441 G Street NW., Washington, DC 20548. When filed by mail, the postmark shall be the date of filing for all submissions to the Office of General Counsel.

(d) *What to file.* The charging party should include in any charge the following information:

(1) Name of the charging party or a clear description of the group or class of persons on whose behalf the charge is being filed;

(2) The names and titles of persons, if any, responsible for actions the charging party wishes to have the Office of General Counsel investigate;

(3) The actions complained about, including dates, reasons given, and internal appeals taken;

(4) The charging party's reasons for believing the actions to be improper;

(5) Remedies sought by the charging party;

(6) Name and address of the representative, if any, who will act for the charging party in any further stages of the matter; and

(7) Signature of the charging party or the charging party's representative.

(e) The General Counsel shall not represent a petitioner when the only issue is attorney fees. When attorney fees are the only issue raised in a charge to the Office of General Counsel, the General Counsel shall transmit the charge to the Board for processing under §§ 28.18 through 28.88 as a petition.

[58 FR 61992, Nov. 23, 1993, as amended at 59 FR 59106, Nov. 16, 1994; 61 FR 36810, July 15, 1996; 68 FR 69298, Dec. 12, 2003; 77 FR 15233, Mar. 15, 2012]

§ 28.12 General Counsel Procedures.

(a) The General Counsel shall serve on the GAO or other charged party a copy of the charge, investigate the matters raised in a charge, refine the issues where appropriate, and attempt to settle all matters at issue.

(b) The General Counsel's investigation may include gathering information from the GAO or other charged party, and interviewing and taking statements from witnesses. Employees of GAO who are requested by the General Counsel to participate in any investigation under these Rules shall be on official time.

(c) Following the investigation, the Office of General Counsel shall provide the charging party with a Right to Petition Letter. Accompanying this letter will be a statement of the General Counsel advising the charging party of the results of the investigation. This statement of the General Counsel is not subject to discovery and may not be introduced into evidence before the Board.

(d)(1) If the General Counsel determines that there are reasonable grounds to believe that the charging party's rights under subchapters III and IV of chapter 7 of title 31, United States Code, have been violated, then the General Counsel shall represent the charging party unless the charging party elects not to be represented by the Office of General Counsel.

(2) If, following the investigation, the General Counsel determines that there are not reasonable grounds to believe that the charging party's rights under subchapters III and IV of chapter 7 of title 31, United States Code, have been violated, then the General Counsel shall not represent the charging party. The charging party may nonetheless file a petition with the Board in accordance with § 28.18.

(3) Any charging party may represent him- or herself or obtain other representation.

(e) When the charging party elects to be represented by the General Counsel, the General Counsel is to direct the representation in the charging party's case. The charging party may also retain a private representative in such cases. However, the role of a private representative is limited to assisting the General Counsel as the General Counsel determines to be appropriate.

(f) When the General Counsel is not participating in a case, the General

Counsel may request permission to intervene with regard to any issue in which the General Counsel finds a significant public interest with respect to the preservation of the merit system.

(g) If 180 days have elapsed since the filing of the charge, and the Office of General Counsel has not completed the investigation and issued a Right to Petition Letter, the charging party may bring his or her case directly to the Board by filing a petition in accordance with §28.18. If a charging party exercises this option to file a petition with the Board without waiting for the completion of the investigation, the Office of General Counsel shall not represent the charging party in proceedings before the Board. The charging party may represent him- or herself or obtain other representation. The Office of General Counsel shall close the investigation of the charge upon being notified by the Clerk of the Board that the charging party has filed a petition with the Board under this paragraph (g).

(h) *Office of General Counsel settlement:* Where the General Counsel under paragraph (a) of this section transmits a settlement which has been agreed to by the parties, the settlement agreement shall be the final disposition of the case.

(i) *Confidentiality:* (1) It is the Office of General Counsel's policy to protect against the disclosure of documents obtained during the investigation, as a means of ensuring that Office's continuing ability to obtain all relevant information. However, if the Office of General Counsel files a petition with the Personnel Appeals Board on behalf of a charging party pursuant to this section, that Office may disclose the identity of witnesses and a synopsis of their expected testimony. Documents to be offered into evidence at the hearing may be disclosed as required by the prehearing disclosure requirements of §28.56.

(2) Unless so ordered by a court of competent jurisdiction, no employee of the Personnel Appeals Board Office of General Counsel shall produce or disclose any information or records acquired as part of the performance of his/her official duties or because of his/her official status. Before producing or disclosing such information or records pursuant to court order, an employee shall notify the General Counsel.

[58 FR 61992, Nov. 23, 1993, as amended at 65 FR 80280, Dec. 21, 2000; 68 FR 69299, Dec. 12, 2003]

§28.13 Special procedure for Reduction in Force.

In the event of a Reduction in Force (RIF) resulting in an individual's separation from employment, an aggrieved employee may choose to file a petition directly with the Personnel Appeals Board, without first filing the charge with the PAB's Office of General Counsel pursuant to §28.11. Pursuant to §28.98, individuals raising discrimination issues in connection with a RIF action need not file a complaint with GAO's Office of Opportunity and Inclusiveness before pursuing a RIF challenge alleging discrimination, either by filing directly with the PAB or by filing a charge with the Board's Office of General Counsel.

[68 FR 69299, Dec. 12, 2003]

Hearing Procedures for Cases Before the Board—General

§28.15 Scope and policy.

The rules in this subpart apply to actions brought by any person, except as otherwise provided in §28.17 (concerning internal petitions of Board employees). These rules also apply to actions brought by the General Counsel, except as otherwise provided in subpart G (concerning corrective action, disciplinary and stay proceedings). It is the policy of the Board that these rules shall be applied in a manner which expedites the processing of each case, but with due regard to the rights of all parties.

[58 FR 61992, Nov. 23, 1993, as amended at 68 FR 69299, Dec. 12, 2003]

§28.16 Revocation, amendment or waiver of rules.

(a) The Board may revoke or amend these regulations by publishing proposed changes within GAO and providing for a comment period of not less than 30 days. Following the comment period, any changes to the rules are final once they are published in the

FEDERAL REGISTER. Notice of publication in the FEDERAL REGISTER must be published throughout GAO.

(b) An administrative judge or the Board may waive a Board regulation in an individual case for good cause shown if application of the regulation is not required by statute.

§ 28.17 Internal petitions of Board employees.

(a) The provisions of the GAO Personnel Act, its implementing regulations, and the Board's procedural rules apply in the same manner to employees of the Board as they do to other GAO employees, with the following exceptions.

(1) The General Counsel serves at the pleasure of the Chair. The General Counsel may not bring any complaint or charge concerning his or her own employment except to allege that he or she has been the victim of prohibited discrimination or a prohibited personnel practice as defined in 31 U.S.C. 732 (b)(2) or (f)(1).

(2) When an employee of the Board believes that he or she has been denied his or her right to equal employment opportunity, the employee shall bring this matter to the attention of the Board's Executive Director or General Counsel. If the matter cannot be resolved within 10 days, the Executive Director shall notify the employee of his or her right to file an EEO complaint. The employee may consult with either the Board's Solicitor or General Counsel and seek advice with regard to procedural matters concerning the filing of an EEO charge. The employee shall have 20 days from service of this notice to file an EEO charge with the PAB Office of General Counsel. Upon receipt of an EEO charge, the General Counsel shall arrange with the Executive Director for processing in accordance with paragraph (b) of this section. If the EEO allegations involve challenge to a RIF-based separation, the employee may choose to expedite the procedures by filing a petition directly with the Board.

(3) When an employee of the Board wishes to raise any other issue that would be subject to the Board's jurisdiction, the employee shall file a charge with the General Counsel and the General Counsel shall arrange with the Executive Director for processing in accordance with paragraph (b) of this section. If the challenged action is a RIF-based separation from employment, the employee may choose to expedite the procedures by filing a petition directly with the Board.

(b) The responsibilities and functions of the Board's General Counsel will be assumed by an attorney who is not a current or former employee of the Board or the GAO. The services of that attorney, who shall be knowledgeable in federal personnel matters, will be paid for by the Board. The attorney will be selected by an impartial body as described below.

(1) If agreed to by the Office of Special Counsel or the EEOC, as appropriate, that body will appoint and detail a person from among its attorneys to perform the functions of the General Counsel.

(2) If the Special Counsel or the EEOC does not agree to such a procedure, an appointment of an attorney will be sought from the Federal Mediation and Conciliation Service (FMCS).

(3) In any event, whoever is so appointed shall possess all of the powers and authority possessed by the General Counsel in employee appeal cases.

(c) The adjudication responsibilities and functions of the Board will be assumed by a person who is not a current or former employee of the Board or the GAO. The services of that person, who shall be knowledgeable in federal personnel matters, will be paid for by the Board. The person will be selected by an impartial body as described below.

(1) If agreed to by the MSPB or the EEOC, as appropriate, that body will appoint and detail one of its administrative law judges (ALJ) or administrative judges (AJ) to perform the Board's adjudicative functions.

(2) If neither the MSPB nor the EEOC agrees to such a procedure, an appointment of an arbitrator will be sought from the FMCS.

(3) In any event, whoever is so appointed shall possess all of the powers and authority possessed by the Board in employee cases. The decision of the administrative law judge, administrative judge or arbitrator shall be a final decision of the Board. The procedure

for judicial review of the decision shall be the same as that described in § 28.90.

(d) Any employee of the Board (other than the General Counsel) who believes that he or she is aggrieved by any personnel matter that is not reviewable by the Board under 31 U.S.C. 753(a) may file a grievance as follows:

(1) *Informal Step.* The employee must discuss the complained of incident with his or her supervisor as soon as possible after the complained of incident.

(2) *Step 1.* If the supervisor is unable to resolve the matter informally to the satisfaction of the employee, then the employee may file a formal grievance with the supervisor. The formal grievance must be filed by the employee with the supervisor within 20 days after the complained of incident. The supervisor must respond to the employee in writing within 10 days.

(3) *Step 2.* (i) If the employee is not satisfied with the supervisor's response, the employee has 10 days in which to appeal to the Chair. In this appeal, the employee must forward to the Chair the formal grievance, the supervisor's response and a brief statement from the employee explaining why the supervisor's response is not satisfactory.

(ii) The Chair or another member designated by the Chair, shall meet with the employee and discuss the matter of concern within 10 days after service of the step 2 appeal. The Chair or designee shall issue a written resolution of the grievance.

(4) *Step 3.* Within 10 days after service of the Chair's resolution or within 60 days after initiating step 2, whichever occurs first, the employee may request that the full Board review the grievance. The decision of the full Board is the final decision in the matter.

[58 FR 61992, Nov. 23, 1993, as amended at 59 FR 59106, Nov. 16, 1994; 61 FR 36810, July 15, 1996; 68 FR 69299, Dec. 12, 2003]

§ 28.18 Filing a petition with the Board.

(a) *Who may file.* Any person who is claiming to be affected adversely by GAO action or inaction that is within the Board's jurisdiction under subchapter IV of chapter 7 of title 31, United States Code, or who is alleging that GAO or a labor organization engaged or is engaging in an unfair labor practice, may file a petition if one of the following is met:

(1) The person has received a Right to Petition Letter from the Board's Office of General Counsel; or

(2) At least 180 days have elapsed from the filing of the charge with the Board's Office of General Counsel and that Office has not issued a Right to Petition Letter; or

(3) The person was separated due to a Reduction in Force and chooses to file a petition directly with the Board, without first filing with the Board's Office of General Counsel, as provided in § 28.13.

(b) *When to file.* (1) Petitions filed pursuant to paragraph (a)(1) of this section must be filed within 30 days after receipt by the charging party of the Right to Petition Letter from the Board's Office of General Counsel.

(2) Petitions filed pursuant to paragraph (a)(2) of this section may be filed at any time after 180 days have elapsed from the filing of the charge with the Board's Office of General Counsel, provided that that Office has not issued a Right to Petition Letter concerning the charge.

(3) Petitions filed pursuant to paragraph (a)(3) of this section must be filed within 30 days after the effective date of the separation due to a Reduction in Force.

(c) *How to file.* (1) A petition may be filed by hand delivery to the office of the Personnel Appeals Board, Room 1566, 441 G Street NW., Washington, DC 20548. It must be received by 4 p.m., Monday through Friday, on the date that it is filed.

(2) A petition may be filed by mail addressed to the Personnel Appeals Board, Room 1566, 441 G Street NW., Washington, DC 20548. When filed by mail, the postmark shall be the date of filing for all submissions to the Board.

(d) *What to file.* The petition shall include the following information:

(1) Name of the petitioner or a clear description of the group or class of persons on whose behalf the petition is being filed;

(2) The names and titles of persons, if any, responsible for actions the petitioner wishes to have the Board review;

(3) The actions being complained about, including dates, reasons given and internal appeals taken;

(4) Petitioner's reasons for believing the actions to be improper;

(5) Remedies sought by the petitioner;

(6) Name and address of the representative, if any, who will act for the petitioner in any further stages of the matter; and

(7) Signature of the petitioner or petitioner's representative.

(e) *Failure to raise a claim or defense.* Failure to raise a claim or defense in the petition shall not bar its submission later unless to do so would prejudice the rights of the other parties or unduly delay the proceedings.

(f) *Non-EEO class actions.* One or more persons may file a petition as representatives of a class in any matter within the Board's jurisdiction. For the purpose of determining whether it is appropriate to treat a petition as a class action, the administrative judge will be guided, but not controlled, by the applicable provisions of the Federal Rules of Civil Procedure. See § 28.97 for EEO class actions.

[58 FR 61992, Nov. 23, 1993, as amended at 59 FR 59106, Nov. 16, 1994; 61 FR 9090, Mar. 7, 1996; 61 FR 36810, July 15, 1996; 65 FR 80280, Dec. 21, 2000; 68 FR 69300, Dec. 12, 2003; 77 FR 15233, Mar. 15, 2012]

§ 28.19 Content of response by charged party.

(a) Within 20 days after service of a copy of a petition, the GAO or other charged party shall file a response containing at least the following:

(1) A statement of the position of the charged party on each allegation set forth therein, including admissions, denials or explanations. If the petition contains numbered paragraphs, the responses should reference the paragraph numbers. If the petition does not contain numbered paragraphs, the responses should quote or otherwise clearly identify the specific allegations of the petition.

(2) Any other defenses to the petition.

(3) Designation of, and signature by, the representative authorized to act for the charged party in the matter.

(b) Failure to raise a claim or defense in the response shall not bar its submission later unless to do so would prejudice the rights of the other parties or unduly delay the proceedings.

[58 FR 61992, Nov. 23, 1993, as amended at 68 FR 69300, Dec. 12, 2003]

§ 28.20 Number of Pleadings, service and response.

(a) *Number.* One original and seven copies of all pleadings (see definition in § 28.3) must be filed with the Board. However, when before a single administrative judge, one original and three copies will be adequate unless informed otherwise.

(b) *Service.* (1) The Board will serve copies of a petition upon the parties to the proceeding by mail and/or by facsimile. The Board will attach a service list indicating the names and addresses of the parties to the proceeding or their designated representatives. The Board will not serve copies of any pleadings, motions, or other submissions by the parties after the initial petition.

(2) The parties shall serve on each other one copy of all pleadings other than the initial petition. Service shall be made by mailing, by facsimile or by delivering personally a copy of the pleading to each party on the service list previously provided by the Board. Each pleading must be accompanied by a certificate of service specifying how and when service was made. It shall be the duty of all parties to notify the Board and one another in writing of any changes in the names or addresses on the service list.

(c) *Time limitations for response to pleadings.* Unless otherwise specified by the administrative judge or this subpart, a party shall file a response to a pleading within 20 days of the service of that pleading upon the party.

(d) Size limitations are set forth at § 28.9(b).

[58 FR 61992, Nov. 23, 1993, as amended at 68 FR 69300, Dec. 12, 2003]

§ 28.21 Amendments to petitions and motions practice.

(a) *Amendments to petitions.* The Board, at its discretion, may allow amendments to a petition as long as all persons who are parties to the proceeding have adequate notice to prepare for the new allegations and if to do so would not prejudice the rights of the other parties or unduly delay the proceedings.

(b) *Motions practice.* (1) When an action is before an administrative judge, motions of the parties shall be filed with the Clerk of the Board and shall be in writing except for oral motions made during the hearing. An original and 3 copies of written motions shall be filed with the Clerk of the Board. An original and 3 copies of responses in opposition to written motions must be filed with the Clerk of the Board within 20 days of service of the motion unless the administrative judge requires a shorter time.

(2) When an action is before the full Board, an original and 7 copies of any motion shall be filed with the Clerk of the Board. An original and 7 copies of any responses in opposition to motions must be filed with the Clerk of the Board within 20 days of service of the motion unless the Board requires a shorter time.

(3) A party filing a motion for extension of time, a motion for postponement of a hearing, or any other procedural motion must first contact the other party to determine whether there is any objection to the motion and must state in the motion whether the other party has any objection.

(4) No motions, responses or other submissions will be accepted for filing by the Clerk of the Board after 4 p.m., Monday through Friday. All written submissions shall be served simultaneously upon the other parties to the proceeding. A certificate of service must be attached showing service by mail, facsimile or personal delivery of the submission to the other parties. Further submissions by either party may be filed only with the approval of the administrative judge or full Board.

(5) All written motions and responses thereto shall include a proposed order, where applicable.

(6) Motions for extension of time will be granted only upon a showing of good cause.

(7) *Oral argument.* The administrative judge may allow oral argument on the motion at his or her discretion.

(c) *Motions for summary judgment.* (1) Either party may move for summary judgment by filing a written motion no later than 14 days prior to the commencement of the hearing or as otherwise ordered by the administrative judge.

(2) Motions for summary judgment must be accompanied by a statement of material facts for which there is no genuine dispute and a statement of reasons in support of the motion. The motion may be supported by documents, affidavits, or other evidence.

(3) Summary judgment will be granted if the pleadings, depositions, answers to interrogatories, admissions, affidavits, if any, and other documents show that there is no genuine issue as to any material fact and that the moving party is entitled to judgment as a matter of law.

(4) A party moving for summary judgment must make a showing sufficient to establish the existence of each element essential to that party's cause of action and for which that party bears the burden of proof.

(5) When a party moves for summary judgment, the Board will evaluate the motion on its own merits, resolving all reasonable inferences against the moving party.

[68 FR 69300, Dec. 12, 2003]

§28.22 Administrative judges.

(a) *Exercise of authority.* Administrative judges may exercise authority as provided in paragraph (b) of this section upon their own initiative or upon the motion of a party, as appropriate.

(b) *Authority.* Administrative judges shall conduct fair and impartial hearings and take all necessary action to avoid delay in the disposition of all proceedings. They shall have all powers necessary to that end unless otherwise limited by law, including, but not limited to, the authority to:

(1) Administer oaths and affirmations;

(2) Issue subpoenas in accordance with §28.46;

(3) Rule upon offers of proof and receive relevant evidence;

(4) Rule upon discovery issues as appropriate under §§28.42 through 28.45;

(5) Convene a hearing as appropriate, regulate the course of the hearing,

maintain decorum and exclude from the hearing any disruptive persons;

(6) Exclude from the hearing any witness, except the petitioner(s), whose later testimony might be colored by testimony of other witnesses, or any persons whose presence might have a chilling effect on a testifying witness;

(7) Rule on all motions, witness and exhibit lists and proposed findings;

(8) Require the filing of memoranda of law and the presentation of oral argument with respect to any question of law;

(9) Order the production of evidence and the appearance of witnesses whose testimony would be relevant, material and not repetitious;

(10) Impose sanctions as provided under § 28.24 of this part;

(11) Hold prehearing conferences for the settlement and simplification of issues; and

(12) Issue initial decisions, as appropriate.

[58 FR 61992, Nov. 23, 1993, as amended at 68 FR 69301, Dec. 12, 2003]

§ 28.23 Disqualification of administrative judges.

(a) In the event that an administrative judge considers himself or herself disqualified, he or she shall withdraw from the case, stating on the record the reasons therefor, and shall immediately notify the Board of the withdrawal.

(b) Any party may file a motion requesting the administrative judge to withdraw on the basis of personal bias or other disqualification and specifically setting forth the reasons for the request. This motion shall be filed as soon as the party has reason to believe there is a basis for disqualification.

(c) The administrative judge shall rule on the withdrawal motion. If the motion is denied, the party requesting withdrawal may take an appeal to the full Board. The notice of appeal, together with a supporting brief, shall be filed within 15 days of service of the denial of the motion. Upon receipt of the appeal, the Board will determine whether a response from the other party or parties is required, and if so, will fix by order the time for the filing of the response.

§ 28.24 Sanctions.

The administrative judge may impose sanctions upon the parties as necessary to serve the ends of justice, including but not limited to the instances set forth in this section.

(a) *Failure to comply with an order or subpoena.* When a party fails to comply with an order or subpoena (including an order for the taking of a deposition, for the production of evidence within the party's control, for an admission, or for production of witnesses), the administrative judge may:

(1) Draw an inference in favor of the requesting party on the issue related to the information sought.

(2) Prohibit the party failing to comply with such order or subpoena from introducing, or otherwise relying upon, evidence relating to the information sought.

(3) Permit the requesting party to introduce secondary evidence concerning the information sought.

(4) Strike any part of the pleadings or other submissions of the party failing to comply with such request.

(b) *Failure to prosecute or defend.* If a party fails to prosecute or defend a petition, the administrative judge may dismiss the action with prejudice or rule for the petitioner.

(c) *Failure to make timely filing.* The administrative judge may refuse to consider any motion or other action which is not filed in a timely fashion in compliance with this subpart.

[58 FR 61992, Nov. 23, 1993, as amended at 68 FR 69301, Dec. 12, 2003]

PARTIES, PRACTITIONERS AND WITNESSES

§ 28.25 Representation.

(a) All parties to a petition may be represented in any matter relating to the petition. The parties shall designate their representatives, if any, in the petition or responsive pleading. Any subsequent changes in representation shall also be in writing, and submitted to the administrative judge and served upon the other parties. Once a party has designated a representative, all documents required by the Board's regulations to be served upon the party shall instead be served upon the representative.

(b) A party may choose any representative so long as the person is willing and available to serve. However, the other party or parties may challenge the representative on the grounds of conflict of interest or conflict of position. This challenge must be made by motion to the administrative judge within 10 days of service of the notice of designation, and shall be ruled upon by the administrative judge prior to any further proceeding in the case. These procedures apply equally to original and subsequent designations of representatives. In the event the selected representative is disqualified, the party affected shall be given a reasonable time to obtain another representative.

(c) The administrative judge, on his or her own motion, may disqualify a party's representative on the grounds described in paragraph (b) of this section.

[58 FR 61992, Nov. 23, 1993, as amended at 68 FR 69301, Dec. 12, 2003]

§ 28.26 Witness fees.

The costs involved in the appearance of witnesses in any Board proceeding shall be allocated as follows:

(a) Persons employed by the GAO shall, upon request by the administrative judge to GAO, be made available to participate in the hearing and shall be in official duty status for this purpose and shall not receive witness fees. Payment of travel and per diem expenses shall be governed by applicable laws and regulations.

(b) Employees of other federal agencies called to testify at a Board hearing shall, at the request of the administrative judge and with the approval of the employing agency, be in official duty status during any period of absence from their normal duties caused by their testimony, and shall not receive witness fees. Payment of travel and per diem expenses shall be governed by applicable laws and regulations. A party planning to call an employee of another federal agency as a witness shall promptly notify the administrative judge of the need to submit to the federal agency a request that the employee be granted official duty status. In the event that the employing agency refuses the request to release the employee-witness in an official duty status, the employee-witness may be paid a witness fee in accordance with paragraph (c) of this section.

(c) Witnesses who are not covered by paragraphs (a) or (b) of this section are entitled to the same witness fees as those paid to subpoenaed witnesses under 28 U.S.C. 1821. The fees shall be paid, in the first instance, by the party requesting the appearance of the witness, subject to a subsequent decision otherwise in accordance with § 28.89, concerning the award of attorneys fees and costs. Such fees shall be tendered to the witness at the time the subpoena is served, or, when the witness appears voluntarily, at the time of appearance. A federal agency or corporation is not required to tender witness fees in advance. Payment of travel and per diem expenses shall be governed by applicable law and regulation.

(d) When the General Counsel is the petitioner or is representing the petitioner, the General Counsel shall pay the witness fees and arrange for the travel and per diem expenses that are required by paragraph (c) of this section.

§ 28.27 Intervenors.

(a) Intervenors are persons who are allowed to participate in a proceeding because the proceeding, or its outcome, may affect their rights or duties.

(b) Any person may, by motion to the administrative judge, request permission to intervene. The motion shall state the reasons why the person should be permitted to intervene. A person alleged to have committed a prohibited personnel practice under 5 U.S.C. 2302(b) may request permission to intervene under this section.

(c) A motion for permission to intervene will be granted where a determination is made by the administrative judge or the Board, where the case is being heard en banc, that the requestor will be affected directly by the outcome of the proceeding. Denial of a motion for intervention may be appealed to the full Board. Such an appeal shall be filed within 10 days of service of the denial of the motion to intervene.

(d) Intervenors who are granted permission to intervene will be considered full parties to the hearing and will have the same rights and duties as a party with two exceptions:

(1) Intervenors will not have an independent right to a hearing.

(2) Intervenors may participate in Board proceedings only on the issues affecting them, as determined by the administrative judge or Board.

[58 FR 61992, Nov. 23, 1993, as amended at 68 FR 69301, Dec. 12, 2003]

§ 28.28 Substitution.

(a) If a petitioner dies or is otherwise unable to pursue the petition, the action may be completed upon substitution of a proper party.

(b) A motion for substitution shall be filed by the proper party within 90 days after the death of the petitioner or other disabling event.

[58 FR 61992, Nov. 23, 1993, as amended at 68 FR 69301, Dec. 12, 2003]

§ 28.29 Consolidation or joinder.

(a) *Explanation.* (1) Consolidation may occur where two or more parties have cases which should be united because they contain identical or similar issues or in such other circumstances as justice requires.

(2) Joinder may occur where one person has two or more petitions pending and they are united for consideration. For example, a single petitioner who has one petition pending challenging a 30-day suspension and another petition pending challenging a subsequent dismissal might have the cases joined.

(b) *Action by administrative judge.* An administrative judge may consolidate or join cases on his or her own initiative or on the motion of a party if to do so would expedite processing of the cases and not adversely affect the interests of the parties.

[58 FR 61992, Nov. 23, 1993, as amended at 68 FR 69301, Dec. 12, 2003]

Discovery

§ 28.40 Statement of purpose.

Proceedings before the Board shall be conducted as expeditiously as possible with due regard to the rights of the parties. Discovery is designed to enable a party to obtain relevant information needed for presentation of the party's case. These regulations are intended to provide a simple method of discovery. They will be interpreted and applied so as to avoid delay and to facilitate adjudication of the case. The parties are expected to initiate and complete needed discovery with a minimum of Board intervention.

§ 28.41 Explanation, scope and methods.

(a) *Explanation.* Discovery is the process apart from the hearing whereby a party may obtain relevant information from another person, including a party, which has not otherwise been provided. Relevant information includes information which appears reasonably calculated to lead to the discovery of admissible evidence. This information is obtained for the purpose of assisting the parties in developing, preparing, and presenting their cases. The Federal Rules of Civil Procedure may be used as a general guide for discovery practices in proceedings before the Board, except as to matters specifically covered by these regulations. The Federal Rules of Civil Procedure shall be interpreted as instructive rather than controlling.

(b) *Scope.* Any person may be examined pursuant to paragraph (c) of this section regarding any nonprivileged matter which is relevant to the issue under review, including the existence, description, nature, custody, condition and location of documents or other tangible things, and the identity and location of persons having knowledge of relevant facts. The information sought must appear reasonably calculated to lead to the discovery of admissible evidence.

(c) *Methods.* Discovery may be obtained by one or more of the methods provided under the Federal Rules of Civil Procedure, including written interrogatories, depositions, production of documents or things for inspection or copying, and requests for admission addressed to parties.

[58 FR 61992, Nov. 23, 1993, as amended at 68 FR 69301, Dec. 12, 2003]

§ 28.42 Discovery procedures and protective orders.

(a) *Discovery from a party.* A party seeking discovery from another party shall initiate the process by serving a request for discovery on the other party. For purposes of discovery under these regulations, a party includes an intervenor.

(1) Each request for discovery shall state the time limit for responding, as prescribed in paragraph (d) of this section.

(2) In the case of a request for deposition of a party, reasonable notice in writing shall be given to every party to the action. The notice shall:

(i) Specify the time and place of the taking of the deposition; and

(ii) Be served on the person to be deposed.

(3) When a request for discovery is directed to an officer or employee of GAO, the agency shall make the officer or employee available on official time for the purpose of responding to the request and shall assist the officer or employee as necessary in providing relevant information that is available to the agency.

(b) *Discovery from a nonparty.* Parties are encouraged to attempt to obtain voluntary discovery from nonparties whenever possible. A party seeking discovery from a nonparty may initiate the process by serving a request for discovery on that nonparty and on all other parties to the proceeding. When a party is unable to obtain voluntary cooperation, the party may request that the administrative judge issue a subpoena by following the procedures set forth in § 28.46.

(c) *Responses to discovery requests.* (1) A party shall answer a discovery request within the time provided by paragraph (d)(2) of this section either by furnishing to the requesting party the information or testimony requested or agreeing to make deponents available to testify within a reasonable time, or by stating an objection to the particular request and the reasons for objection, or by requesting a protective order.

(2) Upon failure or refusal of a party to respond in full to a discovery request, the requesting party may file with the administrative judge a motion to compel discovery. The time limits applicable to a motion to compel are set forth in paragraph (d)(4) of this section. A copy of the motion shall be served on the other parties. The motion shall be accompanied by:

(i) A copy of the original request served on the party from whom discovery was sought and a statement showing the relevancy and materiality of the information sought; and

(ii) A copy of the objections to discovery or, where appropriate, a verified statement that no response has been received.

(3) The party from whom discovery was sought shall respond to the motion to compel within the time limits set forth in paragraph (d)(4) of this section.

(d) *Time limits.* (1) Requests for discovery shall be served within 30 days after the service list is served by the Board on all parties.

(2) A party or nonparty shall respond to a discovery request within 20 days after service of the request on the party or nonparty. Any discovery requests following the initial request shall be served within 10 days of the date of service of the prior response, unless otherwise directed. Deposition witnesses shall give their testimony at the time and place stated in the notice of deposition-taking or in the subpoena, unless the parties agree otherwise.

(3) In responding to a discovery request, a party or nonparty shall respond as fully as possible, except to the extent that the party or nonparty objects to the discovery or requests a protective order. Any objection or request for a protective order shall be filed within the time limits set forth in paragraph (d)(2) of this section. Any objection shall be addressed to the party requesting discovery and shall state the particular grounds for the objection. Any request for a protective order shall state the grounds for the protective order and shall be served on the administrative judge and any other parties to the action. The administrative judge shall rule on the request for a protective order.

(4) Motions for an order compelling discovery shall be filed with the administrative judge within 10 days of the service of objections or within 10 days of the expiration of the time limits for response when no response or an alleged inadequate response is received. Opposition to a motion to compel must

be filed with the administrative judge within 10 days of the date of service of the motion.

(5) Discovery shall be completed by the time designated by the administrative judge, but no later than 65 days after the service of the notice of filing of a petition. A later date may be set by the administrative judge after due consideration of the particular situation including the dates set for hearing and closing of the case record.

[58 FR 61992, Nov. 23, 1993, as amended at 68 FR 69301, Dec. 12, 2003]

§ 28.43 Compelling discovery.

(a) *Motion for an order compelling discovery.* Motions for orders compelling discovery shall be submitted to the administrative judge as set forth at § 28.42(c)(2) and (d)(4) above.

(b) *Content of order.* Any order issued may include, where appropriate:

(1) Provision for notice to the person to be deposed as to the time and place of such deposition.

(2) Such conditions or limitations concerning the conduct or scope of the proceedings or the subject matter as may be necessary to prevent undue delay or to protect any party or deponent from undue expense, embarrassment or oppression.

(3) Limitations upon the time for conducting depositions, answering written interrogatories, or producing documentary evidence.

(4) Other restrictions upon the discovery process as determined by the administrative judge.

(c) Failure to comply with an order compelling discovery may subject the noncomplying party to sanctions under § 28.24.

§ 28.44 Taking of depositions.

Depositions may be taken before any person not interested in the outcome of the proceedings who is authorized by law to administer oaths.

§ 28.45 Admission of facts and genuineness of documents.

(a) Any party may be served with requests for the admission of the genuineness of any relevant documents identified within the request or the truth of any relevant matters of fact or application of law to the facts as set forth in the request.

(b) Within the time period prescribed by § 28.42(d)(2), the party on whom the request is served must submit to the requesting party:

(1) A sworn statement specifically denying, admitting, or expressing a lack of knowledge after making reasonable inquiry regarding the specific matters on which an admission is requested; and/or

(2) An objection to the request for an admission, in whole or in part, on the grounds that the matters contained therein are privileged, irrelevant, or otherwise improper.

(c) Upon a failure or refusal of a party to respond to a request for admissions within the prescribed time period, the request shall be deemed admitted.

SUBPOENAS

§ 28.46 Motion for subpoena.

(a) *Authority to issue subpoenas.* Any member of the Board may issue subpoenas requiring the attendance and testimony of witnesses and the production of documentary or other evidence from any place in the United States or any territory or possession thereof, the Commonwealth of Puerto Rico, or the District of Columbia. Any member of the Board may order the taking of depositions or order responses to written interrogatories.

(b) *Motion.* (1) A motion for the issuance of a subpoena requiring the attendance and testimony of witnesses or the production of documents or other evidence under § 28.46(a) shall be submitted to the administrative judge at least 15 days in advance of the date scheduled for the commencement of the hearing.

(2) If the subpoena is sought as part of the discovery process, the motion shall be submitted to the administrative judge at least 15 days in advance of the date set for the attendance of the witness at a deposition or the production of documents.

(c) *Forms and showing.* Motions for subpoenas shall be submitted in writing to the administrative judge and shall specify with particularity the books, papers, or testimony desired and shall be supported by a showing of general relevance and reasonable scope and a statement of the facts expected to be proven thereby.

[58 FR 61992, Nov. 23, 1993, as amended at 68 FR 69301, Dec. 12, 2003]

§ 28.47 Motion to quash.

Any person against whom a subpoena is directed may file a motion to quash or limit the subpoena setting forth the reasons why the subpoena should not be complied with or why it should be limited in scope. This motion shall be filed with the administrative judge within 20 days after service of the subpoena.

§ 28.48 Service.

Service of a subpoena may be made by a United States Marshal or Deputy Marshal or by any person who is over 18 years of age and not a party to the proceeding.

§ 28.49 Return of service.

When service of a subpoena is effected by a person other than a United States Marshal or Deputy Marshal, that person shall certify on the return of service that service was made either:

(a) In person,

(b) By registered or certified mail, or

(c) By delivery to a responsible person (named) at the residence or place of business (as appropriate) of the person to be served.

§ 28.50 Enforcement.

If a person has been served with a Board subpoena but fails or refuses to comply with its terms, the party seeking compliance may file a written motion for enforcement with the administrative judge or make an oral motion for enforcement while on record at a hearing. The party shall present the return of service and, except where the witness was required to appear before the administrative judge, shall submit affidavit evidence of the failure or refusal to obey the subpoena. The Board may then request the appropriate United States district court to enforce the subpoena.

Hearings

§ 28.55 Scheduling the hearing.

The notice of initial hearing shall fix the date, time and place of hearing. GAO, upon request of the administrative judge, shall provide appropriate hearing space. Motions for postponement by either party shall be made in writing, shall set forth the reasons for the request and shall be granted only upon a showing of good cause. When the parties agree on postponement, motions may be made orally and shall be granted only upon a showing of good cause.

§ 28.56 Hearing procedures, conduct and copies of exhibits.

(a) The Board may designate one or more administrative judges to conduct hearings on appropriate matters.

(b) The hearing will be conducted as an administrative proceeding and, ordinarily, the rules of evidence will not be strictly followed.

(c) Parties will be expected to present their cases in a concise manner limiting the testimony of witnesses and submission of documents to relevant matters.

(d) Any party to a hearing offering exhibits into the record shall submit the original of each such exhibit to the court reporter, two copies to the administrative judge, plus one copy for each opposing party that is separately represented.

(e) Each party to a proceeding shall be responsible for bringing the proper number of copies of an exhibit to the hearing.

(f) Multipage exhibits shall be paginated in the lower right hand corner and the first page shall indicate the total number of pages in the exhibit. Multiple exhibits shall be indexed and tabbed.

(g) No later than the commencement of the hearing, each party shall submit to the administrative judge, to the court reporter, and to the opposing party: (1) A typed list of the witnesses expected to be called to testify; and (2) a typed list of the acronyms (with definitions) expected to be used by the witnesses.

[58 FR 61992, Nov. 23, 1993, as amended at 68 FR 69301, Dec. 12, 2003]

§ 28.57 Public hearings.

(a) Hearings shall be open to the public. However, the administrative judge at his or her discretion, may order a hearing or any part thereof closed, where to do so would be in the best interests of the petitioner, a witness, the public, or other affected persons. Any order closing the hearing shall set forth the reasons for the administrative judge's decision. Any objections thereto shall be made a part of the record.

(b) At the hearing, the petitioner, the petitioner's representative, GAO's legal representative, and a GAO management representative, who is not expected to testify, each have a right to be present. The Agency management representative shall be designated prior to the hearing.

[58 FR 61992, Nov. 23, 1993, as amended at 68 FR 69301, Dec. 12, 2003]

§ 28.58 Transcript.

(a) *Preparation.* A verbatim record made under supervision of the administrative judge shall be kept of every hearing and shall be the sole official record of the proceeding. Upon request, a copy of a transcript of the hearing shall be made available to each party. Additional copies of the transcript shall be made available to a party upon payment of costs. Exceptions to the payment requirement may be granted for good cause shown. A motion for an exception shall be made in writing and accompanied by an affidavit setting forth the reasons for the request and shall be granted upon a showing of good cause. Requests for copies of transcripts shall be directed to the Clerk of the Board. The Clerk of the Board may, by agreement with the person making the request, make arrangements with the official hearing reporter for required services to be charged to the requester.

(b) *Corrections.* Corrections to the official transcript will be permitted. Motions for correction must be submitted within 30 days of service of the transcript upon the party. Corrections of the official transcript will be permitted only when errors of substance are involved and only upon approval of the administrative judge. The administrative judge may make changes at any time with notice to the parties.

§ 28.59 Official record.

The transcript of testimony and the exhibits, together with all papers and motions filed in the proceedings, shall constitute the exclusive and official record.

§ 28.60 Briefs.

(a) *Length.* Principal briefs shall not exceed 60 pages and reply briefs 30 pages, exclusive of tables and pages limited only to quotations of statutes, rules, and the like. Motions to file extended briefs shall be granted only for good cause shown. Briefs in excess of 10 pages shall include an index and a table of authorities.

(b) *Format.* Every brief must be easily readable. Pages must be 8½ × 11 inches with margins at least one inch on all sides. Typewritten briefs must have double spacing between each line of text, except for quoted texts which may be single spaced.

(c) *Number of copies.* An original and 3 copies of each brief shall be filed with the administrative judge and one copy served on each party separately represented. When an action is before the full Board, an original and seven copies of each brief must be filed with the Board and one copy served on each party separately represented.

§ 28.61 Burden and degree of proof.

(a) In appealable actions, as defined by 5 U.S.C. 7701(a), agency action must be sustained by the Board if:

(1) It is a performance-based action and is supported by substantial evidence; or

(2) It is brought under any other provision of law, rule, or regulation as defined by 5 U.S.C. 7701(a) and is supported by a preponderance of evidence.

(b) Notwithstanding paragraph (a) of this section, the agency's decision shall not be sustained if the petitioner:

(1) Shows harmful error in the application of the agency's procedures in arriving at such decision;

(2) Shows that the decision was based on any prohibited personnel practice described in 4 CFR 2.5; or

(3) Shows that the decision was not in accordance with law.

(c) In any other action within the Board's jurisdiction, the petitioner shall have the responsibility of presenting the evidence in support of the action and shall have the burden of proving the allegations of the appeal by a preponderance of the evidence.

(d) *Definitions.* For purposes of this section, the following definitions shall apply:

Harmful error means error by the agency in the application of its procedures which, in the absence or cure of the error, might have caused the agency to reach a conclusion different from the one reached.

Preponderance of the evidence means that degree of relevant evidence which a reasonable person, considering the record as a whole, would accept as sufficient to support a conclusion that the matter asserted is more likely to be true than not true.

Substantial evidence means that degree of relevant evidence which a reasonable person, considering the record as a whole, might accept as adequate to support a conclusion, even though other reasonable persons might disagree. This is a lower standard of proof than preponderance of the evidence.

[58 FR 61992, Nov. 23, 1993, as amended at 68 FR 69302, Dec. 12, 2003]

§ 28.62 Decision on the record.

(a) The parties may agree to forego a hearing and request that the matter be decided by the presiding administrative judge based upon the record submitted.

(b) If the parties agree to forego a hearing under this subpart, the record will close on the date that the administrative judge sets as the final date for the receipt or filing of submissions of the parties. Once the record closes, no additional evidence or argument will be accepted unless the party seeking to submit it demonstrates that the evidence was not available before the record closed.

(c) In matters submitted for decision on the record under this section, the parties bear the same burdens of proof set forth in § 28.61.

(d) A decision obtained under this section is a decision on the merits of the case and is appealable as if the matter had been adjudicated in an evidentiary hearing.

[68 FR 69302, Dec. 12, 2003]

§ 28.63 Closing the record.

(a) When there is a hearing, the record shall be closed at the conclusion of the hearing. However, when the administrative judge allows the parties to submit argument, briefs or documents previously identified for introduction into evidence, the record shall be left open for such time as the administrative judge grants for that purpose.

(b) Once the record is closed, no additional evidence or argument shall be accepted into the record except upon a showing that new and material evidence has become available which was not available despite due diligence prior to the closing of the record. However, the administrative judge shall make part of the record any motions for attorney fees, any supporting documentation, and determinations thereon, and any approved correction to the transcript.

[58 FR 61992, Nov. 23, 1993. Redesignated at 68 FR 69302, Dec. 12, 2003]

EVIDENCE

§ 28.65 Service of documents.

Any document submitted with regard to any pleading, motion, or brief shall be served upon all parties to the proceeding.

§ 28.66 Admissibility.

Evidence or testimony may be excluded from consideration by the administrative judge if it is irrelevant, immaterial, unduly repetitious or protected by privilege. The administrative judge is not bound by formal evidentiary rules but may rely on the Federal Rules of Evidence for guidance.

[68 FR 69302, Dec. 12, 2003]

§ 28.67 Production of statements.

After an individual has given evidence in a proceeding, any party may request a copy of any prior signed statement made by that individual which is relevant to the evidence given. If the party refuses to furnish the statement, the administrative judge may draw an adverse inference from the failure to produce or may exclude the relevant evidence given by the individual from consideration.

§ 28.68 Stipulations.

The parties may stipulate as to any matter of fact. Such a stipulation will satisfy a party's burden of proving the fact alleged.

§ 28.69 Judicial notice.

The administrative judge on his or her own motion or on motion of a party, may take judicial notice of a fact which is not subject to reasonable dispute because it is either: a matter of common knowledge; or a matter capable of accurate and ready determination by resort to sources whose accuracy cannot reasonably be questioned. Judicial notice taken of any fact satisfies a party's burden of proving the fact noticed.

[68 FR 69302, Dec. 12, 2003]

Interlocutory Appeals

§ 28.80 Explanation.

An interlocutory appeal is an appeal to the Board of a ruling made by an administrative judge during the course of a proceeding. This appeal may be permitted by the administrative judge if he or she determines that the issue presented is of such importance to the proceeding that it requires the Board's immediate attention. The Board makes a decision on the issue and the administrative judge acts in accordance with that decision.

§ 28.81 Procedures and criteria for certification.

(a) Interlocutory review by the Board of a ruling by the administrative judge during the course of the proceeding is disfavored and will be permitted only in circumstances where:

(1) The ruling involves an important question of law or policy about which there is substantial ground for difference of opinion; and

(2) An immediate review of the ruling by the Board will materially advance the completion of the proceeding, or denial will cause undue harm to a party or the public.

(b) The administrative judge may, on motion of a party or on his or her own motion, certify an interlocutory ruling to the Board for its immediate consideration. Any such certification shall explain the basis on which the administrative judge concluded that the standards for interlocutory review have been met. If the Board nevertheless determines that the certification does not meet those standards it may decline to accept the certification.

(c) A motion for certification to the Board of an interlocutory ruling by the administrative judge shall be filed within 10 days after service of the ruling upon the parties. The motion shall include arguments in support of both the certification and the determination to be made by the Board. Responses, if any, shall be filed within 10 days after service of the motion.

(d) The grant or denial of a motion for certification of an interlocutory ruling shall not be appealable. The administrative judge shall promptly bring a denial of such a motion, and the reasons therefor, to the attention of the Board. If, upon its consideration of the motion and the underlying record, the Board believes that interlocutory review is warranted, it may grant the motion sua sponte.

(e) Upon its acceptance of a ruling of the administrative judge for interlocutory review, the Board shall issue an order setting forth the procedures that will be followed in the conduct of that review.

(f) Unless otherwise directed by the Board, the stay of any proceedings during the pendency of either a motion for certification or an interlocutory review itself shall be within the discretion of the administrative judge.

(g) The denial of a motion for certification does not affect the right of the parties to challenge interlocutory rulings in the course of the review by the Board of initial or recommended decisions.

BOARD DECISIONS, ATTORNEY'S FEES AND JUDICIAL REVIEW

§28.86 [Reserved]

§28.87 Board procedures; initial decisions.

(a) When a case is heard in the first instance by a single Board member, a panel of members, or a non-member appointed by the Board, an initial decision shall be issued by that member, panel or individual and served upon the parties.

(b) An aggrieved party may seek reconsideration of or may appeal the initial decision in the following manner:

(1) Within 10 days of the service of the initial decision, such a party may file and serve a request for reconsideration with the administrative judge or panel rendering that decision. Filing of the request for reconsideration shall toll the commencement of the 15 day period for filing a notice of appeal with the full Board, pending disposition of the request for reconsideration by the administrative judge or panel. The administrative judge or panel shall determine if a response is required, and if so, will fix by order the time for the filing of the response. A motion for reconsideration will not be granted without providing an opportunity for response.

(2) Within 15 days of the service of the initial decision, such a party may appeal to the full Board by filing and serving a notice of appeal to the Board.

(c) Within 25 days following the filing of a notice of appeal to the full Board, the appellant shall file and serve a supporting brief. That brief shall identify with particularity those findings or conclusions in the initial decision that are challenged and shall refer specifically to the portions of the record and the provisions of statutes or regulations that assertedly support each assignment of error. Within 25 days following the service of the appellant's brief, the appellee may file and serve a responsive brief. Within 10 days following the service of the appellee's responsive brief, the appellant may file and serve a reply brief.

(d) In the absence of a timely appeal, the initial decision shall become the final decision of the Board 30 days following its issuance or the date of the administrative judge's or panel's disposition of a request for reconsideration (whichever comes later) unless, prior to the expiration of the 30 day period, the parties are notified in writing that the full Board intends to review the initial decision in whole or in part on its own motion. Such review sua sponte will normally be conducted only if a majority of the Board concludes that one or more issues of law addressed in the initial decision are of such importance as to warrant consideration by the full Board notwithstanding the absence of appeal. Issues so qualifying shall be identified in the Board's notice and the parties shall be provided an opportunity to brief them prior to the Board's decision.

(e) Oral argument on an appeal or in connection with a sua sponte review shall be held in the discretion of the Board. Any party may request that the Board exercise its discretion in that regard.

(f) Upon appeal or following its review sua sponte, the Board may affirm, reverse, modify or vacate the initial decision in whole or in part. If deemed warranted, the Board may remand the proceeding to the single member or panel for further action, including the reopening of the record for the taking of additional evidence. Unless the full Board expressly retains jurisdiction, the single member or panel shall render, on completion of the remand, a supplemental initial decision which shall be subject to appellate review in the same manner and to the same extent as provided for initial decisions in paragraphs (b), (d) and (g) of this section. If the Board does expressly retain jurisdiction at the time of remand, the single member or panel shall instead render a report to the Board on the remanded matters. Upon receipt of the report, the Board shall determine whether the views of the parties on the content of the report should be obtained in writing and, where necessary, shall fix by order the time for the submission of those views. A decision of the full Board disposing of the proceeding without a remand or, where the Board has expressly retained jurisdiction, following completion of the remand shall be the final decision of the Board and subject to judicial review.

(g) In conducting its examination of the initial decision, the Board may substitute its own findings of fact and conclusions of law, but the Board generally will defer to demeanor-based credibility determinations made in the initial decision. In determining whether some action other than affirmance of the initial decision is required, the Board will also consider whether:

(1) New and material evidence is available that, despite due diligence, was not available when the record was closed;

(2) The initial decision is based on an erroneous interpretation of statute or regulation;

(3) The initial decision is arbitrary, capricious or an abuse of discretion, or otherwise not consistent with law;

(4) The initial decision is not made consistent with required procedures and results in harmful error.

(h) Initial decisions that become final without review by the full Board shall not be binding precedent in any other case.

[58 FR 61992, Nov. 23, 1993, as amended at 68 FR 69302, Dec. 12, 2003]

§ 28.88 Board procedures; enforcement.

(a) All decisions and orders of the Board shall be complied with promptly. Whenever a Board decision or order requires a person or party to take any action, the Board may require such person or party to provide the Board and all parties with a compliance report.

(b) When the Board does not receive a report of compliance in accordance with paragraph (a) of this section, the Solicitor shall make inquiries to determine the status of the compliance report and shall report upon the results of the inquiry to the Board.

(c) Any person and/or the General Counsel may petition the Board for enforcement of a final decision of the Board. The petition shall specifically set forth the reasons why the petitioner believes there is non-compliance.

(d) Upon receipt of a non-compliance report from its Solicitor or of a petition for enforcement of a final decision, the Board may issue a notice to any person to show cause why there was non-compliance. Apart from remedies available to the parties, the Board may seek judicial enforcement of a decision or order issued pursuant to a show cause proceeding.

(e) If the parties enter into a settlement agreement that has been reviewed and approved by the administrative judge, the Board retains jurisdiction to enforce the terms of such settlement agreement.

(f) Any party to a settlement agreement over which the Board retains jurisdiction may petition the Board for enforcement of the terms of such settlement agreement.

[58 FR 61992, Nov. 23, 1993, as amended at 68 FR 69302, Dec. 12, 2003]

§ 28.89 Attorney's fees and costs.

Within 20 days after service of a final decision by the Board, or within 20 days after the date on which an initial decision becomes final pursuant to § 28.87(d), the petitioner, if he or she is the prevailing party, may submit a request for the award of reasonable attorney's fees and costs. GAO may file a response within 20 days after service of the request. Motions for attorney's fees shall be filed in accordance with § 28.21 of these regulations. Rulings on attorney's fees and costs shall be consistent with the standards set forth at 5 U.S.C. 7701(g). The decision of the administrative judge concerning attorney's fees and costs shall be subject to review and shall become final according to the provisions of § 28.87.

[68 FR 69302, Dec. 12, 2003]

§ 28.90 Board procedures; judicial review.

(a) A final decision by the Board under 31 U.S.C. 753(a) (1), (2), (3), (6), (7) or (9) may be appealed to the United States Court of Appeals for the Federal Circuit within 30 days after the petitioner receives notice of the Board's decision.

(b) The Board may designate the Solicitor, the General Counsel or any other qualified individual to represent it in any judicial proceeding involving a Board decision or the interpretation of a Board rule or of the GAO Personnel Act.

[58 FR 61992, Nov. 23, 1993, as amended at 59 FR 59106, Nov. 16, 1994]

Subpart C—Oversight Procedures

§28.91 General.

Pursuant to section 732(f) of Title 31, U.S.C., the Board is authorized to conduct oversight of GAO employment regulations, procedures and practices as they relate to laws prohibiting discrimination in employment on the basis of race, color, religion, national origin, political affiliation, age, sex, marital status, or disability.

§28.92 Oversight of GAO EEO program.

(a) When requested by the Board in the exercise of its oversight responsibility, GAO shall provide:

(1) Such plans, procedures and regulations as GAO may develop in order to eliminate and prevent employment discrimination on the bases enumerated in §28.95;

(2) Reports regarding its efforts to publicize to its employees the procedures to be followed for receiving advice and for filing complaints regarding the enforcement of laws prohibiting discrimination in employment;

(3) Quarterly statistical reports of pre-complaint counseling and of pending complaints, in a manner prescribed by the Board;

(4) An annual report on its equal employment opportunity affirmative action program and its Federal Equal Employment Opportunity Recruitment Program; and

(5) Any other information regarding equal employment opportunity within the GAO that may be required by the Board, in the time frame and format established by the Board after consultation with the Comptroller General or his or her designee.

(b) The Board shall review and evaluate the regulations, procedures and practices of the GAO, including the information filed with it in accordance with paragraph (a) above, and shall:

(1) Require the GAO to make any changes the Board determines are needed due to violations of or inconsistencies with Subchapters III and IV of Chapter 7 of Title 31, U.S.C. or equal employment opportunity laws, and

(2) Report to the Congress on the overall progress being made in effectuating the purposes of Subchapters III and IV of Chapter 7 of Title 31, U.S.C.

Subpart D—Special Procedures; Equal Employment Opportunity (EEO) Cases

§28.95 Purpose and scope.

The procedures in this subpart relate to charges filed against any GAO policies or specific actions which are alleged to involve prohibited discrimination. Prohibited discrimination is defined as any action in violation of:

(a) Section 717 of the Civil Rights Act of 1964, as amended (42 U.S.C. 2000e-16), prohibiting discrimination based on race, color, religion, sex or national origin;

(b) Sections 12 and 15 of the Age Discrimination in Employment Act of 1967 (29 U.S.C. 631, 633a) prohibiting discrimination on account of age;

(c) Section 6(d) of the Fair Labor Standards Act of 1938 (29 U.S.C. 206(d), prohibiting discrimination in wages on the basis of sex;

(d) Title I of the Americans with Disabilities Act of 1990 (42 U.S.C. 12101 *et seq.*) and sections 501 and 505 of the Rehabilitation Act of 1973 (29 U.S.C. 791, 794a) prohibiting discrimination on the basis of disability; or

(e) Any other law prohibiting discrimination in Federal employment on the basis of race, color, religion, age, sex, national origin or disability. 31 U.S.C. 732(f)(2).

[58 FR 61992, Nov. 23, 1993, as amended at 68 FR 69302, Dec. 12, 2003]

§28.96 Applicability of general procedures.

Except where a different procedure is provided for in this subpart, the procedures to be followed by all parties in cases arising under this subpart shall be the general procedures as prescribed in subpart B of this part.

§28.97 Class actions in EEO cases.

(a) Prior to invoking the Board's procedures in a case alleging prohibited discrimination on behalf of a class of

GAO employees or applicants for employment, a complaint must first be filed with GAO in accordance with GAO Order 2713.2.

(b) An appeal from GAO's disposition of any EEO class complaint may be submitted to the Board at the following times:

(1) Within 20 days of receipt of a GAO determination rejecting or canceling the class complaint;

(2) Within 20 days of receipt of a GAO determination accepting the class action, but with modifications that are not satisfactory to the agent of the class;

(3) When a period of more than 180 days has elapsed since the formal class complaint was filed and the GAO has not issued a final decision; or

(4) Within 20 days of receipt of a final GAO decision resolving the complaint if that decision, in whole or in part, has not satisfied the agent for the class.

(c) In EEO class actions, employees shall not file charges with the Board's Office of General Counsel and that Office shall not undertake an independent investigation of a class complaint that has been filed with GAO. However, the General Counsel may request permission to intervene with regard to any issue in which the General Counsel finds a significant public interest with respect to the preservation of the merit system.

(d) An appeal of a GAO disposition of an EEO class complaint shall be decided by the Board based upon a review of the administrative record, including any recommended findings and conclusions, developed in the GAO class complaint process. In such cases, the Board will employ the same standards of review set forth in § 28.87.

(e) The parties to an EEO class complaint do not have a right to a de novo evidentiary hearing before the Board. However, either the class representative or GAO may file a motion requesting an evidentiary hearing, rather than having the Board decide the case upon review of the administrative record already developed by GAO. The Board, in its discretion, may grant such motion or, upon its own review of the administrative record, may direct that a new hearing be conducted. If the Board orders a new evidentiary hearing, the class representative shall file a petition on behalf of the class and the case shall be adjudicated before an administrative judge of this Board pursuant to the procedures applicable to an individual EEO complaint processed under § 28.98 of these regulations. For the purpose of determining whether it is appropriate to treat a petition as a class action, the administrative judge will be guided, but not controlled, by the applicable provisions of the Federal Rules of Civil Procedure.

[58 FR 61992, Nov. 23, 1993, as amended at 68 FR 69303, Dec. 12, 2003]

§ 28.98 Individual charges in EEO cases.

(a) Except as provided in paragraph (c) of this section, a charge alleging prohibited discrimination (as defined in § 28.95) shall not be filed with the Board's General Counsel unless the charging party has first filed a complaint of discrimination with GAO in accordance with GAO Order 2713.2.

(b) A charge relating to GAO's disposition of any individual EEO complaint may be filed with the Board's General Counsel at the following times:

(1) Within 30 days from the receipt by the charging party of a GAO decision rejecting the complaint in whole or part;

(2) Whenever a period of more than 120 days has elapsed since the complaint was filed, and the GAO has not issued a final decision; or

(3) Within 30 days from the receipt by the charging party of a final GAO decision concerning the complaint of discrimination.

(c) *Special rules for adverse and performance based actions.* Where an employee is affected by a removal, suspension for more than 14 days, reduction in grade or pay, or furlough of not more than 30 days (whether due to disciplinary, performance-based or other reasons), and the employee wishes to allege that such action was due in whole or part to prohibited discrimination (as defined in § 28.95), the employee may elect to do either (but not both) of the following:

(1) File a charge directly with the Board's General Counsel within 30 days of the effective date of the personnel

action and raise the issue of discrimination in the course of the proceedings before the Board; or

(2) File a complaint of discrimination with the GAO pursuant to GAO Order 2713.2. If the employee elects to file a complaint of discrimination with GAO, he or she may still seek Board review of the matter by filing a charge with the Board's General Counsel at the times authorized in paragraph (b) of this section. Where a complaint of discrimination filed with GAO relates to non-EEO issues that are within the Board's jurisdiction in addition to EEO-related allegations, the subsequent charge filed with the Board's General Counsel under paragraph (b) of this section shall be considered a timely appeal of the non-EEO issues. An employee will be deemed to have elected the EEO complaint process if the employee files a timely written complaint of discrimination with GAO before filing a charge with the Board's General Counsel. Consultation with an EEO counselor, without filing a written complaint of discrimination, does not constitute an election of the EEO complaint process.

(d) *Special rules for RIF based actions.* An individual alleging discrimination issues in connection with a RIF-based separation may follow the procedures outlined above in paragraph (c) of this section for adverse and performance based actions, or may choose instead a third option. In accordance with the provisions of § 28.13, such an individual may challenge that action by filing directly with the PAB, thus bypassing both the Office of Opportunity and Inclusiveness and the Board's Office of General Counsel.

(e)(1) The charging party shall file the charge with the Board's Office of General Counsel in accordance with § 28.11. That Office shall investigate the charge in accordance with § 28.12.

(2) A charging party challenging a RIF action by filing directly with the PAB shall follow the procedures prescribed in § 28.13 and § 28.18.

[58 FR 61992, Nov. 23, 1993, as amended at 59 FR 59106, Nov. 16, 1994; 61 FR 36811, July 15, 1996; 68 FR 69303, Dec. 12, 2003]

§ 28.99 Petitions to the Board in EEO cases.

(a) The provisions of §§ 28.18 through 28.90, inclusive, shall govern the Board's procedures in processing petitions filed under this subpart.

(b) Remedial action provided in Board orders in these cases may include:

(1) Provision for Agency offers of employment, re-employment or promotion, with or without back pay, when the Board decides such action is required to make whole the individual found to have been discriminated against.

(2) Notification to all GAO employees of the action ordered to be taken to expunge the effect of the discrimination;

(3) Correction of GAO personnel records, as necessary, to reflect the purpose of the Board order; and,

(4) Any other action the Board believes proper to correct the effect of the discrimination found to have occurred.

[58 FR 61992, Nov. 23, 1993, as amended at 68 FR 69303, Dec. 12, 2003]

§ 28.100 [Reserved]

§ 28.101 Termination of Board proceedings when suit is filed in Federal District Court.

Any proceeding before the Board shall be terminated when an employee or applicant who is alleging violation of Title VII of the Civil Rights Act of 1964, as amended, 42 U.S.C. 2000e–16, Title I of the Americans with Disabilities Act of 1990, 42 U.S.C. 12101 *et seq.*, the Age Discrimination in Employment Act, 29 U.S.C. 633a, or the Rehabilitation Act, 29 U.S.C. 791, files suit in Federal District Court on the same cause of action pending before the Personnel Appeals Board.

[68 FR 69303, Dec. 12, 2003]

Subpart E—Special Procedures; Representation Proceedings

§ 28.110 Purpose.

The procedures in this subpart relate to the Board's duty under 31 U.S.C.

753(a) (4) and (5) to determine appropriate units of GAO employees for collective bargaining, to conduct elections in order to determine whether the employees in any such units wish to select a labor organization to represent them in collective bargaining, and, thereafter, to certify labor organizations so selected as the designated exclusive bargaining representative. They are referred to in these regulations as "representation proceedings".

§ 28.111 Scope.

The Board shall consider, decide and order corrective action (as appropriate) in cases arising from the determination of appropriate units of employment for collective bargaining and cases arising from elections and certifications of collective bargaining representatives. Board decisions in these matters will be made with due regard for relevant provisions of GAO Orders and with the objective of insuring that the GAO labor relations program is consistent with Chapter 71 of Title 5, United States Code, which prescribes the standards for the labor relations program in the executive branch.

§ 28.112 Who may file petitions.

(a) Representation petitions may be filed by:

(1) A labor organization which wishes to be designated as the exclusive representative for collective bargaining by the GAO employees in an appropriate unit, or by a labor organization which desires to replace another currently having that status;

(2) An employee or a group of employees (or an individual on his, her or their behalf) desiring a new election to determine whether a labor organization has ceased to represent a majority of employees in a unit;

(3) The GAO if it has a good faith reason to doubt that a majority of employees in the bargaining unit wish to be represented by the labor organization which is currently the exclusive representative of those employees;

(4) The GAO or a labor organization currently recognized as an exclusive representative desiring the Board to clarify an earlier unit determination or certification;

(5) Any person seeking clarification of, or an amendment to, a certification then in effect or any other matter relating to representation.

(b) Notwithstanding the provisions of paragraph (a) of this section, no petition may be filed which seeks representation rights for employees in a unit—

(1) Where an election has been held within the previous 12 calendar months and in such election a majority of the employees voting chose a labor organization for certification as the unit's exclusive representative, or

(2) Where an existing collective bargaining agreement having a term of three years or less is in effect, unless the petition for exclusive recognition is filed not more than 105 days and not less than 60 days before the expiration of the collective bargaining agreement, or

(3) Where an existing collective bargaining agreement having a term of more than three years is in effect, unless the petition for recognition is filed not more than 105 days and not less than 60 days before the third anniversary or any subsequent anniversary of the collective bargaining agreement.

[58 FR 61992, Nov. 23, 1993, as amended at 68 FR 69303, Dec. 12, 2003]

§ 28.113 Contents of representation petitions.

(a) The contents of representation petitions filed under § 28.112(a)(1) (by a labor organization seeking to be designated as or replace an exclusive bargaining representative) shall consist of:

(1) A detailed identification of the unit of employees to which the petition applies, and their geographical location within the GAO, the classifications of employees to be included and excluded, and the number of employees involved;

(2) Names, addresses and officers of any other labor organizations known by the petitioner to be interested in representing employees covered by the petition, including a labor organization which is party to a current collective bargaining agreement covering any employees in the unit;

(3) Name, address, affiliation, if any, and telephone number of the petitioning organization;

(4) A copy of the constitution and bylaws of the organization, a roster of the organization's officers and representatives, and a statement of the organization's objectives, together with a statement that these documents have also been supplied to the GAO;

(5) A declaration by the signer of the petition, under penalties of the Criminal Code (18 U.S.C. 1001), that the petition's contents are true and correct, to the best of his or her knowledge and belief;

(6) The signature of the representative of the petitioner, including title and telephone number; and

(7) Membership cards, dues records, or signed statements by employees indicating their desire to support the petition of the labor organization, or similar evidence acceptable to the Board, showing that at least 30 percent of the employees in the proposed unit support the representation petition.

(b) The contents of petitions filed under §28.112(a)(2) (by an employee or group of employees seeking an election to determine if a labor organization still represents a majority of employees in a unit) shall conform to those provided for in paragraph (a) of this section, except that the information required by paragraphs (a)(4) and (a)(7) of this section need not be supplied. Additionally, a petition under §28.112(a)(2) shall include evidence satisfactory to the Board that at least 30 percent of the employees in the unit support the petition to determine whether the employees wish to continue to be represented by the labor organization currently having bargaining rights.

(c) The contents of petitions filed under §28.112(a)(3) shall conform to those provided in petitions under paragraph (a) of this section except that the information required by paragraphs (a)(4) and (a)(7) of this section need not be supplied. Additionally, such a petition shall include a detailed statement giving the objective considerations which support the GAO's good faith reason for doubting the labor organization's continued status as the exclusive representative.

(d) The contents of petitions filed under §28.112(a)(4) (by GAO or a labor organization seeking clarification of a certification) shall include the information required under paragraph (a) of this section, with the exception of the information required by paragraphs (a)(4) and (a)(7) of this section. Also, instead of the information required in paragraph (a)(1) of this section, the petition shall identify the existing unit and the date the organization was recognized by the GAO or certified as the exclusive representative, and shall explain the changes desired in the unit and the reasons therefor.

(e) Petitions under §28.112(a)(5) (by any person seeking clarification or amendment of a certification, or raising any other representation matter) shall be filed on forms to be supplied by the Board upon request.

[58 FR 61992, Nov. 23, 1993, as amended at 68 FR 69303, Dec. 12, 2003; 76 FR 76874, Dec. 9, 2011]

§28.114 Pre-investigation proceedings.

(a) Upon the filing of a valid petition, the General Counsel may request GAO to notify employees as to the existence of the petition by posting a notice for at least 10 days in locations appropriately selected to reach all employees in the unit covered by the petition. The notice shall include a request that the Board's General Counsel be notified of the existence of any other interested parties.

(b) GAO shall supply the General Counsel with any information in its possession concerning other potentially interested labor organizations, copies of relevant correspondence, and copies of existing or recently expired agreements covering any employees in the unit. The GAO shall also provide a list of employees it believes should be included in the unit together with their classifications and the names and classifications of those employees it proposes to exclude from the unit.

(c) All interested parties shall meet as soon as possible after the expiration of the 10-day posting period and shall attempt to resolve any issues in controversy.

(d) A labor organization may become an intervenor in any representation proceeding by submitting to the General Counsel, within the 10-day period, evidence that it represents at least 10 percent of the employees in the proposed unit or that it is the exclusive representative of the employees involved. Denial of a request to intervene may be appealed to the Board. Such an appeal must be filed within 10 days of service of the General Counsel's determination.

§ 28.115 Processing petitions.

(a) Upon the expiration of the 10-day posting period, and after the General Counsel considers an appropriate period has elapsed for consultation among the parties to resolve or identify issues, the General Counsel shall prepare a report to the Board which may recommend:

(1) Approval of any agreement entered into by the parties during their consultations including an agreement on the appropriate units, on the withdrawal of the petition, or on a joint request to conduct an election to determine which labor organization, if any, the employees select to be their exclusive bargaining representative;

(2) Dismissal of the petition as being without merit; or

(3) Issuance of a notice of hearing for the purpose of disposing of the remaining issues raised in the petition.

(b) The General Counsel's report shall be supplied to all interested parties, and, unless all parties agree to a shorter period, they shall have 15 days during which to file any response with the Board.

(c) The Board, as expeditiously as feasible after the expiration of the period specified in paragraph (b) of this section, but no later than 30 days thereafter, shall either approve the report and order appropriate steps to carry out its recommendations, or remand it to the General Counsel with further instructions.

(d) Where a hearing is ordered, an administrative judge shall be designated by the Board. The report of the administrative judge shall include Findings of Fact and Recommendations.

(e) After receiving the report from the administrative judge, and after providing the parties with an opportunity for comment, the Board shall issue a Decision and Order determining the appropriate unit, directing an election, dismissing the petition or making some other appropriate disposition of the matter.

(f) Final Decisions and Orders issued by the Board based on hearings held in accordance with paragraphs (d) and (e) of this section shall not be considered final decisions subject to appeal before the Circuit Courts of Appeal.

§ 28.116 Conduct of elections.

(a) The Board shall supervise any election it orders to be conducted, but may delegate ministerial functions relating to an election to any qualified independent organization; to members of the Board's full-time staff; or to temporary employees hired for this purpose.

(b) Appropriate notices setting forth details of the election shall be posted by GAO as directed by the Board.

(c) The Board shall, through its agents chosen to conduct the election:

(1) Provide the opportunity for all qualified voters to indicate their choices in secrecy;

(2) Offer qualified voters the opportunity to vote for any labor organization on the ballot, or to reject all labor organizations;

(3) Permit all parties to observe all aspects of the election procedure other than any which would interfere with the secrecy of the ballot;

(4) Provide for all parties to challenge the eligibility of any voters, and to impound the ballots of such voters, subject to later determination of eligibility should the number of challenges potentially affect the results;

(5) Certify to all parties the results of the election.

(d) Upon receiving a report of the results of the election, the Board shall:

(1) If necessary rule on the challenges and adjust the results accordingly;

(2) Formally announce the results and, where appropriate, designate a labor organization as the exclusive collective bargaining agent, or withdraw such a designation;

(3) Order a runoff or an additional election, if the Board deems it appropriate, where the results of the original election are inconclusive because no choice on the ballot has secured a majority of the valid votes cast. Not more than one additional and one runoff election may be held.

(i) *Runoff election.* The Board may order a runoff election where one or more of the labor organizations on the ballot has received the vote of at least 30 percent of the employees eligible to vote, but none has gained a majority of the votes cast. The runoff election will be between the two choices receiving the largest and the second largest number of votes in the original election.

(ii) *Additional election.* The Board may order an additional election where there is a tie vote between all of the choices on the ballot or where a runoff election is not feasible because there is a tie between the choices receiving the second most votes in the original election. The additional election will include all the choices that appeared on the original ballot.

Subpart F—Special Procedures; Unfair Labor Practices

§ 28.120 Authority of the Board.

(a) The procedures in this subpart relate in part to the Board's function, under 31 U.S.C. 753(a)(6), to "consider and order corrective or disciplinary action in a case arising from * * * a matter appealable to the Board under the labor-management relations program under (31 U.S.C. 732(e)(2)) including a labor practice prohibited under (31 U.S.C. 732(e)(1))."

(b) The system so established by the Comptroller General is required to provide that each employee of the GAO has the right to form, join or assist, or not form, join or assist an employee organization, freely and without penalty or reprisal, and for a labor-management relations program consistent with Chapter 71 of Title 5, U.S.C. (31 U.S.C. 732(e)).

§ 28.121 Unfair labor practices; Board procedures.

(a) Unfair labor practices are defined at GAO Order 2711.1. An allegation that a provision of GAO Order 2711.1 is inconsistent with Chapter 71 of Title 5, United States Code, and thereby denies to an employee or labor organization rights comparable to those granted by Chapter 71 of Title 5, United States Code, may also be raised under the unfair labor practice procedure.

(b) An allegation that unfair labor practices have been committed shall be subject to the procedures appearing in subpart B of this part for the filing of charges, investigation by the General Counsel, and the Board's disposition, except as set forth in paragraphs (c) and (d) of this section.

(c) Except as provided in paragraph (d) of this section, no petition may be filed based on any alleged unfair labor practice which occurred more than 6 months before the filing of an unfair labor practice charge with the charged party, as provided in paragraph 15e of GAO Order 2711.1, or more than 9 months before the filing of a charge with the Office of General Counsel.

(d) If the Board determines that the charging party was prevented from filing the charge during the 6-month period referred to in paragraph (c) of this section by reason of:

(1) Any failure of the charged party to perform a duty owed to the charging party; or

(2) Any concealment which prevented discovery of the alleged unfair labor practice during the 6-month period; the charge will be considered timely filed, provided it was filed with the charged party during the 6-month period beginning on the day of the discovery of the alleged unfair labor practice by the charging party.

[58 FR 61992, Nov. 23, 1993, as amended at 68 FR 69303, Dec. 12, 2003]

§ 28.122 Negotiability issues.

Where the GAO and an exclusive bargaining representative disagree on whether a matter is subject to negotiation as part of the requirement to bargain in good faith, the matter shall be appealable to the Board under the following procedures:

(a) When, in connection with negotiations, a proposal is declared nonnegotiable, the party submitting the proposal shall, prior to the close of negotiations, submit to the other party a Request for Formal Negotiability Determination reciting the proposal in question. The party declaring the proposal nonnegotiable shall, within ten (10) days, deliver to the other party a Formal Negotiability Determination stating the basis for the Determination.

(b) A Formal Negotiability Determination may be appealed to the Board within 20 days of its service by filing a Petition for Review with the Board. A complete statement of argument from the petitioner should accompany the Petition for Review.

(c) The Board shall serve the Respondent with a copy of the Petition for Review and accompanying argument. Respondent shall reply to the Petition for Review within 20 days of its service upon respondent.

(d) One or more members of the Board shall review the arguments, hold a hearing if the administrative judge deems it necessary, and issue a decision.

(e) The decision shall become final in accordance with § 28.87.

[58 FR 61992, Nov. 23, 1993, as amended at 68 FR 69303, Dec. 12, 2003]

§ 28.123 Standards of conduct for labor organizations.

(a) The GAO shall only accord recognition to labor organizations that are free from corrupt influences and from influences opposed to basic democratic principles. An organization is not required to prove it is free from such influence if it is subject to governing requirements calling for the maintenance of:

(1) Democratic procedures;

(2) Freedom from totalitarian influence;

(3) Independence on the part of its agents and officers from any business or financial interests which represent conflicts of interest or potential conflicts of interest; and

(4) Fiscal integrity.

(b) A labor organization which has or seeks recognition as a representative of employees under this chapter shall file financial and other reports with the Board and comply with trusteeship and election standards.

(c) A labor organization which has or seeks recognition under these Rules shall adhere to principles enunciated in the Regulations issued by the Assistant Secretary of Labor for Employment Standards regarding standards of conduct for labor organizations in the public sector. Complaints of violations of this section shall be filed with the Board. In any matter arising under this section, the Board may require a labor organization to cease and desist from violations of this section and require it to take such actions as it considers appropriate to carry out the policies of this section.

(d) This chapter does not authorize participation in the management of a labor organization or acting as a representative of a labor organization by a management official, a supervisor, or a confidential employee, or by any employee if the participation or activity would result in a conflict or apparent conflict of interest or would otherwise be incompatible with law or with the official duties of the employee.

(e) In the case of any labor organization which by omission or commission has willfully and intentionally called or participated in a strike, work stoppage or slowdown, or picketed in a manner which interfered with the operations of a government agency, or has condoned such activity, the Board shall, upon an appropriate finding it has made of such a violation—

(1) Revoke the recognition status of the labor organization; or

(2) Take any other appropriate disciplinary action.

(f) The General Counsel may charge a labor organization with violations of this section. The Board shall conduct proceedings with regard to such charge and may require a labor organization to take such actions as it deems necessary to carry out the policies of this section.

[58 FR 61992, Nov. 23, 1993, as amended at 68 FR 69303, Dec. 12, 2003]

§ 28.124 Review of arbitration awards.

(a) *Filing an exception.* (1) Either party to arbitration, conducted pursuant to a grievance procedure under a collective bargaining agreement, may file with the Board an exception to the arbitrator's award rendered pursuant to the arbitration.

(2) The time limit for filing an exception to an arbitration award is 30 days from the service of the award on the filing party.

(3) An opposition to the exception may be filed by a party within 30 days after the service of the exception.

(4) A copy of the exception and any opposition shall be served on the other party.

(b) *Content of exception.* An exception must be a dated, self-contained document which sets forth in full:

(1) A statement of the grounds on which review is requested;

(2) Evidence or rulings bearing on the issues before the Board;

(3) Arguments in support of the stated grounds, together with specific reference to the pertinent documents and citations of authorities;

(4) A legible copy of the award of the arbitrator and legible copies of other pertinent documents; and

(5) The name and address of the arbitrator.

(c) *Grounds for review.* (1) The Board will review an arbitrator's award to which an exception has been filed to determine if the award is deficient—

(i) Because it is contrary to any law, rule or regulation; or

(ii) On other grounds similar to those applied by Federal courts in private sector labor-management relations.

(2) The Board will not consider an exception where:

(i) The award relates to an action based on unacceptable performance covered under 5 U.S.C. 4303;

(ii) The award relates to a removal, suspension for more than 14 days, reduction in grade, reduction in pay, or furlough of 30 days or less covered under 5 U.S.C. 7512; or

(iii) the exception is based on a GAO rule which was not introduced into the record submitted to the arbitrator.

(d) *Board decision.* The Board shall issue its decision and order taking such action and making such recommendations concerning the award as it considers necessary, consistent with applicable laws, rules, or regulations.

Subpart G—Corrective Action, Disciplinary and Stay Proceedings

§28.130 General authority.

The procedures in this subpart relate to the Board's functions "to consider, decide and order corrective or disciplinary action (as appropriate) in cases arising" from any area within the Board's jurisdiction.

§28.131 Corrective action proceedings.

(a) When information comes to the attention of the General Counsel suggesting that a prohibited personnel practice may have occurred, exists or is to be taken, the General Counsel shall investigate the matter to the extent necessary to determine whether there are reasonable grounds to believe that a prohibited personnel practice has occurred, exists or is to be taken.

(b) If the General Counsel terminates any investigation under this section which is not also the subject of a charge, the General Counsel shall prepare and transmit to any person on whose allegation the investigation was initiated, a written statement notifying the person of the termination of the investigation and the reasons therefore.

(c) If the General Counsel determines that there are reasonable grounds to believe that a prohibited personnel practice has occurred, exists or is to be taken which requires corrective action and which is not also the subject of a charge, the General Counsel shall report the determination together with any findings or recommendations to the GAO.

(d) If, after a reasonable period, GAO has not taken the corrective action recommended, the Board's Office of General Counsel may file a petition with the Board. Such petition shall be processed in accordance with §§28.19 through 28.25.

[58 FR 61992, Nov. 23, 1993, as amended at 68 FR 69303, Dec. 12, 2003]

§28.132 Disciplinary proceedings.

(a) If the General Counsel determines after any investigation under 31 U.S.C. 752(b) that disciplinary action should be initiated against an employee, the General Counsel shall prepare a written complaint against the employee containing his or her determination, together with a statement of the supporting facts, and present the complaint and the statement to the employee and the Board in accordance with paragraphs (b) and (c) of this section.

(b) In the case of an employee in a confidential, policy making, policy-determining, or policy-advocating position appointed by the President, by and with the advice and consent of the Senate, the complaint and statement referred to in paragraph (a) of this section, with any response by the employee, shall be presented to the Congress for appropriate action in lieu of being presented under paragraph (d) of this section.

(c) Any employee against whom a complaint has been presented to the Board under paragraph (a) of this section is entitled to:

(1) A reasonable time to answer orally and in writing and to furnish affidavits and other documentary evidence in support of the answer;

(2) Be represented by an attorney or other representative;

(3) A hearing before the Board or a member designated by the Board;

(4) Have a transcript kept of any hearing under paragraph (c)(3) of this section; and

(5) A written decision and reasons therefor at the earliest practicable date, including a copy of a final decision ordering disciplinary action.

(d) A final order of the Board may order disciplinary action consisting of removal, reduction in grade, debarment from GAO employment for a period not to exceed 5 years, suspension, reprimand, or an assessment of civil penalty not to exceed $1,000.

(e) An employee subject to a final decision ordering disciplinary action under this section may obtain judicial review of the order in the U.S. Court of Appeals for the Federal Circuit in accordance with 31 U.S.C. 755.

[58 FR 61992, Nov. 23, 1993, as amended at 68 FR 69304, Dec. 12, 2003]

§ 28.133 Stay proceedings.

(a) Prior to the effective date of any proposed personnel action, the Board's General Counsel may request, ex parte, the issuance of an initial stay of the proposed personnel action for a period not to exceed 30 days if the General Counsel believes that the proposed personnel action arises out of a prohibited personnel practice. The request shall be in writing and shall specify the nature of the action to be stayed and the basis for the General Counsel's belief. The Board's Office of General Counsel shall serve a copy of the request on the GAO. Within three business days of its filing, the request shall be granted by the Board member designated by the Board Chair to entertain the request unless that Board member determines that the request either:

(1) Fails to satisfy the requirements of this paragraph or

(2) On its face, conclusively establishes that the proposed personnel action did not arise out of an alleged prohibited personnel practice as specified by the General Counsel.

(b) The Board's General Counsel may request the issuance of either:

(1) Further temporary stays for the purpose of allowing additional time to pursue its investigation or

(2) A permanent stay for the purpose of staying the proposed personnel action until a final decision is rendered.

(c) Requests for stays under paragraph (b) of this section shall be received by both the Board and the GAO no less than 10 days before the expiration of any stay then in effect. Any response from GAO to the request shall be received by both the Board and the Board's Office of General Counsel no less than three days before the expiration of any stay then in effect. Any request for stay under this paragraph shall be decided by the Board member who issued the prior stay under paragraph (a) of this section, unless the Board Chair determines that it should be decided by the Board en banc. The Board member, or Board en banc, may require further briefing, oral argument, submission of affidavits or other documentary evidence, or may conduct an evidentiary hearing before rendering a decision. Any stay then in effect may be extended, sua sponte, for a period not to exceed 30 days to enable the Board member, or Board en banc, a reasonable opportunity to render a decision.

(d) A temporary stay under paragraph (b)(1) of this section may be issued if the Board member, or Board en banc, determines that under all of the circumstances the interests of justice would be served by providing more time for the Board's Office of General Counsel to pursue the investigation.

However, the duration of any single temporary stay shall not exceed the amount of time reasonably necessary to acquire sufficient information to support a request for a permanent stay in the exercise of a high degree of diligence and, in no event, shall any single temporary stay exceed 60 days except as provided under paragraph (c) of this section for the purpose of allowing time to render a decision.

(e) In determining whether a permanent stay under paragraph (b)(2) of this section should be issued, the Board member, or Board en banc, shall:

(1) Assess the evidence adduced by each side as to whether the proposed personnel action arises out of an alleged prohibited personnel practice as specified by the Board's General Counsel;

(2) Assess the nature and gravity of any harm that could inure to each side if the request for permanent stay is either granted or denied; and

(3) Balance the assessments conducted under paragraphs (e)(1) and (2) of this section.

(f) Any order issued by a member of the Board granting or denying, in whole or in part, a stay request under paragraph (b) shall be subject to review by the Board en banc on the filing and service of a notice of appeal, accompanied by a supporting brief, within 10 days of the service of that order. Responsive briefs shall be filed and served within 10 days of service of the appeal.

(g) A motion to vacate a stay order may be filed at any time. A stay order issued by the Board en banc may not be vacated by a single Board member.

[58 FR 61992, Nov. 23, 1993, as amended at 68 FR 69304, Dec. 12, 2003]

Subpart H—Appeals by Members of the Senior Executive Service

§ 28.140 Personnel actions involving SES members.

Members of the GAO Senior Executive Service (SES) may appeal adverse actions relating to misconduct, malfeasance or similar action to the Board in accordance with Subpart B of this part. Members of the GAO SES who allege that they have been subjected to a personnel action that constitutes a prohibited personnel practice or prohibited discrimination may appeal to the Board in accordance with subpart B or subpart D of this part respectively.

§ 28.141 Performance based actions.

A career appointee removed from SES to a GAO position outside the SES for less than fully successful executive performance shall, upon notice of such removal, be entitled, upon request, to an informal hearing before a member of the Board designated by the Chair of the Board.

(a) At the informal hearing, the career appointee and/or a representative and the agency may appear and present documentary evidence and argument.

(b) The Board member will determine which, if any, witnesses will be allowed to testify. As a general rule, no cross-examination of witnesses will be allowed. The Board member will have discretion to allow cross-examination of witnesses in exceptional circumstances.

(c) The informal hearing shall not give the career appointee the right to initiate an action with the Board under another provision of these rules, nor need the removal action be delayed as a result of the granting of such hearing.

Subpart I—Ex Parte Communications

§ 28.145 Policy.

It is the policy of the Board to regulate strictly ex parte communications between members of the Board and their decision-making personnel and any interested party to a proceeding before the Board.

§ 28.146 Explanation and definitions.

(a) Ex parte communications are oral or written communications between decision-making personnel of the Board and an interested party to a proceeding without providing the other parties to the proceeding a chance to participate. The only ex parte communications that are prohibited are those that involve the merits of the case or those that violate other rules requiring submissions to be in writing. Accordingly, interested parties may make inquiries about such matters as the status of a case, when it will be heard, and the method for transmitting evidence to the Board. Such communications should be directed to the Clerk of the Board. Parties may not inquire about such matters as what defense they should use or whether their evidence is adequate, make a submission orally which is required to be in writing, or otherwise inquire as to the merits of a pending case.

(b) In this subpart—

(1) "Interested party" includes:

(i) Any party, including the General Counsel of the Board, or representative of a party involved in a proceeding before the Board;

(ii) Any person desiring to intervene in any proceeding before the Board; or

(iii) Any other person who might be affected by the outcome of a proceeding before the Board.

(2) "Decision-making personnel" means the Board, a panel of Board members, a Board member, an administrative judge, and/or an employee of the Board, who reasonably can be expected to participate in the decision-making process of the Board.

[58 FR 61992, Nov. 23, 1993, as amended at 68 FR 69304, Dec. 12, 2003]

§ 28.147 Prohibited communications.

Ex parte communications concerning the merits of any matter before the Board for adjudication, or which would otherwise violate rules requiring written submissions, are prohibited from the time the interested party involved has knowledge that the matter may be considered by the Board until the Board has rendered a final decision on the case.

§ 28.148 Reporting of communications.

Any communication made in violation of this section shall be made part of the record in the proceeding and an opportunity for rebuttal allowed. If the communication was oral, a memorandum stating the substance of the discussion shall be placed in the record.

§ 28.149 Sanctions.

The following sanctions shall be available for violations of this Subpart:

(a) The Board, a panel of Board members, a Board member or an administrative judge, as necessary, may, in the interest of justice, require the offending party to show cause why his or her claim, interest, motion or petition should not be dismissed, denied or otherwise adversely affected.

(b) The Board, a panel of Board members, a Board member or an administrative judge, as necessary, may invoke such sanctions against any offending party as may be appropriate under the circumstances.

Subpart J—Statement of Policy or Guidance

§ 28.155 Statement of policy or guidance.

Upon petition by any person, or on its own motion, the Board may issue statements of policy or guidance. In determining whether to issue such a statement, the criteria to be considered by the Board will include, but not be limited to, the following:

(a) Whether the question presented can more appropriately be resolved by other means;

(b) Where other means are available, whether a Board statement would prevent the proliferation of cases;

(c) Whether the resolution of the question presented would have general applicability;

(d) Whether the question currently confronts the parties as part of their employee-management relationship;

(e) Whether the question is presented jointly by the parties involved; and

(f) Whether the issuance by the Board of a statement of policy or guidance would promote the purposes of the General Accounting Office Personnel Act.

Subpart K—Access to Records

SOURCE: 68 FR 69304, Dec. 12, 2003, unless otherwise noted.

§ 28.160 Request for records.

(a) Individuals may request access to records pertaining to them that are maintained as described in 4 CFR part 83, by addressing inquiry to the PAB General Counsel either by mail or by appearing in person at the Personnel Appeals Board Office of General Counsel, Room 1562, 441 G Street NW., Washington, DC 20548, during business hours on a regular business day. Requests in writing should be clearly and prominently marked "Privacy Act Request." Requests for copies of records shall be subject to duplication fees set forth in 4 CFR 83.17.

(b) Individuals making a request in person shall be required to present satisfactory proof of identity, preferably a document bearing the individual's photograph. Requests by mail or submitted other than in person should contain sufficient information to enable the General Counsel to determine with reasonable certainty that the requester and the subject of the record are one and the same. To assist in this process, individuals should submit their names and addresses, dates and places of birth, social security number, and any other known identifying information such as an agency file number or identification number and a description of the circumstances under which the records were compiled.

(c) *Exemptions from disclosure.* The Personnel Appeals Board General Counsel and the Personnel Appeals Board, in deciding what records are exempt from disclosure, will follow the policies set forth in 4 CFR part 83.

[68 FR 69304, Dec. 12, 2003, as amended at 77 FR 15233, Mar. 15, 2012]

§28.161 Denial of access to information—Appeals.

(a) If a request for access to information under §28.160 is denied, the General Counsel shall give the requester the following information:

(1) The General Counsel's name and business mailing address;

(2) The date of the denial;

(3) The reasons for the denial, including citation of appropriate authorities; and

(4) The individual's right to appeal the denial as set forth in paragraphs (b) and (c) of this section.

(b) Any individual whose request for access to records of the PAB General Counsel has been denied in whole or in part by the General Counsel may, within 30 days of receipt of the denial, challenge that decision by filing a written request for review of the decision with the Personnel Appeals Board, Room 1566, 441 G Street NW., Washington, DC 20548.

(c) The appeal shall describe:

(1) The initial request made by the individual for access to records;

(2) The General Counsel's decision denying the request; and

(3) The reasons why that decision should be modified by the Board.

(d) The Board, en banc, may in its discretion render a decision based on the record, may request oral argument, or may conduct an evidentiary hearing.

[68 FR 69304, Dec. 12, 2003, as amended at 77 FR 15233, Mar. 15, 2012]

PART 29 [RESERVED]

SUBCHAPTERS C–D [RESERVED]

SUBCHAPTER E—STANDARDIZED FISCAL PROCEDURES

PART 75—CERTIFICATES AND APPROVALS OF BASIC VOUCHERS AND INVOICES

AUTHORITY: 31 U.S.C. 711 and 3511.

§ 75.1 Contractors' and vendors' certificates.

(a) The Government Accountability Office no longer requires that a certificate as to correctness and nonpayment be executed on the bills and invoices of contractors and vendors, with the exception that carriers, or other corporations, agencies, or persons furnishing transportation and accessorial services to the Government must continue to execute the certificates as provided in chapter 101 of 41 CFR part 41. Pending the eventual elimination of the contractors' and vendors' certificates from all other standard voucher forms, the certificates on such other forms need no longer be executed. However, the elimination of this requirement does not dispense with the necessity for the specific certification of facts required by certain contracts.

(b) The omission of the certificate from bills or invoices submitted for payment to Government agencies does not in any manner lessen the responsibility of contractors and vendors in complying with all statutory requirements applicable to transactions with the Government, nor will it be construed as mitigating their liability for asserting false, fictitious, or fraudulent claims against the United States, penalties for which are set forth in 18 U.S.C. 287.

[22 FR 10906, Dec. 28, 1957, as amended at 47 FR 50843, Nov. 10, 1982; 47 FR 56980, Dec. 22, 1982]

SUBCHAPTER F—RECORDS

PART 81—PUBLIC AVAILABILITY OF GOVERNMENT ACCOUNTABILITY OFFICE RECORDS

AUTHORITY: 31 U.S.C. 711.

SOURCE: 68 FR 33832, June 6, 2003, unless otherwise noted.

§ 81.1 Purpose and scope of part.

(a) This part implements the policy of the U.S. Government Accountability Office (GAO) with respect to the public availability of GAO records, except as set forth in paragraph (b) of this section. While GAO is not subject to the Freedom of Information Act (5 U.S.C. 552), GAO's disclosure policy follows the spirit of the act consistent with its duties and functions and responsibility to the Congress. Application of this act to GAO is not to be inferred from the provisions of these regulations.

(b) GAO published testimonies, reports, decisions, special publications, or listings of publications are not included within the scope of this part. These documents may be obtained from the GAO Web site, *http://www.gao.gov*, or by telephone at 202–512–6000, TDD 202–512–2537, or 1–866–801–7077 (toll free). These publications may be downloaded free of charge from the GAO Web site. Paper copies requested from GAO are subject to a printing, shipping, and handling fee.

(c) Requests for all other GAO records are within the scope of this part and should be submitted to GAO as directed in paragraph (a) of § 81.4.

[68 FR 33832, June 6, 2003, as amended at 76 FR 12550, Mar. 8, 2011]

§ 81.2 Administration.

(a) GAO's Chief Quality Officer administers this part and may promulgate such supplemental rules or regulations as may be necessary.

(b) Requests for records of GAO's Office of Inspector General (OIG) shall be processed by the Counsel to the Inspector General in accordance with this part. The Inspector General shall decide any administrative appeals of decisions of the Counsel to the Inspector General concerning such requests. However, if any of the requested records of the OIG originated in GAO, the Counsel to the Inspector General shall refer the requester to GAO's Chief Quality Officer for processing of the request for those records in accordance with this part. With regard to any public request to inspect or copy records of the OIG, other than records that originated in GAO, in this part the term "Counsel to the Inspector General" is to be substituted for "Chief Quality Officer" and the term "Inspector General" is to be substituted for "Comptroller General". All requests to inspect or obtain a copy of an identifiable record of the OIG must be submitted in writing to the Counsel to the Inspector General, U.S. Government Accountability Office, Suite 1808, 441 G Street NW., Washington, DC 20548 or emailed to *OIGRecordsRequest@gao.gov*.

[76 FR 12550, Mar. 8, 2011, as amended at 82 FR 51753, Nov. 8, 2017]

§ 81.3 Definitions.

As used in this part:

(a) *Identifiable* means a reasonably specific description of a particular record sought, such as the date of the record, subject matter, agency or person involved, etc., which will permit location or retrieval of the record.

(b) *Records* includes all books, papers, manuals, maps, photographs, reports, and other documentary materials, regardless of physical form or characteristics, including electronically created or maintained materials, under the control of GAO in pursuance of law or in connection with the transaction of public business. As used in this part, the term "records" is limited to an existing record under GAO's control and does not include compiling or procuring records, library or museum material made, acquired, or preserved solely for reference or exhibition purposes, or extra copies of documents preserved only for convenience of reference.

(c) *Records available to the public* means records which may be examined or copied or of which copies may be obtained, in accordance with this part, by the public or representatives of the press regardless of interest and without specific justification.

(d) *Disclose* or *disclosure* means making available for examination or copying, or furnishing a copy.

(e) *Person* includes an individual, partnership, corporation, association, or public or private organization other than a Federal agency.

(f) *Compelling need* means that a failure to obtain requested records on an expedited basis could reasonably be expected to pose an imminent threat to the life or physical safety of an individual, or the records are needed urgently, with respect to a request made by a person primarily engaged in disseminating information, for the requester to inform the public concerning actual or alleged Federal Government activity.

§ 81.4 Requests for identifiable records.

(a) A request to inspect or obtain a copy of an identifiable record of GAO must be submitted in writing to the Chief Quality Officer, U.S. Government Accountability Office, 441 G Street, NW., Washington, DC 20548. Requests also may be emailed to *recordsrequest@gao.gov*. The Chief Quality Officer will either acknowledge or honor the request within 20 days of receipt.

(b) The Chief Quality Officer will honor requests for expedited processing before all other requests in cases in which the person requesting the records demonstrates a compelling need. A demonstration of compelling need shall be made by a statement certified by the requester to be true and correct to the best of the requester's knowledge and belief.

(c) In the event of an objection or doubt as to the propriety of providing the requester with a copy of the record sought, every effort will be made to resolve such problems as quickly as possible, including consultation with appropriate GAO elements. If it is determined that the record should be withheld, the Chief Quality Officer shall inform the requester in writing that the request has been denied, shall identify the material withheld, and shall explain the basis for the denial.

(d) A person whose request is denied in whole or part may administratively appeal the denial within 60 days after the date of the denial by submitting a letter to the Comptroller General of the United States at the address listed in paragraph (a) of this section, explaining why the denial of the request was unwarranted.

[68 FR 33832, June 6, 2003, as amended at 76 FR 12550, Mar. 8, 2011]

§ 81.5 Records originating outside GAO, records of interviews, or records involving work in progress.

(a) It is the policy of GAO not to provide records from its files that originate in another agency or nonfederal organization to persons who may not be entitled to obtain the records from the originator. In such instances, requesters will be referred to the person or organization that originated the records.

(b) It is the policy of GAO that prior to the release of a record of interview created by GAO in connection with an audit, evaluation, or investigation of a program, activity, or funding of a government entity, GAO will notify the agency from which an interview was obtained of the request. GAO will provide that agency with a reasonable opportunity to indicate whether the record of interview or portions thereof should be exempt from disclosure and the reason(s) for the exemption. The public disclosure of a record of interview remains within the discretion of GAO's Chief Quality Officer, but GAO will consider the views of the agency and the exemptions provided for under § 81.6 or any other law or regulation in deciding whether to release all or portions of a record of interview.

(c) In order to avoid disruption of work in progress, and in the interests of fairness to those who might be adversely affected by the release of information which has not been fully reviewed to assure its accuracy and completeness, it is the policy of GAO not to provide records which are part of ongoing reviews or other current projects. In response to such requests, GAO will inform the requester of the estimated completion date of the review or project so that the requester may then ask for the records. At that time, the records may be released unless exempt from disclosure under §81.6.

[68 FR 33832, June 6, 2003, as amended at 72 FR 50643, Sept. 4, 2007]

§81.6 Records which may be exempt from disclosure.

The public disclosure of GAO records contemplated by this part does not apply to records, or parts thereof, within any of the categories listed below. Unless precluded by law, the Chief Quality Officer may nevertheless release records within these categories.

(a) Records relating to work performed in response to a congressional request (unless authorized by the congressional requester), congressional correspondence, and congressional contact memoranda.

(b) Records specifically required by an Executive Order to be kept secret in the interest of national defense or foreign policy. An example of this category is a record classified under Executive Order 12958, Classified National Security Information.

(c) *Records related solely to the internal personnel rules and practices of an agency.* This category includes, in addition to internal matters of personnel administration, internal rules and practices which cannot be disclosed without prejudice to the effective performance of an agency function. Examples within the purview of this exemption are guidelines and procedures for auditors, investigators, or examiners, and records concerning an agency's security practices or procedures.

(d) Records specifically exempted from disclosure by statute provided that such statute:

(1) Requires that the matters be withheld from the public in such a manner as to leave no discretion on the issue, or

(2) Establishes particular criteria for withholding or refers to particular types of matters to be withheld.

(e) *Records containing trade secrets and commercial or financial information obtained from a person that are privileged or confidential.* This exemption may include, but is not limited to, business sales statistics, inventories, customer lists, scientific or manufacturing processes or development information.

(f) *Personnel and medical files and similar files the disclosure of which could constitute a clearly unwarranted invasion of personal privacy.* This exemption excludes from disclosure all personnel and medical files, and all private or personal information contained in other files, which, if disclosed to the public, would amount to a clearly unwarranted invasion of the privacy of any person. An example of such other files within the exemption would be files compiled to evaluate candidates for security clearance.

(g) Records compiled for law enforcement purposes that originate in another agency, or records prepared for referral to and/or provided by GAO or the OIG to another agency for law enforcement purposes.

(h) Records having information contained in or related to examination, operation, or condition reports prepared by, on behalf of, or for the use of an agency responsible for the regulation or supervision of financial institutions.

(i) Records containing geological and geophysical information and data (including maps) concerning wells.

(j) *Inter-agency or intra-agency memoranda, letters, or other materials that are part of the deliberative process.* For example, this exemption includes internal communications such as GAO or other agency draft reports, and those portions of internal drafts, memoranda and workpapers containing opinions, recommendations, advice, or evaluative remarks of GAO employees. This exemption seeks to avoid the inhibiting of internal communications, and the premature disclosure of documents which would be detrimental to an agency decision making.

(k) Records in addition to those described in paragraph (j) of this section containing information customarily subject to protection as privileged in a court or other proceedings, such as information protected by the doctor-patient, attorney-work product, or lawyer-client privilege.

(l) Records GAO has obligated itself not to disclose, including but not limited to, records for which GAO officials have made a pledge of confidentiality, and records the release of which would adversely impact significant property interests or negatively affect public safety.

(m) *Unsolicited records containing information submitted by any person to GAO in confidence.* Records obtained by the GAO Forensic Audits and Special Investigations (GAO FraudNet) are an example of records that could contain information covered by this exemption.

[68 FR 33832, June 6, 2003, as amended at 72 FR 50644, Sept. 4, 2007; 76 FR 12550, Mar. 8, 2011; 82 FR 51753, Nov. 8, 2017]

§ 81.7 Fees and charges.

(a) No fee or charge will be made for:

(1) Records provided under this part when the direct costs involve less than one hour of search time and 50 pages of photocopying.

(2) Staff-hours spent in resolving any legal or policy questions pertaining to the request.

(3) Copies of records, including those certified as true copies, furnished for official use to a federal government officer or employee.

(4) Copies of pertinent records furnished to a party having a direct and immediate interest in a matter pending before GAO, when necessary or desirable to the performance of a GAO function.

(b) The fees and charges described below will be assessed for the direct costs of search, review, and reproduction of records available to the public under this part.

(1) The cost for reproduction per page shall be 20 cents.

(2) The cost for a certification of authenticity shall be $10 for each certificate.

(3) Manual search and review for records by office personnel will be assessed at $12, $25, or $45 per hour, depending on the rate of pay of the individual actually conducting the search or review, and the complexity of the search.

(4) Other direct costs related to the request may be charged for such items as computer searches.

(5) Except as noted immediately below, requesters generally will be charged only for document duplication. However, there may be times when a search charge will be added, for example, if records are not described with enough specificity to enable them to be located within one hour. Requesters seeking records for commercial use will be charged for document duplication, search, and review costs. Additionally, representatives of the news media, in support of a news gathering or dissemination function, and education or noncommercial scientific institutions not seeking records for commercial use will be charged only for document duplication, unless such request requires extraordinary search or review.

(c) GAO shall notify the requester if an advance deposit is required.

(d) Fees and charges shall be paid by check or money order payable to the U.S. Government Accountability Office.

(e) The Chief Quality Officer may waive or reduce the fees under this section upon a determination that disclosure of the records requested is in the public interest, is likely to contribute significantly to public understanding of the operations or activities of the government, and is not primarily in the commercial interest of the requester. Persons seeking a waiver or fee reduction may be required to submit a statement setting forth the intended purpose for which the records are requested, indicate how disclosure will primarily benefit the public and, in appropriate cases, explain why the volume of records requested is necessary. Determinations pursuant to this paragraph are solely within the discretion of GAO.

§ 81.8 Public reading facility.

GAO maintains a public reading facility in the Law Library at the Government Accountability Office Building, 441 G Street, NW., Washington, DC. To determine if a record is part of the public reading facility collection and to schedule an appointment to visit the facility, contact the Library reference desk at 202–512–2585. The facility is open to the public from 8:30 a.m. to 4 p.m. except Saturdays, Sundays, and Federal holidays.

[68 FR 33832, June 6, 2003, as amended at 76 FR 12550, Mar. 8, 2011]

PART 82—FURNISHING RECORDS OF THE GOVERNMENT ACCOUNTABILITY OFFICE IN JUDICIAL PROCEEDINGS

AUTHORITY: 31 U.S.C. 711, 713, 714, 718, 3523, 2524, 2526, and 3529.

§82.1 Court subpoenas or requests.

(a) A subpoena or request from a court for records of the Government Accountability Office should be directed to the Comptroller General of the United States and served upon the Records Management and Services Officer, Office of Information Systems and Services.

(b) In honoring a court subpoena or request original records may be presented for examination but must not be presented as evidence or otherwise used in any manner by reason of which they may lose their identity as official records of the Government Accountability Office. They must not be marked or altered, or their value as evidence impaired, destroyed, or otherwise affected. In lieu of the original records, certified copies will be presented for evidentiary purposes since they are admitted in evidence equally with the originals (31 U.S.C. 704).

[33 FR 358, Jan. 10, 1968, as amended at 45 FR 84955, Dec. 24, 1980; 47 FR 56980, Dec. 22, 1982]

§82.2 Fees and charges.

The provisions of §81.7 of this chapter are applicable to this part; however, where the charging of fees is appropriate, they need not be collected in advance.

[33 FR 358, Jan. 10, 1968, as amended at 47 FR 56980, Dec. 22, 1982]

PART 83—PRIVACY PROCEDURES FOR PERSONNEL RECORDS

AUTHORITY: 31 U.S.C. 711(1); Memorandum of Understanding between the U.S. Office of Personnel Management, the National Archives and Records Service of the General Services Administration and the U.S. Government Accountability Office; 4 CFR part 81; 5 CFR parts 294–297; and 31 U.S.C. 731, *et seq.*

SOURCE: 50 FR 13162, Apr. 3, 1985, unless otherwise noted.

§83.1 Purpose and scope of part.

This part describes the policy and prescribes the procedures of the U.S. Government Accountability Office (GAO) with respect to maintaining and protecting the privacy of GAO personnel records. While GAO is not subject to the Privacy Act (Act) (5 U.S.C. 552a), GAO's policy is to conduct its activities in a manner that is consistent with the spirit of the Act and its duties, functions, and responsibilities to the Congress. Application of the Privacy Act to GAO is not to be inferred from the provisions of these regulations. These regulations are designed to safeguard individuals against invasions of personal privacy by requiring GAO, except as otherwise provided by law, to—

(a) Protect privacy interests of individuals by imposing requirements of accuracy, relevance, and confidentiality for the maintenance and disclosure of personnel records;

(b) Inform individuals of the existence of systems of personnel records maintained by GAO containing personal information; and

(c) Inform individuals of the right to see and challenge the contents of personnel records containing information about them.

This part applies to all systems of personnel records (as defined in § 83.3(g)) for which GAO is responsible.

§ 83.2 Administration.

The administration of this part is the duty and responsibility of the Director, Personnel, U.S. Government Accountability Office, 441 G Street NW., Washington, D.C. 20548. To this end, the Director, Personnel, in consultation with the Office of the General Counsel, is authorized to issue such supplemental regulations or procedural directives as may be necessary and appropriate.

(a) The Director, Personnel, shall have general responsibility and authority for implementing this part, including—

(1) Approving all systems of personnel records to be maintained by GAO (whether physically located in GAO's Office of Personnel or elsewhere), including the contents and uses of such systems, accounting methods, and security methods; and

(2) Responding to an individual's request to gain access to or amend his or her own personnel records.

(b) The Director, Personnel, may delegate within GAO any of his functions under this part.

§ 83.3 Definitions.

As used in this part:

(a) *Individual* means a citizen of the United States or an alien lawfully admitted for permanent residence;

(b) *Information* means papers, records, photographs, magnetic storage media, micro storage media, and other documentary materials, regardless of physical form or characteristics, containing data about an individual and required by GAO in pursuance of law or in connection with the discharge of official business, as defined by statute, regulation, or administrative procedure;

(c) *Maintain* includes to collect, to use, or to disseminate;

(d) *Personnel record* means any record concerning an individual which is maintained pursuant to GAO's personnel management process or personnel policy setting process;

(e) *Record* means any item, collection, or grouping of information about an individual that is maintained by GAO, including, but not limited to, education, financial transactions, medical history, criminal history, or employment history, that contains the name or other identifying particular assigned to the individual, such as a fingerprint, voice print, or a photograph;

(f) *Routine use* means the disclosure of a record for a purpose which is compatible with the purpose for which it was collected;

(g) *System of personnel records* means a group of personnel records under the control of GAO from which information is retrieved by the name of the individual or by some identifying number, symbol, or other indentifying particular assigned to the individual; and,

(h) *System manager* means the Director of Personnel, his designee, or other GAO official designated by the Comptroller General, who has the authority to decide matters relative to systems of personnel records maintained by GAO.

§ 83.4 Conditions of disclosure.

GAO shall not disclose any record that is contained in a system of personnel records by any means of communication to any person or organization, including another agency, without the prior written consent of the individual to whom the record pertains, unless disclosure of the record would be:

(a) To those officers and employees of GAO who have a need for the record in the performance of their duties; or

(b) Required under regulations implementing the public availability of GAO records published at part 81 of this chapter, or authorized under § 83.5; or

(c) For a routine use as defined in § 83.3(f); or

(d) To a recipient who has provided GAO with advance adequate written assurance that the record will be used solely as a statistical research or reporting record, and the record is to be transferred in a form that is not individually identifiable; or

(e) To another agency or an instrumentality of any governmental jurisdiction within or under the control of the United States for a civil or criminal law enforcement activity if the activity is authorized by law, if the head of the agency or instrumentality has made a written request to GAO specifying the particular record desired and the law enforcement activity for which the record is sought; or

(f) To any person pursuant to a showing of compelling circumstances affecting the health or safety of an individual (not necessarily the data subject) if upon such disclosure notification is transmitted to the last known address of the subject of the personnel record; or

(g) To either House of Congress, or, to the extent of matter within its jurisdiction, any committee or subcommittee of Congress; or

(h) Pursuant to the order of a court of competent jurisdiction or in connection with any judicial or quasi-judicial proceedings; or

(i) To the Bureau of the Census for purposes of planning or carrying out a census or survey or related activity pursuant to the provisions of Title 13, United States Code; or

(j) To the National Archives of the United States as a record which has sufficient historical or other value to warrant its continued preservation by the U.S. Government, or for evaluation by the Administrator of General Services or his designee to determine whether the record has such value; or

(k) To a consumer reporting agency in accordance with 31 U.S.C. 3711(f).

§ 83.5 Specific disclosure of information.

(a) This section governs responses to a member of the public, prospective employers, and law enforcement officials, for access to information covered by this part. It does not limit in any way other disclosures of information pursuant to other provisions of this part.

(b) The following information about most present and former GAO employees is available to the public:

(1) Name;

(2) Present and past position titles;

(3) Present and past grades;

(4) Present and past salaries; and

(5) Present and past duty stations (which include room numbers, shop designations, or other identifying information regarding buildings or places of employment.

(c) Disclosure of the above information will not be made where the information requested is a list of present or past position titles, grades, salaries, and/or duty stations of Government employees which, as determined by the Director, Personnel, is:

(1) Selected in such a way as to constitute a clearly unwarranted invasion of personal privacy because the nature of the request calls for a response that would reveal more about the employees on whom information is sought than the five enumerated items; or

(2) Would otherwise be protected from mandatory disclosure under an exemption of part 81 of this title concerning the public availability of GAO records.

(d) In addition to the information that may be made available under paragraph (a) of this section, GAO may make available the following information to a prospective employer of a GAO employee or former GAO employee:

(1) Tenure of employment;

(2) Civil service status;

(3) Length of service in GAO and the Government; and

(4) When separated, the date and reason for separation shown on the required standard form.

(e) In addition to the information to be made available under paragraph (a) of this section, the home address of an employee shall be made available to a police or court official on receipt of a proper request stating that an indictment has been returned against the employee or that complaint, information, accusation, or other writ involving nonsupport or a criminal offense has been filed against the employee and the employee's address is needed for service of a summons, warrant, subpoena, or other legal process.

(f) Except as provided in paragraphs (a) through (e) of this section, and except as provided in this part, information required to be included in an Official Personnel Folder is not available to the public and is protected from disclosure by § 81.6(f) of this chapter.

(g) *Personnel Appeal Files.* (Those records maintained by the Government Accountability Office Personnel Appeals Board of petitions or appeals filed with the Board by GAO employees, former employees, or applicants for employment. Such records do not include any of the investigative files or reports of the Personnel Appeals Board General Counsel. See 4 CFR 28.18(c)). GAO, upon receipt of a request which identifies the individual from whose file the information is sought, shall disclose the following information from a Personnel Appeal File to a member of the public, except when the disclosure would constitute a clearly unwarranted invasion of personal privacy:

(1) Confirmation of the name of the individual from whose file the information is sought and the names of the other parties concerned;

(2) The status of the case;

(3) The decision on the case;

(4) The nature of the action appealed; and

(5) With the consent of the parties concerned, other reasonably identified information from the file.

(h) *Leave records.* The annual and sick leave record of an employee, or information from these records, is not to be made available to the public by GAO or other Government agency.

(i) *Examinations and related subjects.* Information concerning the results of examinations will be released only to the individual concerned, and to those parties explicitly designated in writing by the individual. The names of applicants for GAO positions or eligibles on GAO or civil service registers, certificates, employment lists, or other lists of eligibles, or their ratings or relative standings are not information available to the public.

(j) *Investigations.* (1) Upon written request, GAO will disclose to the parties concerned any report of personnel investigation under its control, or an extract of the report, to the extent the report is involved in a processed before GAO. For the purpose of this paragraph, the "parties concerned" means the Government employee involved in the proceeding, his or her representative designated in writing, and the representative of GAO involved in the proceeding. Where GAO obtains reports of personnel investigations or information from such reports from other government agencies on condition that it not release such data, GAO will refer parties requesting such information to the originating agency where their request will be processed.

(2) GAO will not make a report of investigation or information from a report under its control available to the public or to witnesses, except as otherwise required under GAO regulations implementing the public availability of records published at part 81 of this chapter.

§ 83.6 Accounting of certain disclosures.

(a) With respect to each system of personnel records, GAO shall, except for disclosures made under §§ 83.4(a) and 83.4(b), keep an accurate accounting of—

(1) The date, nature, and purpose of disclosure of a record to any person; and

(2) The name and address of the person, agency, or organization to whom the disclosure is made.

(b) Such accounting shall be retained for at least 3 years or the life of the record, whichever is longer, after the disclosure for which the accounting is made.

(c) Except for disclosures made under § 83.4(e), the accounting shall be available upon written request to the individual named in the record.

§ 83.7 GAO policy and requirements.

(a) GAO shall maintain in its personnel records only such information about an individual as is relevant and necessary to accomplish an authorized official purpose. Authority to maintain personnel records does not constitute authority to maintain information in the record merely because a need for it may develop in the future. Both Government-wide and internal agency personnel records shall contain only information concerning an individual that is relevant and necessary to accomplish GAO's personnel management objectives as required by statute, GAO internal directive, or formal agreements between GAO and other Federal agencies.

(b) GAO shall make every reasonable effort to collect information about an individual directly from that individual when the information may result in adverse determinations about the individual's rights, benefits, and privileges under Federal programs. Factors to be considered in determining whether to collect the data from the individual concerned or a third party are:

(1) The nature of the information is such that it can only be obtained from another party;

(2) The cost of collecting the information directly from the individual is unreasonable when compared with the cost of collecting it from another party;

(3) There is virtually no risk that information collected from other parties, if inaccurate, could result in a determination adverse to the individual concerned;

(4) The information supplied by an individual must be verified by another party; or

(5) Provisions are made, to the greatest extent practical, to verify information collected from another party with the individual concerned.

(c) GAO shall inform each individual whom it asks to supply information for a personnel record, on the form which it uses to collect the information or on a separate form that can be retained by the individual, of—

(1) The authority for the solicitation of the information and whether disclosure of such information is mandatory or voluntary;

(2) The principal purpose or purposes for which the information is intended to be used;

(3) The routine uses which may be made of the information, as published pursuant to paragraph (d)(4) of this section; and

(4) The effects, if any, of not providing all or any part of the requested information;

(d) Subject to the provisions of paragraph (i) of this section, GAO shall publish in the FEDERAL REGISTER, upon establishment or revision, a notice of the existence and character of its systems of personnel records. Such notice shall include—

(1) The name and location(s) of each system of personnel records;

(2) The categories of individuals about whom records are maintained in each such system;

(3) The categories of records maintained in each system of personnel records;

(4) Each routine use of the records contained in each system of personnel records, including the categories of users and the purpose(s) of such use;

(5) The policies and practices of GAO regarding storage, retrievability, access controls, retention, and disposal of the records;

(6) The title and business address of the GAO official who is responsible for maintaining each system of personnel records;

(7) GAO procedures whereby an individual can ascertain whether a system of personnel records contains a record pertaining to the individual;

(8) Procedures whereby an individual can request access to any record pertaining to him contained in any system of personnel records, and how the individual may contest its content; and

(9) The categories of sources of records in each system of personnel records.

(e) GAO shall maintain all records which it uses in making any determination about any individual with such accuracy, relevancy, timeliness, and completeness as is reasonably necessary to assure fairness to the individual in the determination;

(f) GAO shall, prior to disseminating any record about an individual to any person other than a Federal agency, make all reasonable efforts to reassure that such records are accurate, complete, timely, and relevant for GAO's purposes;

(g) GAO shall make reasonable efforts to serve notice on an individual or his authorized representative when any personnel record on such individual is being made available to any person under compulsory legal process as soon as practicable after service of the subpoena or other legal process;

(h) GAO shall establish rules of conduct for persons involved in the design, development, operation, or maintenance of any system of personnel records or files or in maintaining any record, and to instruct each person with respect to such rules and requirements of this part, including any other rules and procedures adopted pursuant to this part;

(i)(1) GAO shall establish and maintain appropriate administrative, technical and physical safeguards to ensure the security and confidentiality of personnel records. At a minimum, these controls shall require that all persons whose official duties require access to and use of personnel records be responsible and accountable for safeguarding those records and for ensuring that the records are secured whenever they are not in use or under the direct control of authorized persons. Generally, personnel records should be held, processed, or stored only where facilities and conditions are adequate to prevent unauthorized access;

(2) Except for access by the data subject, only employees whose official duties require and authorize access shall be allowed to handle and use personnel records, in whatever form or media the records might appear. To the extent feasible, entry into personnel record storage areas shall be similarly limited. Documentation of the removal of records from storage areas must be kept so that adequate control procedures can be established to assure that removed records are returned intact on a timely basis and properly controlled during such period of removal.

(3) In addition to following the above security requirements, managers of automated personnel records shall establish and maintain administrative, technical, physical, and security safeguards for data about individuals in automated records, including input and output documents, reports, punched cards, magnetic tapes, disks, and on-line computer storage. As a minimum, the safeguards must be sufficient to:

(i) Prevent careless, accidental, or unintentional disclosure, modification, or destruction of identifiable personal data;

(ii) Minimize the risk of improper access, modification, or destruction of identifiable personnel data;

(iii) Prevent casual entry by persons who have no official reason for access to such data;

(iv) Minimize the risk of unauthorized disclosure where use is made of identifiable personal data in testing of computer programs;

(v) Control the flow of data into, through, and from computer operations;

(vi) Adequately protect identifiable data from environmental hazards and unnecessary exposure; and

(vii) Assure adequate internal audit procedures to comply with these procedures.

(4) The disposal of identifiable personal data in automated files is to be accomplished in such a manner as to make the data unobtainable to unauthorized personnel. Unneeded personal data stored on reusable media, such as magnetic tapes and disks, must be erased prior to release of the media for reuse.

(j) At least 30 days prior to publication of information under paragraph (d)(4) of this section, GAO shall publish in the FEDERAL REGISTER notice of any new use or intended use of the information in the system, and provide an opportunity for interested persons to submit written data, views, or arguments to GAO.

§ 83.8 Standards of conduct.

(a) GAO employees whose official duties involve the maintenance and handling of personnel records shall not disclose information from any personnel record unless disclosure is part of their official duties or required by statute, regulation, or internal procedure.

(b) Any GAO employee who makes an unauthorized disclosure of personnel records or a disclosure of information derived from such records, knowing that such disclosure is unauthorized, or otherwise knowingly violates these regulations, shall be subject to appropriate disciplinary action. GAO employees are prohibited from using personnel information not available to the public, obtained through official duties, for commercial solicitation or sale, or for personal gain. Any employee who knowingly violates this prohibition shall be subject to appropriate disciplinary action.

§83.9 Social Security number.

(a) GAO may not require individuals to disclose their Social Security Number (SSN) unless disclosure would be required—

(1) Under Federal statute; or

(2) Under any statute, executive order, or regulation that authorizes any Federal, State, or local agency maintaining a system of records that was in existence and operating prior to January 1, 1975, to request the SSN as a necessary means of verifying the identity of an individual.

(b) Individuals asked to voluntarily provide their SSN shall suffer no penalty or denial of benefits for refusing to provide it.

(c) When GAO requests an individual to disclose his or her SSN, it shall inform that individual whether that disclosure is mandatory or voluntary, by what statutory or other authority such number is solicited, and what uses will be made of it.

§83.10 First Amendment rights.

Personnel records or entries thereon describing how individuals exercise rights guaranteed by the First Amendment to the United States Constitution are prohibited, unless expressly authorized by statute or by the individual concerned, or unless pertinent to and within the scope of an authorized law enforcement activity. These rights include, but are not limited to, free exercise of religious and political beliefs, freedom of speech and the press, and freedom to assemble and to petition the Government.

§83.11 Official Personnel Folder.

(a) GAO shall establish and maintain an Official Personnel Folder for each of its employees, except as provided in the GAO/U.S. OPM/GSA Memorandum of Understanding (see subsection (b)). Except as provided for in Federal Personnel Manual (FPM) Supplement 293-31 there will be only one Official Personnel Folder maintained for each employee.

(b) *GAO/U.S. OPM/GSA Memorandum of Understanding.* The Memorandum of Understanding agreed to by the U.S. Government Accountability Office, the U.S. Office of Personnel Management (U.S. OPM), and the National Archives and Records Service of the General Services Administration (GSA), Appendix I, constitutes the official and sole agreement concerning the continuity and coordination of the Official Personnel Folder.

(c) GAO policy is to assure continuity and coordination of the Official Personnel Folder when a person, for whom an Official Personnel Folder has been established, separates from GAO, or transfers to or from GAO from or to a Federal agency subject to regulations of the U.S. OPM relating to Official Personnel Folders. GAO will maximize the pooling of information between itself and those Federal agencies subject to U.S. OPM rules and regulations concerning the Official Personnel Folder so that a GAO employee may transfer to and from other Federal agencies with one complete and informative Official Personnel Folder.

(d) *Ownership of Official Personnel Folder.* (1) The Official Personnel Folders of individuals whose employment with GAO terminated prior to October 1, 1980, are the records of U.S. OPM and are under the jurisdiction and control of U.S. OPM.

(2) The Official Personnel Folders of current GAO employees whose GAO employment began on or after October 1, 1980, and who have had no previous employment by an executive branch agency of the Federal government shall be under the jurisdiction and control of, and are the records of GAO. GAO shall retain jurisdiction over such records even when they are transferred to an executive branch agency.

(3) The Official Personnel Folders of current GAO employees who were employed prior to October 1, 1980, by either GAO or an executive branch agency shall be under the control of GAO, but those records established prior to October 1, 1980, by GAO, and all records

established as a result of employment by an executive branch agency shall remain under the jurisdiction of, and be part of the records of, U.S. OPM.

(4) GAO will maintain those Official Personnel Folders containing records of employment by an executive branch Federal agency, or by GAO prior to October 1, 1980, in compliance with regulations of the U.S. OPM in accordance with the procedures contained in the Memorandum of Understanding and the provisions of regulations of U.S. OPM contained in 5 CFR parts 293, 294, and 297, as well as the provisions of FPM Chapters 293, 294, and 297.

(e) *Maintenance and content of Folder.* GAO shall maintain in the Official Personnel Folder the reports of selection and other personnel actions named in section 2951 of title 5, United States Code. The Folder shall also contain permanent records affecting the employee's status and service as required by U.S. OPM instructions and as designated in FPM Supplement 293–31.

(f) *Use of existing Folders upon transfer or reemployment.* In accordance with paragraph (a) of this section, GAO shall request the transfer of the Official Personnel Folder for a person who was previously employed with a Federal agency that maintains such a Folder. The Folder so obtained shall be used in lieu of establishing a new Official Personnel Folder.

(1) When a person for whom an Official Personnel Folder has been established transfers from GAO to another Federal agency that maintains the Folder, GAO shall, on request, transfer the Folder to the new employing agency.

(2) Before transferring the Official Personnel Folder, GAO shall—

(i) Remove those records of a temporary nature filed on the left side of the Folder; and

(ii) Ensure that all permanent documents of the Folder are complete, correct, and present in the Folder in accordance with FPM Supplement 293–31.

(g) *Disposition of Folders of former Federal employees.* (1) Folders containing the personnel records of individuals separated from employment with GAO will be retained by GAO for 30 days after separation, and may be retained for an additional 60 days. Thereafter, the Folder shall be transferred to the same location and in the same manner as Official Personnel Folders of persons separated from Federal agencies which are subject to U.S. OPM regulations in accordance with the Memorandum of Understanding.

(2) GAO shall remove temporary records from the Folder before it is transferred in accordance with guidelines applicable to Federal agencies which are subject to U.S. OMP regulations.

(3) If a former GAO employee is reappointed in the Federal service, the employee's Folder shall, upon request, be transferred to the new employing agency.

(h) *Access requests and amendments to the Official Personnel Folder.* Requests for access to, disclosure from, correction of, or amendments to documents contained in the Official Personnel Folder will be made in accordance with the Memorandum of Understanding.

§ 83.12 Procedures for individual access to records.

(a) Upon written request by any individual outside of GAO or upon written or oral request by any officer or employee of GAO to gain access to his or her record or to any information pertaining to the individual which is contained in a system of personnel records, and not otherwise exempted, GAO shall permit the individual and upon the individual's request a person of his or her own choosing to accompany him or her, to review the record and have a copy made of all or any portion thereof in a form comprehensible to him or her, except that GAO may require the individual to furnish a written statement authorizing discussion of that individual's record in the accompanying person's presence. When access to the records has been granted by a system manager or designee:

(1) Inspection in person may be made in the office designated in the system notice during the hours specified by GAO.

(2) Upon the determination of the designated GAO official, records may be transferred to a GAO office more convenient to the data subject to review.

(3) Generally, GAO will not furnish certified copies of records. Where certified copies of records are to be furnished, they may be mailed at the request of the data subject or, as determined by GAO, only after payment of any fee levied in accordance with §83.17 is received.

(4) In no event shall original records be made available for review by the individual except in the presence of a system manager or designee.

(b) The general identifying information items that the designated GAO official may ask to be furnished before a specific inquiry is granted include:

(1) Full name, signature, and home address;

(2) Picture identification card;

(3) The current or last place and dates of Federal employment, if appropriate; and

(4) Social security number (for those systems of records retrieved by this identifier).

(c) A request or inquiry from someone other than the individual to whom the information pertains shall contain such documents or copies of documents that establish the relationship or authorize access as follows:

(1) When the requester is the parent or legal guardian of a data subject who is a minor, the requester shall identify the relationship with the data subject and furnish a certified or authenticated (e.g. notarized) copy of any document establishing parentage or appointment as legal guardian.

(2) Where the requester is the legal guardian of a data subject who has been declared incompetent by the courts, the requester shall identify the relationship with the data subject and furnish a certified or authenticated copy of the court's appointment of guardianship.

(3) Where the requester is a representative of the data subject, the requester shall identify the relationship with the data subject or the data subject's parent or legal guardian, and furnish documentation designating the representative as having the authority to act on behalf of the data subject.

(d) When the requester appears in person and cannot be identified by sight and signature, proof of identity is required as follows:

(1) When a request is from the data subject, the means of proof, in order of preference, are:

(i) A document bearing the individual's photograph and signature (for example, driver's license, passport, or military or civilian identification card); or

(ii) Two documents bearing the individual's signature (for example, Medicare card, unemployment insurance book, employer identification card, major credit card, professional, draft, or union membership card).

(2) When a request is made by the parent, legal guardian, or authorized representative of the data subject, the means of identifying the requester and his or her authority for acting on behalf of the data subject shall be as prescribed in paragraph (c) of this section. In addition, the requester shall establish the identity of the data subject by requiring the identifying information in paragraph (b) of this section.

(e) When a written inquiry or request is received from the data subject, or from the data subject's parent, legal guardian, or authorized representative, it should be signed and—

(1) For an inquiry, contain sufficient identifying information about the data subject to permit searching of the record system(s) and to permit response; and

(2) For an access request—

(i) From the data subject, contain sufficient information to locate the record and establish that the requester and the data subject are the same (e.g. matching signatures); or

(ii) From the data subject's parent, legal guardian, or authorized representative, contain sufficient information to locate the record, match identity with the data subject, and such documentation of association or authorization as is prescribed in paragraphs (c) and (d) of this section.

(f) The signed request from the data subject, or from the data subject's parent, legal guardian, or authorized representative specified in paragraph (c) of this section shall be sufficient proof of identity of the requester, unless for good cause, the system manager or designee determines that there is a need to require some notarized or certified evidence of the identity of the requester.

§ 83.13 Inquiries.

(a) General inquiries to request assistance in identifying which system of records may contain a record about an individual may be made in person or by mail to the Director, Personnel.

(b) An inquiry that requests GAO to determine if it has, in a given system of personnel records, a record about the inquirer, should be addressed to the official identified in the FEDERAL REGISTER notice for that system. Inquirers should specify the name of the system of personnel records, if known, as published in the FEDERAL REGISTER. Such inquiries should contain the identifying data prescribed in § 83.12 before a search can be made of that particular system of records.

§ 83.14 Denial of access requests.

(a) If an access request is denied, the official denying the request shall give the requester the following information:

(1) The official's name, position title, and business mailing address;

(2) The date of the denial;

(3) The reasons for the denial, including citation of appropriate sections of this or any other applicable part; and

(4) The individual's opportunities for further administrative consideration, including the name, position title, and address of the GAO official (see paragraph (c) of this section) responsible for such further review.

(b) Denial of a request for access to records will be made only by the official GAO designee and only upon a determination that:

(1) The record is subject to an exemption under § 83.21 when the system manager has elected to invoke the exemption; or

(2) The record is information compiled in reasonable anticipation of a civil action or proceeding; or

(3) The data subject or authorized representative of the data subject refuses to abide by procedures for gaining access to records.

(c) A request for administrative review of a denial shall be made to the Assistant Comptroller General for Human Resources, U.S. Government Accountability Office, 441 G Street, NW, Washington, D.C. 20548. The Assistant Comptroller General shall acknowledge receipt of a request for administrative review of a denial of access within 10 working days after receipt of the request. If it is not possible to reach a decision within an additional 10 working days, the requester shall be informed of the approximate date (within 30 working days) when such a decision may be expected.

(d) In reaching a decision, the Assistant Comptroller General will review the criteria prescribed in this section which were cited as the basis for denying access, and may seek additional information as deemed necessary.

§ 83.15 Request for amendment of record.

(a) Individuals may request the amendment of their records in writing or in person by contacting the system manager or designee indicated in the notice of systems of records published by GAO in the FEDERAL REGISTER. Time limits will be measured from receipt at the proper office.

(b) A request for amendment should include the following:

(1) The precise identification of the records sought to be amended, deleted, or added.

(2) A statement of the reasons for the request, with all available documents and material that substantiate the request.

(c) GAO shall permit an individual to request amendment of a record pertaining to the individual. Not later than 10 working days after the date of receipt of such request, the designated GAO official shall acknowledge in writing such request and, promptly, either—

(1) Make any correction of any portion thereof which the individual believes is not accurate, relevant, timely, or complete; or

(2) Inform the individual of the refusal to amend the record in accordance with his or her request, the reason for the refusal, and the name and business address of the GAO official responsible for the refusal.

(3) The GAO offical shall permit an individual who disagrees with the refusal by the designated GAO official to

amend his or her record to request review of such refusal. A request for administrative review of a denial shall be made in accordance with §83.16.

(4) In any disclosure containing information about which the individual has filed a statement of disagreement, occurring after the filing of the statement under §83.16(d), GAO shall clearly note any portion of the record which is disputed and provide copies of a concise statement of the reasons for not making the amendments requested, to persons or other agencies to whom the disputed record has been disclosed.

(5) Nothing in this section shall allow an individual access to any information compiled in reasonable anticipation of a civil action or proceeding.

(d) If necessary, the official authorized to rule on a request for amendment may seek additional information pertinent to the request to assure that a fair, equitable, and accurate decision is reached.

(e) The following criteria will be considered by the system manager or designee in reviewing initial requests for amendment of records:

(1) The sufficiency of the evidence submitted by the data subject;

(2) The factual accuracy of the information submitted and the information in the record;

(3) The relevancy, necessity, timeliness, and completeness of the information in light of the purpose for which it was collected;

(4) The degree of possibility that denial of the request could result in unfair determinations adverse to the data subject;

(5) The character of record sought to be amended;

(6) The propriety and feasibility of complying with specific means of amendment requested by the data subject; and

(7) The possible involvement of the record in a judicial or quasi-judicial process.

§83.16 Administrative review of request for amendment of record.

(a) A request for administrative review of GAO's denial to amend a record in GAO's system of personnel records shall be addressed to the Assistant Comptroller General for Human Resources, U.S. Government Accountability Office, 441 G Street, NW, Washington, D.C. 20548. The Assistant Comptroller General shall acknowledge receipt of a request for administrative review of a denial of amendment within 10 working days.

(b) If a decision cannot be made within an additional 10-day period, a letter will be sent within that time explaining the delay and furnishing an expected date for the decision. A decision on the request must be made within 30 working days after receipt of the request. Only for good cause shown, and at the discretion of the Assistant Comptroller General for Human Resources can this time limit be extended. Any extension requires written notification to the requester explaining the reason for the extension and furnishing a new expected date for the decision. Generally, such extension shall be for no more than an additional 30 working days.

(c) When a request for administrative review of an amendment denial is submitted, the individual must provide a copy of the original request for amendment, a copy of the initial denial, and a statement of the specific reasons why the initial denial is believed to be in error.

(d) An individual requesting an amendment of a record has the burden of supplying information in support of the propriety and necessity of the amendment request. The decision on the request will then be rendered based on a review of the data submitted. The GAO official is not required to gather supporting evidence for the individual and will have the right to verify the evidence which the individual submits.

(e) Amendment of a record will be denied upon a determination by the system manager or designee that:

(1) The record is subject to an exemption from the provisions of this part, allowing amendment of records;

(2) The information submitted by the data subject is not accurate, relevant, or of sufficient probative value;

(3) The amendment would violate a statute or regulation;

(4) The individual refuses to provide information which is necessary to process the request to amend the record; or

(5) The record for which amendment is requested is a record presented in a judicial or quasi-judicial proceeding, or maintained in anticipation of being used in a judicial or quasi-judicial proceeding, when such record is or will become available to the individual under that proceeding.

(f) If, after review, the Assistant Comptroller General for Human Resources also refuses to amend the record in accordance with the request, the individual will be permitted to file with the system manager or designee of the system of records concerned a concise statement setting forth the reasons for his or her disagreement. Any such statement of disagreement will be treated in accordance with paragraph (c)(4) of §83.15.

§83.17 Fees.

(a) Generally, GAO's policy is to provide the first copy of any record or portion thereof, furnished as a result of this part, at no cost to the data subject or authorized representative. However, in cases where GAO deems it appropriate (for example, where the record is voluminous), the system manager or designee in his or her discretion may charge a fee when the cost for copying the record (at a rate of 20 cents per page) would be in excess of ten dollars ($10).

(b) There shall be no fees charged or collected from a data subject for the following:

(1) Search for or retrieval of the data subject's records;

(2) Review of the records;

(3) Making a copy of a record when it is a necessary part of the process of making the record available for review;

(4) Copying at the initiative of GAO without a request from the individual;

(5) Transportation of the record; and

(6) Making a copy of an amended record to provide the individual with evidence of the amendment.

(c) Certification of authenticity shall be $10 for each certificate, which fee may be waived in the discretion of the system manager or designee.

§83.18 Rights of legal guardians.

For the purposes of this part, the parent of any minor, or the legal guardian of any individual who has been declared to be incompetent due to physical or mental incapacity or age by a court of competent jurisdiction, may act on behalf of the individual.

§83.19 Government contractors.

When GAO provides by a contract for the operation by or on behalf of GAO of a system of personnel records to accomplish a function of GAO, GAO shall, consistent with its authority, cause the requirements of this part to be applied to such system. Any such contractor and any employee of such contractor, if such contract is agreed to on or after the effective date of this section, shall be considered, for the purposes of this part, to be an employee of GAO. Contractor employees will be required to observe the confidentiality requirements of this part. Violations of this part by contractor employees may be a sufficient ground for contract termination.

§83.20 Mailing lists.

An individual's name and address may not be sold or rented by GAO unless such action is specifically authorized by law. This provision shall not be construed to require the withholding of names and addresses otherwise permitted to be made public.

§83.21 Exemptions.

(a) All personnel records are exempted from §§83.6(c), 83.12, 83.13, 83.14, and 83.15, relating to making an accounting of disclosures available to the data subject or his authorized representative and access to and amendment of the records and other sections relating to procedural requirements of the above-cited sections if the record is:

(1) Specifically authorized under criteria established by an Executive order to be kept secret in the interest of national defense or foreign policy and is in fact classified pursuant to such Executive order. *See* 31 U.S.C. 716(e)(1) and 718(b)(3) concerning the applicability of these requirements to GAO.

(2) Investigatory material compiled for law enforcement purposes: *Provided, however*, That if any individual is denied any right, privilege, or benefit that he would otherwise be entitled to by Federal law, or for which he would otherwise be eligible, as a result of the

maintenance of such material, such material shall be provided to such individual, except to the extent that the disclosure of such material would reveal the identity of a source who furnished information to the Government under an express promise that the identity of the source would be held in confidence, or, prior to the effective date of this section, under an express or implied promise that the identity of the source would be held in confidence;

(3) Maintained in connection with providing protection services to the President of the United States or other individuals pursuant to section 3056 of Title 18, United States Code;

(4) Required by statute to be maintained and used solely as statistical records;

(5) Investigatory material compiled solely for the purposes of determining suitability, eligibility, or qualifications for Federal civilian employment, military service, Federal contracts, or access to classified information, but only to the extent that the disclosure of such material would reveal the identity of the source who furnished information to the Government under an express promise that the identity of the source would be held in confidence, or, prior to the effective date of this section, under an express or implied promise that the identity of the source would be held in confidence (*see* § 83.5(j)(1) for the procedure to be used to obtain investigative data originated by other Government agencies);

(6) Testing or examination material used solely to determine individual qualifications for appointment or promotion in the Federal service the disclosure of which would compromise the objectivity or fairness of the testing or examination process; or

(7) Evaluation material used to determine potential for promotion in the armed services, but only to the extent that the disclosure of such material would reveal the identity of a source who furnished information to the Government under an express promise that the identity of the source would be held in confidence, or, prior to the effective date of this section, under an express or implied promise that the identity of the source would be held in confidence.

Appendix I to Part 83—Memorandum of Understanding

This memorandum of understanding constitutes an agreement between the U.S. Office of Personnel Management (OPM), the National Archives and Records Service of the General Services Administration (NARS), and the U.S. Government Accountability Office (GAO) concerning:

(1) The maintenance of the Official Personnel Folder (OPF) of an individual who has been employed in a position subject to the provisions of Title 5, U.S.C. and to the regulations and procedures issued by OPM to govern the Federal civil service, and also in a position subject to the GAO Personnel Act of 1980 (Pub. L. 96–191) and its implementing regulations and procedures;

(2) The exchange of personnel documents and data between the Federal civil service administered by OPM and the personnel system administered by GAO;

(3) The establishment of procedures for processing requests for access to, disclosure from, and amendment of documents in the OPF of an individual who has service under both personnel systems;

(4) The establishment of procedures to be followed by the National Personnel Records Center (NPRC) when responding to requests pertaining to separated employees in any of the following circumstances:

(a) When the OPF contains documentation resulting from employment in both systems;

(b) When a request is received for transfer of an OPF between systems;

(c) When processing a request for an OPF, and that OPF contains only records of GAO employment since October 1, 1980;

(5) The agreement of the parties to consult and cooperate in matters relating to the establishment and revision of personnel procedures which may have mutual effect so as to insure the sharing of essential information while minimizing the recordkeeping burden of all three parties.

SUBCHAPTER G [RESERVED]

PARTS 84–199 [RESERVED]

FINDING AIDS

A list of CFR titles, subtitles, chapters, subchapters and parts and an alphabetical list of agencies publishing in the CFR are included in the CFR Index and Finding Aids volume to the Code of Federal Regulations which is published separately and revised annually.

Table of CFR Titles and Chapters

(Revised as of January 1, 2019)

Title 1—General Provisions

Title 2—Grants and Agreements

Title 2—Grants and Agreements—Continued

Chap.

XXVII Small Business Administration (Parts 2700—2799)

XXVIII Department of Justice (Parts 2800—2899)

XXIX Department of Labor (Parts 2900—2999)

XXX Department of Homeland Security (Parts 3000—3099)

XXXI Institute of Museum and Library Services (Parts 3100—3199)

XXXII National Endowment for the Arts (Parts 3200—3299)

XXXIII National Endowment for the Humanities (Parts 3300—3399)

XXXIV Department of Education (Parts 3400—3499)

XXXV Export-Import Bank of the United States (Parts 3500—3599)

XXXVI Office of National Drug Control Policy, Executive Office of the President (Parts 3600—3699)

XXXVII Peace Corps (Parts 3700—3799)

LVIII Election Assistance Commission (Parts 5800—5899)

LIX Gulf Coast Ecosystem Restoration Council (Parts 5900—5999)

Title 3—The President

I Executive Office of the President (Parts 100—199)

Title 4—Accounts

I Government Accountability Office (Parts 1—199)

Title 5—Administrative Personnel

I Office of Personnel Management (Parts 1—1199)

II Merit Systems Protection Board (Parts 1200—1299)

III Office of Management and Budget (Parts 1300—1399)

IV Office of Personnel Management and Office of the Director of National Intelligence (Parts 1400—1499)

V The International Organizations Employees Loyalty Board (Parts 1500—1599)

VI Federal Retirement Thrift Investment Board (Parts 1600—1699)

VIII Office of Special Counsel (Parts 1800—1899)

IX Appalachian Regional Commission (Parts 1900—1999)

XI Armed Forces Retirement Home (Parts 2100—2199)

XIV Federal Labor Relations Authority, General Counsel of the Federal Labor Relations Authority and Federal Service Impasses Panel (Parts 2400—2499)

XVI Office of Government Ethics (Parts 2600—2699)

XXI Department of the Treasury (Parts 3100—3199)

XXII Federal Deposit Insurance Corporation (Parts 3200—3299)

XXIII Department of Energy (Parts 3300—3399)

XXIV Federal Energy Regulatory Commission (Parts 3400—3499)

XXV Department of the Interior (Parts 3500—3599)

XXVI Department of Defense (Parts 3600—3699)

Chap.	
XXVIII	Department of Justice (Parts 3800—3899)
XXIX	Federal Communications Commission (Parts 3900—3999)
XXX	Farm Credit System Insurance Corporation (Parts 4000—4099)
XXXI	Farm Credit Administration (Parts 4100—4199)
XXXIII	Overseas Private Investment Corporation (Parts 4300—4399)
XXXIV	Securities and Exchange Commission (Parts 4400—4499)
XXXV	Office of Personnel Management (Parts 4500—4599)
XXXVI	Department of Homeland Security (Parts 4600—4699)
XXXVII	Federal Election Commission (Parts 4700—4799)
XL	Interstate Commerce Commission (Parts 5000—5099)
XLI	Commodity Futures Trading Commission (Parts 5100—5199)
XLII	Department of Labor (Parts 5200—5299)
XLIII	National Science Foundation (Parts 5300—5399)
XLV	Department of Health and Human Services (Parts 5500—5599)
XLVI	Postal Rate Commission (Parts 5600—5699)
XLVII	Federal Trade Commission (Parts 5700—5799)
XLVIII	Nuclear Regulatory Commission (Parts 5800—5899)
XLIX	Federal Labor Relations Authority (Parts 5900—5999)
L	Department of Transportation (Parts 6000—6099)
LII	Export-Import Bank of the United States (Parts 6200—6299)
LIII	Department of Education (Parts 6300—6399)
LIV	Environmental Protection Agency (Parts 6400—6499)
LV	National Endowment for the Arts (Parts 6500—6599)
LVI	National Endowment for the Humanities (Parts 6600—6699)
LVII	General Services Administration (Parts 6700—6799)
LVIII	Board of Governors of the Federal Reserve System (Parts 6800—6899)
LIX	National Aeronautics and Space Administration (Parts 6900—6999)
LX	United States Postal Service (Parts 7000—7099)
LXI	National Labor Relations Board (Parts 7100—7199)
LXII	Equal Employment Opportunity Commission (Parts 7200—7299)
LXIII	Inter-American Foundation (Parts 7300—7399)
LXIV	Merit Systems Protection Board (Parts 7400—7499)
LXV	Department of Housing and Urban Development (Parts 7500—7599)
LXVI	National Archives and Records Administration (Parts 7600—7699)
LXVII	Institute of Museum and Library Services (Parts 7700—7799)
LXVIII	Commission on Civil Rights (Parts 7800—7899)
LXIX	Tennessee Valley Authority (Parts 7900—7999)
LXX	Court Services and Offender Supervision Agency for the District of Columbia (Parts 8000—8099)
LXXI	Consumer Product Safety Commission (Parts 8100—8199)
LXXIII	Department of Agriculture (Parts 8300—8399)

Title 5—Administrative Personnel—Continued

Title 6—Domestic Security

Title 7—Agriculture

Chap.	
IX	Agricultural Marketing Service (Marketing Agreements and Orders; Fruits, Vegetables, Nuts), Department of Agriculture (Parts 900—999)
X	Agricultural Marketing Service (Marketing Agreements and Orders; Milk), Department of Agriculture (Parts 1000—1199)
XI	Agricultural Marketing Service (Marketing Agreements and Orders; Miscellaneous Commodities), Department of Agriculture (Parts 1200—1299)
XIV	Commodity Credit Corporation, Department of Agriculture (Parts 1400—1499)
XV	Foreign Agricultural Service, Department of Agriculture (Parts 1500—1599)
XVI	Rural Telephone Bank, Department of Agriculture (Parts 1600—1699)
XVII	Rural Utilities Service, Department of Agriculture (Parts 1700—1799)
XVIII	Rural Housing Service, Rural Business-Cooperative Service, Rural Utilities Service, and Farm Service Agency, Department of Agriculture (Parts 1800—2099)
XX	Local Television Loan Guarantee Board (Parts 2200—2299)
XXV	Office of Advocacy and Outreach, Department of Agriculture (Parts 2500—2599)
XXVI	Office of Inspector General, Department of Agriculture (Parts 2600—2699)
XXVII	Office of Information Resources Management, Department of Agriculture (Parts 2700—2799)
XXVIII	Office of Operations, Department of Agriculture (Parts 2800—2899)
XXIX	Office of Energy Policy and New Uses, Department of Agriculture (Parts 2900—2999)
XXX	Office of the Chief Financial Officer, Department of Agriculture (Parts 3000—3099)
XXXI	Office of Environmental Quality, Department of Agriculture (Parts 3100—3199)
XXXII	Office of Procurement and Property Management, Department of Agriculture (Parts 3200—3299)
XXXIII	Office of Transportation, Department of Agriculture (Parts 3300—3399)
XXXIV	National Institute of Food and Agriculture (Parts 3400—3499)
XXXV	Rural Housing Service, Department of Agriculture (Parts 3500—3599)
XXXVI	National Agricultural Statistics Service, Department of Agriculture (Parts 3600—3699)
XXXVII	Economic Research Service, Department of Agriculture (Parts 3700—3799)
XXXVIII	World Agricultural Outlook Board, Department of Agriculture (Parts 3800—3899)
XLI	[Reserved]
XLII	Rural Business-Cooperative Service and Rural Utilities Service, Department of Agriculture (Parts 4200—4299)

Title 8—Aliens and Nationality

Chap.

Chap.	
I	Department of Homeland Security (Immigration and Naturalization) (Parts 1—499)
V	Executive Office for Immigration Review, Department of Justice (Parts 1000—1399)

Title 9—Animals and Animal Products

Chap.	
I	Animal and Plant Health Inspection Service, Department of Agriculture (Parts 1—199)
II	Grain Inspection, Packers and Stockyards Administration (Packers and Stockyards Programs), Department of Agriculture (Parts 200—299)
III	Food Safety and Inspection Service, Department of Agriculture (Parts 300—599)

Title 10—Energy

Chap.	
I	Nuclear Regulatory Commission (Parts 0—199)
II	Department of Energy (Parts 200—699)
III	Department of Energy (Parts 700—999)
X	Department of Energy (General Provisions) (Parts 1000—1099)
XIII	Nuclear Waste Technical Review Board (Parts 1300—1399)
XVII	Defense Nuclear Facilities Safety Board (Parts 1700—1799)
XVIII	Northeast Interstate Low-Level Radioactive Waste Commission (Parts 1800—1899)

Title 11—Federal Elections

Chap.	
I	Federal Election Commission (Parts 1—9099)
II	Election Assistance Commission (Parts 9400—9499)

Title 12—Banks and Banking

Chap.	
I	Comptroller of the Currency, Department of the Treasury (Parts 1—199)
II	Federal Reserve System (Parts 200—299)
III	Federal Deposit Insurance Corporation (Parts 300—399)
IV	Export-Import Bank of the United States (Parts 400—499)
V	(Parts 500—599) [Reserved]
VI	Farm Credit Administration (Parts 600—699)
VII	National Credit Union Administration (Parts 700—799)
VIII	Federal Financing Bank (Parts 800—899)
IX	Federal Housing Finance Board (Parts 900—999)
X	Bureau of Consumer Financial Protection (Parts 1000—1099)
XI	Federal Financial Institutions Examination Council (Parts 1100—1199)
XII	Federal Housing Finance Agency (Parts 1200—1299)
XIII	Financial Stability Oversight Council (Parts 1300—1399)

Title 12—Banks and Banking—Continued

Chap.

XIV Farm Credit System Insurance Corporation (Parts 1400—1499)

XV Department of the Treasury (Parts 1500—1599)

XVI Office of Financial Research (Parts 1600—1699)

XVII Office of Federal Housing Enterprise Oversight, Department of Housing and Urban Development (Parts 1700—1799)

XVIII Community Development Financial Institutions Fund, Department of the Treasury (Parts 1800—1899)

Title 13—Business Credit and Assistance

I Small Business Administration (Parts 1—199)

III Economic Development Administration, Department of Commerce (Parts 300—399)

IV Emergency Steel Guarantee Loan Board (Parts 400—499)

V Emergency Oil and Gas Guaranteed Loan Board (Parts 500—599)

Title 14—Aeronautics and Space

I Federal Aviation Administration, Department of Transportation (Parts 1—199)

II Office of the Secretary, Department of Transportation (Aviation Proceedings) (Parts 200—399)

III Commercial Space Transportation, Federal Aviation Administration, Department of Transportation (Parts 400—1199)

V National Aeronautics and Space Administration (Parts 1200—1299)

VI Air Transportation System Stabilization (Parts 1300—1399)

Title 15—Commerce and Foreign Trade

SUBTITLE A—OFFICE OF THE SECRETARY OF COMMERCE (PARTS 0—29)

SUBTITLE B—REGULATIONS RELATING TO COMMERCE AND FOREIGN TRADE

I Bureau of the Census, Department of Commerce (Parts 30—199)

II National Institute of Standards and Technology, Department of Commerce (Parts 200—299)

III International Trade Administration, Department of Commerce (Parts 300—399)

IV Foreign-Trade Zones Board, Department of Commerce (Parts 400—499)

VII Bureau of Industry and Security, Department of Commerce (Parts 700—799)

VIII Bureau of Economic Analysis, Department of Commerce (Parts 800—899)

IX National Oceanic and Atmospheric Administration, Department of Commerce (Parts 900—999)

XI National Technical Information Service, Department of Commerce (Parts 1100—1199)

Title 15—Commerce and Foreign Trade—Continued

Chap.	
XIII	East-West Foreign Trade Board (Parts 1300—1399)
XIV	Minority Business Development Agency (Parts 1400—1499)
	SUBTITLE C—REGULATIONS RELATING TO FOREIGN TRADE AGREEMENTS
XX	Office of the United States Trade Representative (Parts 2000—2099)
	SUBTITLE D—REGULATIONS RELATING TO TELECOMMUNICATIONS AND INFORMATION
XXIII	National Telecommunications and Information Administration, Department of Commerce (Parts 2300—2399) [Reserved]

Title 16—Commercial Practices

I	Federal Trade Commission (Parts 0—999)
II	Consumer Product Safety Commission (Parts 1000—1799)

Title 17—Commodity and Securities Exchanges

I	Commodity Futures Trading Commission (Parts 1—199)
II	Securities and Exchange Commission (Parts 200—399)
IV	Department of the Treasury (Parts 400—499)

Title 18—Conservation of Power and Water Resources

I	Federal Energy Regulatory Commission, Department of Energy (Parts 1—399)
III	Delaware River Basin Commission (Parts 400—499)
VI	Water Resources Council (Parts 700—799)
VIII	Susquehanna River Basin Commission (Parts 800—899)
XIII	Tennessee Valley Authority (Parts 1300—1399)

Title 19—Customs Duties

I	U.S. Customs and Border Protection, Department of Homeland Security; Department of the Treasury (Parts 0—199)
II	United States International Trade Commission (Parts 200—299)
III	International Trade Administration, Department of Commerce (Parts 300—399)
IV	U.S. Immigration and Customs Enforcement, Department of Homeland Security (Parts 400—599) [Reserved]

Title 20—Employees' Benefits

I	Office of Workers' Compensation Programs, Department of Labor (Parts 1—199)
II	Railroad Retirement Board (Parts 200—399)
III	Social Security Administration (Parts 400—499)

Title 20—Employees' Benefits—Continued

Chap.

IV Employees' Compensation Appeals Board, Department of Labor (Parts 500—599)

V Employment and Training Administration, Department of Labor (Parts 600—699)

VI Office of Workers' Compensation Programs, Department of Labor (Parts 700—799)

VII Benefits Review Board, Department of Labor (Parts 800—899)

VIII Joint Board for the Enrollment of Actuaries (Parts 900—999)

IX Office of the Assistant Secretary for Veterans' Employment and Training Service, Department of Labor (Parts 1000—1099)

Title 21—Food and Drugs

I Food and Drug Administration, Department of Health and Human Services (Parts 1—1299)

II Drug Enforcement Administration, Department of Justice (Parts 1300—1399)

III Office of National Drug Control Policy (Parts 1400—1499)

Title 22—Foreign Relations

I Department of State (Parts 1—199)

II Agency for International Development (Parts 200—299)

III Peace Corps (Parts 300—399)

IV International Joint Commission, United States and Canada (Parts 400—499)

V Broadcasting Board of Governors (Parts 500—599)

VII Overseas Private Investment Corporation (Parts 700—799)

IX Foreign Service Grievance Board (Parts 900—999)

X Inter-American Foundation (Parts 1000—1099)

XI International Boundary and Water Commission, United States and Mexico, United States Section (Parts 1100—1199)

XII United States International Development Cooperation Agency (Parts 1200—1299)

XIII Millennium Challenge Corporation (Parts 1300—1399)

XIV Foreign Service Labor Relations Board; Federal Labor Relations Authority; General Counsel of the Federal Labor Relations Authority; and the Foreign Service Impasse Disputes Panel (Parts 1400—1499)

XV African Development Foundation (Parts 1500—1599)

XVI Japan-United States Friendship Commission (Parts 1600—1699)

XVII United States Institute of Peace (Parts 1700—1799)

Title 23—Highways

I Federal Highway Administration, Department of Transportation (Parts 1—999)

Chap.

II National Highway Traffic Safety Administration and Federal Highway Administration, Department of Transportation (Parts 1200—1299)

III National Highway Traffic Safety Administration, Department of Transportation (Parts 1300—1399)

Title 24—Housing and Urban Development

SUBTITLE A—OFFICE OF THE SECRETARY, DEPARTMENT OF HOUSING AND URBAN DEVELOPMENT (PARTS 0—99)

SUBTITLE B—REGULATIONS RELATING TO HOUSING AND URBAN DEVELOPMENT

I Office of Assistant Secretary for Equal Opportunity, Department of Housing and Urban Development (Parts 100—199)

II Office of Assistant Secretary for Housing-Federal Housing Commissioner, Department of Housing and Urban Development (Parts 200—299)

III Government National Mortgage Association, Department of Housing and Urban Development (Parts 300—399)

IV Office of Housing and Office of Multifamily Housing Assistance Restructuring, Department of Housing and Urban Development (Parts 400—499)

V Office of Assistant Secretary for Community Planning and Development, Department of Housing and Urban Development (Parts 500—599)

VI Office of Assistant Secretary for Community Planning and Development, Department of Housing and Urban Development (Parts 600—699) [Reserved]

VII Office of the Secretary, Department of Housing and Urban Development (Housing Assistance Programs and Public and Indian Housing Programs) (Parts 700—799)

VIII Office of the Assistant Secretary for Housing—Federal Housing Commissioner, Department of Housing and Urban Development (Section 8 Housing Assistance Programs, Section 202 Direct Loan Program, Section 202 Supportive Housing for the Elderly Program and Section 811 Supportive Housing for Persons With Disabilities Program) (Parts 800—899)

IX Office of Assistant Secretary for Public and Indian Housing, Department of Housing and Urban Development (Parts 900—1699)

XII Office of Inspector General, Department of Housing and Urban Development (Parts 2000—2099)

XV Emergency Mortgage Insurance and Loan Programs, Department of Housing and Urban Development (Parts 2700—2799) [Reserved]

XX Office of Assistant Secretary for Housing—Federal Housing Commissioner, Department of Housing and Urban Development (Parts 3200—3899)

XXIV Board of Directors of the HOPE for Homeowners Program (Parts 4000—4099) [Reserved]

XXV Neighborhood Reinvestment Corporation (Parts 4100—4199)

Title 25—Indians

Chap.

I Bureau of Indian Affairs, Department of the Interior (Parts 1—299)

II Indian Arts and Crafts Board, Department of the Interior (Parts 300—399)

III National Indian Gaming Commission, Department of the Interior (Parts 500—599)

IV Office of Navajo and Hopi Indian Relocation (Parts 700—899)

V Bureau of Indian Affairs, Department of the Interior, and Indian Health Service, Department of Health and Human Services (Part 900—999)

VI Office of the Assistant Secretary, Indian Affairs, Department of the Interior (Parts 1000—1199)

VII Office of the Special Trustee for American Indians, Department of the Interior (Parts 1200—1299)

Title 26—Internal Revenue

I Internal Revenue Service, Department of the Treasury (Parts 1—End)

Title 27—Alcohol, Tobacco Products and Firearms

I Alcohol and Tobacco Tax and Trade Bureau, Department of the Treasury (Parts 1—399)

II Bureau of Alcohol, Tobacco, Firearms, and Explosives, Department of Justice (Parts 400—699)

Title 28—Judicial Administration

I Department of Justice (Parts 0—299)

III Federal Prison Industries, Inc., Department of Justice (Parts 300—399)

V Bureau of Prisons, Department of Justice (Parts 500—599)

VI Offices of Independent Counsel, Department of Justice (Parts 600—699)

VII Office of Independent Counsel (Parts 700—799)

VIII Court Services and Offender Supervision Agency for the District of Columbia (Parts 800—899)

IX National Crime Prevention and Privacy Compact Council (Parts 900—999)

XI Department of Justice and Department of State (Parts 1100—1199)

Title 29—Labor

Subtitle A—Office of the Secretary of Labor (Parts 0—99)

Subtitle B—Regulations Relating to Labor

I National Labor Relations Board (Parts 100—199)

Title 29—Labor—Continued

Chap.

Chap.	
II	Office of Labor-Management Standards, Department of Labor (Parts 200—299)
III	National Railroad Adjustment Board (Parts 300—399)
IV	Office of Labor-Management Standards, Department of Labor (Parts 400—499)
V	Wage and Hour Division, Department of Labor (Parts 500—899)
IX	Construction Industry Collective Bargaining Commission (Parts 900—999)
X	National Mediation Board (Parts 1200—1299)
XII	Federal Mediation and Conciliation Service (Parts 1400—1499)
XIV	Equal Employment Opportunity Commission (Parts 1600—1699)
XVII	Occupational Safety and Health Administration, Department of Labor (Parts 1900—1999)
XX	Occupational Safety and Health Review Commission (Parts 2200—2499)
XXV	Employee Benefits Security Administration, Department of Labor (Parts 2500—2599)
XXVII	Federal Mine Safety and Health Review Commission (Parts 2700—2799)
XL	Pension Benefit Guaranty Corporation (Parts 4000—4999)

Title 30—Mineral Resources

I	Mine Safety and Health Administration, Department of Labor (Parts 1—199)
II	Bureau of Safety and Environmental Enforcement, Department of the Interior (Parts 200—299)
IV	Geological Survey, Department of the Interior (Parts 400—499)
V	Bureau of Ocean Energy Management, Department of the Interior (Parts 500—599)
VII	Office of Surface Mining Reclamation and Enforcement, Department of the Interior (Parts 700—999)
XII	Office of Natural Resources Revenue, Department of the Interior (Parts 1200—1299)

Title 31—Money and Finance: Treasury

	SUBTITLE A—OFFICE OF THE SECRETARY OF THE TREASURY (PARTS 0—50)
	SUBTITLE B—REGULATIONS RELATING TO MONEY AND FINANCE
I	Monetary Offices, Department of the Treasury (Parts 51—199)
II	Fiscal Service, Department of the Treasury (Parts 200—399)
IV	Secret Service, Department of the Treasury (Parts 400—499)
V	Office of Foreign Assets Control, Department of the Treasury (Parts 500—599)
VI	Bureau of Engraving and Printing, Department of the Treasury (Parts 600—699)
VII	Federal Law Enforcement Training Center, Department of the Treasury (Parts 700—799)

Title 31—Money and Finance: Treasury—Continued

Chap.

VIII Office of Investment Security, Department of the Treasury (Parts 800—899)

IX Federal Claims Collection Standards (Department of the Treasury—Department of Justice) (Parts 900—999)

X Financial Crimes Enforcement Network, Department of the Treasury (Parts 1000—1099)

Title 32—National Defense

SUBTITLE A—DEPARTMENT OF DEFENSE

I Office of the Secretary of Defense (Parts 1—399)

V Department of the Army (Parts 400—699)

VI Department of the Navy (Parts 700—799)

VII Department of the Air Force (Parts 800—1099)

SUBTITLE B—OTHER REGULATIONS RELATING TO NATIONAL DEFENSE

XII Defense Logistics Agency (Parts 1200—1299)

XVI Selective Service System (Parts 1600—1699)

XVII Office of the Director of National Intelligence (Parts 1700—1799)

XVIII National Counterintelligence Center (Parts 1800—1899)

XIX Central Intelligence Agency (Parts 1900—1999)

XX Information Security Oversight Office, National Archives and Records Administration (Parts 2000—2099)

XXI National Security Council (Parts 2100—2199)

XXIV Office of Science and Technology Policy (Parts 2400—2499)

XXVII Office for Micronesian Status Negotiations (Parts 2700—2799)

XXVIII Office of the Vice President of the United States (Parts 2800—2899)

Title 33—Navigation and Navigable Waters

I Coast Guard, Department of Homeland Security (Parts 1—199)

II Corps of Engineers, Department of the Army, Department of Defense (Parts 200—399)

IV Saint Lawrence Seaway Development Corporation, Department of Transportation (Parts 400—499)

Title 34—Education

SUBTITLE A—OFFICE OF THE SECRETARY, DEPARTMENT OF EDUCATION (PARTS 1—99)

SUBTITLE B—REGULATIONS OF THE OFFICES OF THE DEPARTMENT OF EDUCATION

I Office for Civil Rights, Department of Education (Parts 100—199)

II Office of Elementary and Secondary Education, Department of Education (Parts 200—299)

III Office of Special Education and Rehabilitative Services, Department of Education (Parts 300—399)

Title 34—Education—Continued

Chap.

IV Office of Career, Technical and Adult Education, Department of Education (Parts 400—499)

V Office of Bilingual Education and Minority Languages Affairs, Department of Education (Parts 500—599) [Reserved]

VI Office of Postsecondary Education, Department of Education (Parts 600—699)

VII Office of Educational Research and Improvement, Department of Education (Parts 700—799) [Reserved]

SUBTITLE C—REGULATIONS RELATING TO EDUCATION

XI (Parts 1100—1199) [Reserved]

XII National Council on Disability (Parts 1200—1299)

Title 35 [Reserved]

Title 36—Parks, Forests, and Public Property

I National Park Service, Department of the Interior (Parts 1—199)

II Forest Service, Department of Agriculture (Parts 200—299)

III Corps of Engineers, Department of the Army (Parts 300—399)

IV American Battle Monuments Commission (Parts 400—499)

V Smithsonian Institution (Parts 500—599)

VI [Reserved]

VII Library of Congress (Parts 700—799)

VIII Advisory Council on Historic Preservation (Parts 800—899)

IX Pennsylvania Avenue Development Corporation (Parts 900—999)

X Presidio Trust (Parts 1000—1099)

XI Architectural and Transportation Barriers Compliance Board (Parts 1100—1199)

XII National Archives and Records Administration (Parts 1200—1299)

XV Oklahoma City National Memorial Trust (Parts 1500—1599)

XVI Morris K. Udall Scholarship and Excellence in National Environmental Policy Foundation (Parts 1600—1699)

Title 37—Patents, Trademarks, and Copyrights

I United States Patent and Trademark Office, Department of Commerce (Parts 1—199)

II U.S. Copyright Office, Library of Congress (Parts 200—299)

III Copyright Royalty Board, Library of Congress (Parts 300—399)

IV National Institute of Standards and Technology, Department of Commerce (Parts 400—599)

Title 38—Pensions, Bonuses, and Veterans' Relief

I Department of Veterans Affairs (Parts 0—199)

II Armed Forces Retirement Home (Parts 200—299)

Title 39—Postal Service

Chap.

I United States Postal Service (Parts 1—999)

III Postal Regulatory Commission (Parts 3000—3099)

Title 40—Protection of Environment

I Environmental Protection Agency (Parts 1—1099)

IV Environmental Protection Agency and Department of Justice (Parts 1400—1499)

V Council on Environmental Quality (Parts 1500—1599)

VI Chemical Safety and Hazard Investigation Board (Parts 1600—1699)

VII Environmental Protection Agency and Department of Defense; Uniform National Discharge Standards for Vessels of the Armed Forces (Parts 1700—1799)

VIII Gulf Coast Ecosystem Restoration Council (Parts 1800—1899)

Title 41—Public Contracts and Property Management

SUBTITLE A—FEDERAL PROCUREMENT REGULATIONS SYSTEM [NOTE]

SUBTITLE B—OTHER PROVISIONS RELATING TO PUBLIC CONTRACTS

50 Public Contracts, Department of Labor (Parts 50–1—50–999)

51 Committee for Purchase From People Who Are Blind or Severely Disabled (Parts 51–1—51–99)

60 Office of Federal Contract Compliance Programs, Equal Employment Opportunity, Department of Labor (Parts 60–1—60–999)

61 Office of the Assistant Secretary for Veterans' Employment and Training Service, Department of Labor (Parts 61–1—61–999)

62—100 [Reserved]

SUBTITLE C—FEDERAL PROPERTY MANAGEMENT REGULATIONS SYSTEM

101 Federal Property Management Regulations (Parts 101–1—101–99)

102 Federal Management Regulation (Parts 102–1—102–299)

103—104 [Reserved]

105 General Services Administration (Parts 105–1—105–999)

109 Department of Energy Property Management Regulations (Parts 109–1—109–99)

114 Department of the Interior (Parts 114–1—114–99)

115 Environmental Protection Agency (Parts 115–1—115–99)

128 Department of Justice (Parts 128–1—128–99)

129—200 [Reserved]

SUBTITLE D—OTHER PROVISIONS RELATING TO PROPERTY MANAGEMENT [RESERVED]

SUBTITLE E—FEDERAL INFORMATION RESOURCES MANAGEMENT REGULATIONS SYSTEM [RESERVED]

SUBTITLE F—FEDERAL TRAVEL REGULATION SYSTEM

300 General (Parts 300–1—300–99)

301 Temporary Duty (TDY) Travel Allowances (Parts 301–1—301–99)

Title 41—Public Contracts and Property Management—Continued

Chap.

302 Relocation Allowances (Parts 302–1—302–99)

303 Payment of Expenses Connected with the Death of Certain Employees (Part 303–1—303–99)

304 Payment of Travel Expenses from a Non-Federal Source (Parts 304–1—304–99)

Title 42—Public Health

I Public Health Service, Department of Health and Human Services (Parts 1—199)

II—III [Reserved]

IV Centers for Medicare & Medicaid Services, Department of Health and Human Services (Parts 400—699)

V Office of Inspector General-Health Care, Department of Health and Human Services (Parts 1000—1099)

Title 43—Public Lands: Interior

SUBTITLE A—OFFICE OF THE SECRETARY OF THE INTERIOR (PARTS 1—199)

SUBTITLE B—REGULATIONS RELATING TO PUBLIC LANDS

I Bureau of Reclamation, Department of the Interior (Parts 400—999)

II Bureau of Land Management, Department of the Interior (Parts 1000—9999)

III Utah Reclamation Mitigation and Conservation Commission (Parts 10000—10099)

Title 44—Emergency Management and Assistance

I Federal Emergency Management Agency, Department of Homeland Security (Parts 0—399)

IV Department of Commerce and Department of Transportation (Parts 400—499)

Title 45—Public Welfare

SUBTITLE A—DEPARTMENT OF HEALTH AND HUMAN SERVICES (PARTS 1—199)

SUBTITLE B—REGULATIONS RELATING TO PUBLIC WELFARE

II Office of Family Assistance (Assistance Programs), Administration for Children and Families, Department of Health and Human Services (Parts 200—299)

III Office of Child Support Enforcement (Child Support Enforcement Program), Administration for Children and Families, Department of Health and Human Services (Parts 300—399)

IV Office of Refugee Resettlement, Administration for Children and Families, Department of Health and Human Services (Parts 400—499)

Title 45—Public Welfare—Continued

Chap.	
V	Foreign Claims Settlement Commission of the United States, Department of Justice (Parts 500—599)
VI	National Science Foundation (Parts 600—699)
VII	Commission on Civil Rights (Parts 700—799)
VIII	Office of Personnel Management (Parts 800—899)
IX	Denali Commission (Parts 900—999)
X	Office of Community Services, Administration for Children and Families, Department of Health and Human Services (Parts 1000—1099)
XI	National Foundation on the Arts and the Humanities (Parts 1100—1199)
XII	Corporation for National and Community Service (Parts 1200—1299)
XIII	Administration for Children and Families, Department of Health and Human Services (Parts 1300—1399)
XVI	Legal Services Corporation (Parts 1600—1699)
XVII	National Commission on Libraries and Information Science (Parts 1700—1799)
XVIII	Harry S. Truman Scholarship Foundation (Parts 1800—1899)
XXI	Commission of Fine Arts (Parts 2100—2199)
XXIII	Arctic Research Commission (Parts 2300—2399)
XXIV	James Madison Memorial Fellowship Foundation (Parts 2400—2499)
XXV	Corporation for National and Community Service (Parts 2500—2599)

Title 46—Shipping

I	Coast Guard, Department of Homeland Security (Parts 1—199)
II	Maritime Administration, Department of Transportation (Parts 200—399)
III	Coast Guard (Great Lakes Pilotage), Department of Homeland Security (Parts 400—499)
IV	Federal Maritime Commission (Parts 500—599)

Title 47—Telecommunication

I	Federal Communications Commission (Parts 0—199)
II	Office of Science and Technology Policy and National Security Council (Parts 200—299)
III	National Telecommunications and Information Administration, Department of Commerce (Parts 300—399)
IV	National Telecommunications and Information Administration, Department of Commerce, and National Highway Traffic Safety Administration, Department of Transportation (Parts 400—499)
V	The First Responder Network Authority (Parts 500—599)

Title 48—Federal Acquisition Regulations System

Chap.

1 Federal Acquisition Regulation (Parts 1—99)

2 Defense Acquisition Regulations System, Department of Defense (Parts 200—299)

3 Department of Health and Human Services (Parts 300—399)

4 Department of Agriculture (Parts 400—499)

5 General Services Administration (Parts 500—599)

6 Department of State (Parts 600—699)

7 Agency for International Development (Parts 700—799)

8 Department of Veterans Affairs (Parts 800—899)

9 Department of Energy (Parts 900—999)

10 Department of the Treasury (Parts 1000—1099)

12 Department of Transportation (Parts 1200—1299)

13 Department of Commerce (Parts 1300—1399)

14 Department of the Interior (Parts 1400—1499)

15 Environmental Protection Agency (Parts 1500—1599)

16 Office of Personnel Management, Federal Employees Health Benefits Acquisition Regulation (Parts 1600—1699)

17 Office of Personnel Management (Parts 1700—1799)

18 National Aeronautics and Space Administration (Parts 1800—1899)

19 Broadcasting Board of Governors (Parts 1900—1999)

20 Nuclear Regulatory Commission (Parts 2000—2099)

21 Office of Personnel Management, Federal Employees Group Life Insurance Federal Acquisition Regulation (Parts 2100—2199)

23 Social Security Administration (Parts 2300—2399)

24 Department of Housing and Urban Development (Parts 2400—2499)

25 National Science Foundation (Parts 2500—2599)

28 Department of Justice (Parts 2800—2899)

29 Department of Labor (Parts 2900—2999)

30 Department of Homeland Security, Homeland Security Acquisition Regulation (HSAR) (Parts 3000—3099)

34 Department of Education Acquisition Regulation (Parts 3400—3499)

51 Department of the Army Acquisition Regulations (Parts 5100—5199)

52 Department of the Navy Acquisition Regulations (Parts 5200—5299)

53 Department of the Air Force Federal Acquisition Regulation Supplement (Parts 5300—5399) [Reserved]

54 Defense Logistics Agency, Department of Defense (Parts 5400—5499)

57 African Development Foundation (Parts 5700—5799)

61 Civilian Board of Contract Appeals, General Services Administration (Parts 6100—6199)

99 Cost Accounting Standards Board, Office of Federal Procurement Policy, Office of Management and Budget (Parts 9900—9999)

Title 49—Transportation

Chap.

SUBTITLE A—OFFICE OF THE SECRETARY OF TRANSPORTATION (PARTS 1—99)

SUBTITLE B—OTHER REGULATIONS RELATING TO TRANSPORTATION

I Pipeline and Hazardous Materials Safety Administration, Department of Transportation (Parts 100—199)

II Federal Railroad Administration, Department of Transportation (Parts 200—299)

III Federal Motor Carrier Safety Administration, Department of Transportation (Parts 300—399)

IV Coast Guard, Department of Homeland Security (Parts 400—499)

V National Highway Traffic Safety Administration, Department of Transportation (Parts 500—599)

VI Federal Transit Administration, Department of Transportation (Parts 600—699)

VII National Railroad Passenger Corporation (AMTRAK) (Parts 700—799)

VIII National Transportation Safety Board (Parts 800—999)

X Surface Transportation Board (Parts 1000—1399)

XI Research and Innovative Technology Administration, Department of Transportation (Parts 1400—1499) [Reserved]

XII Transportation Security Administration, Department of Homeland Security (Parts 1500—1699)

Title 50—Wildlife and Fisheries

I United States Fish and Wildlife Service, Department of the Interior (Parts 1—199)

II National Marine Fisheries Service, National Oceanic and Atmospheric Administration, Department of Commerce (Parts 200—299)

III International Fishing and Related Activities (Parts 300—399)

IV Joint Regulations (United States Fish and Wildlife Service, Department of the Interior and National Marine Fisheries Service, National Oceanic and Atmospheric Administration, Department of Commerce); Endangered Species Committee Regulations (Parts 400—499)

V Marine Mammal Commission (Parts 500—599)

VI Fishery Conservation and Management, National Oceanic and Atmospheric Administration, Department of Commerce (Parts 600—699)

Alphabetical List of Agencies Appearing in the CFR

(Revised as of January 1, 2019)

Agency	CFR Title, Subtitle or Chapter
Administrative Conference of the United States	1, III
Advisory Council on Historic Preservation	36, VIII
Advocacy and Outreach, Office of	7, XXV
Afghanistan Reconstruction, Special Inspector General for	5, LXXXIII
African Development Foundation	22, XV
Federal Acquisition Regulation	48, 57
Agency for International Development	2, VII; 22, II
Federal Acquisition Regulation	48, 7
Agricultural Marketing Service	7, I, IX, X, XI
Agricultural Research Service	7, V
Agriculture, Department of	2, IV; 5, LXXIII
Advocacy and Outreach, Office of	7, XXV
Agricultural Marketing Service	7, I, IX, X, XI
Agricultural Research Service	7, V
Animal and Plant Health Inspection Service	7, III; 9, I
Chief Financial Officer, Office of	7, XXX
Commodity Credit Corporation	7, XIV
Economic Research Service	7, XXXVII
Energy Policy and New Uses, Office of	2, IX; 7, XXIX
Environmental Quality, Office of	7, XXXI
Farm Service Agency	7, VII, XVIII
Federal Acquisition Regulation	48, 4
Federal Crop Insurance Corporation	7, IV
Food and Nutrition Service	7, II
Food Safety and Inspection Service	9, III
Foreign Agricultural Service	7, XV
Forest Service	36, II
Grain Inspection, Packers and Stockyards Administration	7, VIII; 9, II
Information Resources Management, Office of	7, XXVII
Inspector General, Office of	7, XXVI
National Agricultural Library	7, XLI
National Agricultural Statistics Service	7, XXXVI
National Institute of Food and Agriculture	7, XXXIV
Natural Resources Conservation Service	7, VI
Operations, Office of	7, XXVIII
Procurement and Property Management, Office of	7, XXXII
Rural Business-Cooperative Service	7, XVIII, XLII
Rural Development Administration	7, XLII
Rural Housing Service	7, XVIII, XXXV
Rural Telephone Bank	7, XVI
Rural Utilities Service	7, XVII, XVIII, XLII
Secretary of Agriculture, Office of	7, Subtitle A
Transportation, Office of	7, XXXIII
World Agricultural Outlook Board	7, XXXVIII
Air Force, Department of	32, VII
Federal Acquisition Regulation Supplement	48, 53
Air Transportation Stabilization Board	14, VI
Alcohol and Tobacco Tax and Trade Bureau	27, I
Alcohol, Tobacco, Firearms, and Explosives, Bureau of	27, II
AMTRAK	49, VII
American Battle Monuments Commission	36, IV
American Indians, Office of the Special Trustee	25, VII
Animal and Plant Health Inspection Service	7, III; 9, I

Agency	CFR Title, Subtitle or Chapter
Appalachian Regional Commission	5, IX
Architectural and Transportation Barriers Compliance Board	36, XI
Arctic Research Commission	45, XXIII
Armed Forces Retirement Home	5, XI
Army, Department of	32, V
Engineers, Corps of	33, II; 36, III
Federal Acquisition Regulation	48, 51
Bilingual Education and Minority Languages Affairs, Office of	34, V
Blind or Severely Disabled, Committee for Purchase from People Who Are	41, 51
Broadcasting Board of Governors	22, V
Federal Acquisition Regulation	48, 19
Career, Technical, and Adult Education, Office of	34, IV
Census Bureau	15, I
Centers for Medicare & Medicaid Services	42, IV
Central Intelligence Agency	32, XIX
Chemical Safety and Hazardous Investigation Board	40, VI
Chief Financial Officer, Office of	7, XXX
Child Support Enforcement, Office of	45, III
Children and Families, Administration for	45, II, III, IV, X, XIII
Civil Rights, Commission on	5, LXVIII; 45, VII
Civil Rights, Office for	34, I
Council of the Inspectors General on Integrity and Efficiency	5, XCVIII
Court Services and Offender Supervision Agency for the District of Columbia	5, LXX
Coast Guard	33, I; 46, I; 49, IV
Coast Guard (Great Lakes Pilotage)	46, III
Commerce, Department of	2, XIII; 44, IV; 50, VI
Census Bureau	15, I
Economic Analysis, Bureau of	15, VIII
Economic Development Administration	13, III
Emergency Management and Assistance	44, IV
Federal Acquisition Regulation	48, 13
Foreign-Trade Zones Board	15, IV
Industry and Security, Bureau of	15, VII
International Trade Administration	15, III; 19, III
National Institute of Standards and Technology	15, II; 37, IV
National Marine Fisheries Service	50, II, IV
National Oceanic and Atmospheric Administration	15, IX; 50, II, III, IV, VI
National Technical Information Service	15, XI
National Telecommunications and Information Administration	15, XXIII; 47, III, IV
National Weather Service	15, IX
Patent and Trademark Office, United States	37, I
Secretary of Commerce, Office of	15, Subtitle A
Commercial Space Transportation	14, III
Commodity Credit Corporation	7, XIV
Commodity Futures Trading Commission	5, XLI; 17, I
Community Planning and Development, Office of Assistant Secretary for	24, V, VI
Community Services, Office of	45, X
Comptroller of the Currency	12, I
Construction Industry Collective Bargaining Commission	29, IX
Consumer Financial Protection Bureau	5, LXXXIV; 12, X
Consumer Product Safety Commission	5, LXXI; 16, II
Copyright Royalty Board	37, III
Corporation for National and Community Service	2, XXII; 45, XII, XXV
Cost Accounting Standards Board	48, 99
Council on Environmental Quality	40, V
Court Services and Offender Supervision Agency for the District of Columbia	5, LXX; 28, VIII
Customs and Border Protection	19, I
Defense Contract Audit Agency	32, I
Defense, Department of	2, XI; 5, XXVI; 32, Subtitle A; 40, VII
Advanced Research Projects Agency	32, I
Air Force Department	32, VII

Agency	CFR Title, Subtitle or Chapter
Army Department	32, V; 33, II; 36, III; 48, 51
Defense Acquisition Regulations System	48, 2
Defense Intelligence Agency	32, I
Defense Logistics Agency	32, I, XII; 48, 54
Engineers, Corps of	33, II; 36, III
National Imagery and Mapping Agency	32, I
Navy Department	32, VI; 48, 52
Secretary of Defense, Office of	2, XI; 32, I
Defense Contract Audit Agency	32, I
Defense Intelligence Agency	32, I
Defense Logistics Agency	32, XII; 48, 54
Defense Nuclear Facilities Safety Board	10, XVII
Delaware River Basin Commission	18, III
Denali Commission	45, IX
Disability, National Council on	5, C; 34, XII
District of Columbia, Court Services and Offender Supervision Agency for the	5, LXX; 28, VIII
Drug Enforcement Administration	21, II
East-West Foreign Trade Board	15, XIII
Economic Analysis, Bureau of	15, VIII
Economic Development Administration	13, III
Economic Research Service	7, XXXVII
Education, Department of	2, XXXIV; 5, LIII
Bilingual Education and Minority Languages Affairs, Office of	34, V
Career, Technical, and Adult Education, Office of	34, IV
Civil Rights, Office for	34, I
Educational Research and Improvement, Office of	34, VII
Elementary and Secondary Education, Office of	34, II
Federal Acquisition Regulation	48, 34
Postsecondary Education, Office of	34, VI
Secretary of Education, Office of	34, Subtitle A
Special Education and Rehabilitative Services, Office of	34, III
Educational Research and Improvement, Office of	34, VII
Election Assistance Commission	2, LVIII; 11, II
Elementary and Secondary Education, Office of	34, II
Emergency Oil and Gas Guaranteed Loan Board	13, V
Emergency Steel Guarantee Loan Board	13, IV
Employee Benefits Security Administration	29, XXV
Employees' Compensation Appeals Board	20, IV
Employees Loyalty Board	5, V
Employment and Training Administration	20, V
Employment Policy, National Commission for	1, IV
Employment Standards Administration	20, VI
Endangered Species Committee	50, IV
Energy, Department of	2, IX; 5, XXIII; 10, II, III, X
Federal Acquisition Regulation	48, 9
Federal Energy Regulatory Commission	5, XXIV; 18, I
Property Management Regulations	41, 109
Energy, Office of	7, XXIX
Engineers, Corps of	33, II; 36, III
Engraving and Printing, Bureau of	31, VI
Environmental Protection Agency	2, XV; 5, LIV; 40, I, IV, VII
Federal Acquisition Regulation	48, 15
Property Management Regulations	41, 115
Environmental Quality, Office of	7, XXXI
Equal Employment Opportunity Commission	5, LXII; 29, XIV
Equal Opportunity, Office of Assistant Secretary for	24, I
Executive Office of the President	3, I
Environmental Quality, Council on	40, V
Management and Budget, Office of	2, Subtitle A; 5, III, LXXVII; 14, VI; 48, 99
National Drug Control Policy, Office of	2, XXXVI; 21, III
National Security Council	32, XXI; 47, 2

Agency	CFR Title, Subtitle or Chapter
Presidential Documents	3
Science and Technology Policy, Office of	32, XXIV; 47, II
Trade Representative, Office of the United States	15, XX
Export-Import Bank of the United States	2, XXXV; 5, LII; 12, IV
Family Assistance, Office of	45, II
Farm Credit Administration	5, XXXI; 12, VI
Farm Credit System Insurance Corporation	5, XXX; 12, XIV
Farm Service Agency	7, VII, XVIII
Federal Acquisition Regulation	48, 1
Federal Aviation Administration	14, I
Commercial Space Transportation	14, III
Federal Claims Collection Standards	31, IX
Federal Communications Commission	5, XXIX; 47, I
Federal Contract Compliance Programs, Office of	41, 60
Federal Crop Insurance Corporation	7, IV
Federal Deposit Insurance Corporation	5, XXII; 12, III
Federal Election Commission	5, XXXVII; 11, I
Federal Emergency Management Agency	44, I
Federal Employees Group Life Insurance Federal Acquisition Regulation	48, 21
Federal Employees Health Benefits Acquisition Regulation	48, 16
Federal Energy Regulatory Commission	5, XXIV; 18, I
Federal Financial Institutions Examination Council	12, XI
Federal Financing Bank	12, VIII
Federal Highway Administration	23, I, II
Federal Home Loan Mortgage Corporation	1, IV
Federal Housing Enterprise Oversight Office	12, XVII
Federal Housing Finance Agency	5, LXXX; 12, XII
Federal Housing Finance Board	12, IX
Federal Labor Relations Authority	5, XIV, XLIX; 22, XIV
Federal Law Enforcement Training Center	31, VII
Federal Management Regulation	41, 102
Federal Maritime Commission	46, IV
Federal Mediation and Conciliation Service	29, XII
Federal Mine Safety and Health Review Commission	5, LXXIV; 29, XXVII
Federal Motor Carrier Safety Administration	49, III
Federal Prison Industries, Inc.	28, III
Federal Procurement Policy Office	48, 99
Federal Property Management Regulations	41, 101
Federal Railroad Administration	49, II
Federal Register, Administrative Committee of	1, I
Federal Register, Office of	1, II
Federal Reserve System	12, II
Board of Governors	5, LVIII
Federal Retirement Thrift Investment Board	5, VI, LXXVI
Federal Service Impasses Panel	5, XIV
Federal Trade Commission	5, XLVII; 16, I
Federal Transit Administration	49, VI
Federal Travel Regulation System	41, Subtitle F
Financial Crimes Enforcement Network	31, X
Financial Research Office	12, XVI
Financial Stability Oversight Council	12, XIII
Fine Arts, Commission of	45, XXI
Fiscal Service	31, II
Fish and Wildlife Service, United States	50, I, IV
Food and Drug Administration	21, I
Food and Nutrition Service	7, II
Food Safety and Inspection Service	9, III
Foreign Agricultural Service	7, XV
Foreign Assets Control, Office of	31, V
Foreign Claims Settlement Commission of the United States	45, V
Foreign Service Grievance Board	22, IX
Foreign Service Impasse Disputes Panel	22, XIV
Foreign Service Labor Relations Board	22, XIV
Foreign-Trade Zones Board	15, IV
Forest Service	36, II
General Services Administration	5, LVII; 41, 105

Agency	CFR Title, Subtitle or Chapter
Contract Appeals, Board of	48, 61
Federal Acquisition Regulation	48, 5
Federal Management Regulation	41, 102
Federal Property Management Regulations	41, 101
Federal Travel Regulation System	41, Subtitle F
General	41, 300
Payment From a Non-Federal Source for Travel Expenses	41, 304
Payment of Expenses Connected With the Death of Certain Employees	41, 303
Relocation Allowances	41, 302
Temporary Duty (TDY) Travel Allowances	41, 301
Geological Survey	30, IV
Government Accountability Office	4, I
Government Ethics, Office of	5, XVI
Government National Mortgage Association	24, III
Grain Inspection, Packers and Stockyards Administration	7, VIII; 9, II
Gulf Coast Ecosystem Restoration Council	2, LIX; 40, VIII
Harry S. Truman Scholarship Foundation	45, XVIII
Health and Human Services, Department of	2, III; 5, XLV; 45, Subtitle A
Centers for Medicare & Medicaid Services	42, IV
Child Support Enforcement, Office of	45, III
Children and Families, Administration for	45, II, III, IV, X, XIII
Community Services, Office of	45, X
Family Assistance, Office of	45, II
Federal Acquisition Regulation	48, 3
Food and Drug Administration	21, I
Indian Health Service	25, V
Inspector General (Health Care), Office of	42, V
Public Health Service	42, I
Refugee Resettlement, Office of	45, IV
Homeland Security, Department of	2, XXX; 5, XXXVI; 6, I; 8, I
Coast Guard	33, I; 46, I; 49, IV
Coast Guard (Great Lakes Pilotage)	46, III
Customs and Border Protection	19, I
Federal Emergency Management Agency	44, I
Human Resources Management and Labor Relations Systems	5, XCVII
Immigration and Customs Enforcement Bureau	19, IV
Transportation Security Administration	49, XII
HOPE for Homeowners Program, Board of Directors of	24, XXIV
Housing and Urban Development, Department of	2, XXIV; 5, LXV; 24, Subtitle B
Community Planning and Development, Office of Assistant Secretary for	24, V, VI
Equal Opportunity, Office of Assistant Secretary for	24, I
Federal Acquisition Regulation	48, 24
Federal Housing Enterprise Oversight, Office of	12, XVII
Government National Mortgage Association	24, III
Housing—Federal Housing Commissioner, Office of Assistant Secretary for	24, II, VIII, X, XX
Housing, Office of, and Multifamily Housing Assistance Restructuring, Office of	24, IV
Inspector General, Office of	24, XII
Public and Indian Housing, Office of Assistant Secretary for	24, IX
Secretary, Office of	24, Subtitle A, VII
Housing—Federal Housing Commissioner, Office of Assistant Secretary for	24, II, VIII, X, XX
Housing, Office of, and Multifamily Housing Assistance Restructuring, Office of	24, IV
Immigration and Customs Enforcement Bureau	19, IV
Immigration Review, Executive Office for	8, V
Independent Counsel, Office of	28, VII
Independent Counsel, Offices of	28, VI
Indian Affairs, Bureau of	25, I, V
Indian Affairs, Office of the Assistant Secretary	25, VI

Agency	CFR Title, Subtitle or Chapter
Indian Arts and Crafts Board	25, II
Indian Health Service	25, V
Industry and Security, Bureau of	15, VII
Information Resources Management, Office of	7, XXVII
Information Security Oversight Office, National Archives and Records Administration	32, XX
Inspector General	
Agriculture Department	7, XXVI
Health and Human Services Department	42, V
Housing and Urban Development Department	24, XII, XV
Institute of Peace, United States	22, XVII
Inter-American Foundation	5, LXIII; 22, X
Interior, Department of	2, XIV
American Indians, Office of the Special Trustee	25, VII
Endangered Species Committee	50, IV
Federal Acquisition Regulation	48, 14
Federal Property Management Regulations System	41, 114
Fish and Wildlife Service, United States	50, I, IV
Geological Survey	30, IV
Indian Affairs, Bureau of	25, I, V
Indian Affairs, Office of the Assistant Secretary	25, VI
Indian Arts and Crafts Board	25, II
Land Management, Bureau of	43, II
National Indian Gaming Commission	25, III
National Park Service	36, I
Natural Resource Revenue, Office of	30, XII
Ocean Energy Management, Bureau of	30, V
Reclamation, Bureau of	43, I
Safety and Enforcement Bureau, Bureau of	30, II
Secretary of the Interior, Office of	2, XIV; 43, Subtitle A
Surface Mining Reclamation and Enforcement, Office of	30, VII
Internal Revenue Service	26, I
International Boundary and Water Commission, United States and Mexico, United States Section	22, XI
International Development, United States Agency for	22, II
Federal Acquisition Regulation	48, 7
International Development Cooperation Agency, United States	22, XII
International Joint Commission, United States and Canada	22, IV
International Organizations Employees Loyalty Board	5, V
International Trade Administration	15, III; 19, III
International Trade Commission, United States	19, II
Interstate Commerce Commission	5, XL
Investment Security, Office of	31, VIII
James Madison Memorial Fellowship Foundation	45, XXIV
Japan–United States Friendship Commission	22, XVI
Joint Board for the Enrollment of Actuaries	20, VIII
Justice, Department of	2, XXVIII; 5, XXVIII; 28, I, XI; 40, IV
Alcohol, Tobacco, Firearms, and Explosives, Bureau of	27, II
Drug Enforcement Administration	21, II
Federal Acquisition Regulation	48, 28
Federal Claims Collection Standards	31, IX
Federal Prison Industries, Inc.	28, III
Foreign Claims Settlement Commission of the United States	45, V
Immigration Review, Executive Office for	8, V
Independent Counsel, Offices of	28, VI
Prisons, Bureau of	28, V
Property Management Regulations	41, 128
Labor, Department of	2, XXIX; 5, XLII
Employee Benefits Security Administration	29, XXV
Employees' Compensation Appeals Board	20, IV
Employment and Training Administration	20, V
Employment Standards Administration	20, VI
Federal Acquisition Regulation	48, 29
Federal Contract Compliance Programs, Office of	41, 60

Agency	CFR Title, Subtitle or Chapter
Federal Procurement Regulations System	41, 50
Labor-Management Standards, Office of	29, II, IV
Mine Safety and Health Administration	30, I
Occupational Safety and Health Administration	29, XVII
Public Contracts	41, 50
Secretary of Labor, Office of	29, Subtitle A
Veterans' Employment and Training Service, Office of the Assistant Secretary for	41, 61; 20, IX
Wage and Hour Division	29, V
Workers' Compensation Programs, Office of	20, I, VII
Labor-Management Standards, Office of	29, II, IV
Land Management, Bureau of	43, II
Legal Services Corporation	45, XVI
Libraries and Information Science, National Commission on	45, XVII
Library of Congress	36, VII
Copyright Royalty Board	37, III
U.S. Copyright Office	37, II
Local Television Loan Guarantee Board	7, XX
Management and Budget, Office of	5, III, LXXVII; 14, VI; 48, 99
Marine Mammal Commission	50, V
Maritime Administration	46, II
Merit Systems Protection Board	5, II, LXIV
Micronesian Status Negotiations, Office for	32, XXVII
Military Compensation and Retirement Modernization Commission	5, XCIX
Millennium Challenge Corporation	22, XIII
Mine Safety and Health Administration	30, I
Minority Business Development Agency	15, XIV
Miscellaneous Agencies	1, IV
Monetary Offices	31, I
Morris K. Udall Scholarship and Excellence in National Environmental Policy Foundation	36, XVI
Museum and Library Services, Institute of	2, XXXI
National Aeronautics and Space Administration	2, XVIII; 5, LIX; 14, V
Federal Acquisition Regulation	48, 18
National Agricultural Library	7, XLI
National Agricultural Statistics Service	7, XXXVI
National and Community Service, Corporation for	2, XXII; 45, XII, XXV
National Archives and Records Administration	2, XXVI; 5, LXVI; 36, XII
Information Security Oversight Office	32, XX
National Capital Planning Commission	1, IV, VI
National Counterintelligence Center	32, XVIII
National Credit Union Administration	5, LXXXVI; 12, VII
National Crime Prevention and Privacy Compact Council	28, IX
National Drug Control Policy, Office of	2, XXXVI; 21, III
National Endowment for the Arts	2, XXXII
National Endowment for the Humanities	2, XXXIII
National Foundation on the Arts and the Humanities	45, XI
National Geospatial-Intelligence Agency	32, I
National Highway Traffic Safety Administration	23, II, III; 47, VI; 49, V
National Imagery and Mapping Agency	32, I
National Indian Gaming Commission	25, III
National Institute of Food and Agriculture	7, XXXIV
National Institute of Standards and Technology	15, II; 37, IV
National Intelligence, Office of Director of	5, IV; 32, XVII
National Labor Relations Board	5, LXI; 29, I
National Marine Fisheries Service	50, II, IV
National Mediation Board	5, CI; 29, X
National Oceanic and Atmospheric Administration	15, IX; 50, II, III, IV, VI
National Park Service	36, I
National Railroad Adjustment Board	29, III
National Railroad Passenger Corporation (AMTRAK)	49, VII
National Science Foundation	2, XXV; 5, XLIII; 45, VI
Federal Acquisition Regulation	48, 25
National Security Council	32, XXI

Agency	CFR Title, Subtitle or Chapter
Selective Service System	32, XVI
Small Business Administration	2, XXVII; 13, I
Smithsonian Institution	36, V
Social Security Administration	2, XXIII; 20, III; 48, 23
Soldiers' and Airmen's Home, United States	5, XI
Special Counsel, Office of	5, VIII
Special Education and Rehabilitative Services, Office of	34, III
State, Department of	2, VI; 22, I; 28, XI
Federal Acquisition Regulation	48, 6
Surface Mining Reclamation and Enforcement, Office of	30, VII
Surface Transportation Board	49, X
Susquehanna River Basin Commission	18, VIII
Tennessee Valley Authority	5, LXIX; 18, XIII
Trade Representative, United States, Office of	15, XX
Transportation, Department of	2, XII; 5, L
Commercial Space Transportation	14, III
Emergency Management and Assistance	44, IV
Federal Acquisition Regulation	48, 12
Federal Aviation Administration	14, I
Federal Highway Administration	23, I, II
Federal Motor Carrier Safety Administration	49, III
Federal Railroad Administration	49, II
Federal Transit Administration	49, VI
Maritime Administration	46, II
National Highway Traffic Safety Administration	23, II, III; 47, IV; 49, V
Pipeline and Hazardous Materials Safety Administration	49, I
Saint Lawrence Seaway Development Corporation	33, IV
Secretary of Transportation, Office of	14, II; 49, Subtitle A
Transportation Statistics Bureau	49, XI
Transportation, Office of	7, XXXIII
Transportation Security Administration	49, XII
Transportation Statistics Bureau	49, XI
Travel Allowances, Temporary Duty (TDY)	41, 301
Treasury, Department of the	2, X;5, XXI; 12, XV; 17, IV; 31, IX
Alcohol and Tobacco Tax and Trade Bureau	27, I
Community Development Financial Institutions Fund	12, XVIII
Comptroller of the Currency	12, I
Customs and Border Protection	19, I
Engraving and Printing, Bureau of	31, VI
Federal Acquisition Regulation	48, 10
Federal Claims Collection Standards	31, IX
Federal Law Enforcement Training Center	31, VII
Financial Crimes Enforcement Network	31, X
Fiscal Service	31, II
Foreign Assets Control, Office of	31, V
Internal Revenue Service	26, I
Investment Security, Office of	31, VIII
Monetary Offices	31, I
Secret Service	31, IV
Secretary of the Treasury, Office of	31, Subtitle A
Truman, Harry S. Scholarship Foundation	45, XVIII
United States and Canada, International Joint Commission	22, IV
United States and Mexico, International Boundary and Water Commission, United States Section	22, XI
U.S. Copyright Office	37, II
Utah Reclamation Mitigation and Conservation Commission	43, III
Veterans Affairs, Department of	2, VIII; 38, I
Federal Acquisition Regulation	48, 8
Veterans' Employment and Training Service, Office of the Assistant Secretary for	41, 61; 20, IX
Vice President of the United States, Office of	32, XXVIII
Wage and Hour Division	29, V
Water Resources Council	18, VI
Workers' Compensation Programs, Office of	20, I, VII
World Agricultural Outlook Board	7, XXXVIII

List of CFR Sections Affected

All changes in this volume of the Code of Federal Regulations (CFR) that were made by documents published in the FEDERAL REGISTER since January 1, 2014 are enumerated in the following list. Entries indicate the nature of the changes effected. Page numbers refer to FEDERAL REGISTER pages. The user should consult the entries for chapters, parts and subparts as well as sections for revisions.

For changes to this volume of the CFR prior to this listing, consult the annual edition of the monthly List of CFR Sections Affected (LSA). The LSA is available at www.govinfo.gov. For changes to this volume of the CFR prior to 2001, see the "List of CFR Sections Affected, 1949–1963, 1964–1972, 1973–1985, and 1986–2000" published in 11 separate volumes. The "List of CFR Sections Affected 1986–2000" is available at www.govinfo.gov.

2014

(No regulations published)

2015

4 CFR

80 FR Page

Chapter II

Chapter II Removed 36231

2016

(No regulations published)

2017

4 CFR

82 FR Page

Chapter I

81.2 Existing text designated as (a); (b) added 51753

81.6 (g) revised 51753

2018

4 CFR

83 FR Page

Chapter I

21.0 (a)(2) introductory text, (b)(2), and (c) amended; (a)(2)(A), (B), (f), and (g) redesignated as (a)(2)(i), (ii), (g), and (h); new (g) revised 13823

4 CFR—Continued

83 FR Page

Chapter I—Continued

21.1 (b) and (c)(1) revised; (g) and (h) amended 13823

21.2 (a)(1), (2), and (3) amended 13823

21.3 Heading, (a), (c), (d), (e), (g), and (i) revised; (f) and (h) amended 13823

21.4 (b), (c), and (d) redesignated as (c), (d), and (e); (a), new (c), and new (d) amended; new (b) added 13824

21.5 (a), (b)(2), and (d) through (g) amended; (b) heading, (1), (3), and (h) revised; (l) and (m) added 13824

21.6 Revised 13824

21.7 (a) amended; (e) revised 13825

21.8 (e), (f)(2), and (3) revised; (f) heading, (4), (5), and (6) added 13825

21.9 (a) revised 13825

21.10 (a), (d)(1), (2), and (e) revised; (c) amended 13825

21.11 (b) revised 13825

21.12 (b) revised 13825

21.13 (b) revised 13825

21.14 (b) revised; (c) amended 13825

○

www.ingramcontent.com/pod-product-compliance
Lightning Source LLC
Chambersburg PA
CBHW062005200326
41519CB00017B/4681

* 9 7 8 1 6 4 0 2 4 4 9 1 7 *